GOD SHED HIS GRACE ON THEE

GOD SHED HIS GRACE ON THEE

Moving Remembrances of 50 American Catholics

COMPILED AND INTRODUCED BY

Carol DeChant

GOD SHED HIS GRACE ON THEE
Moving Remembrances of 50 American Catholics
Compiled and Introduced by Carol DeChant

Edited by Gregory F. Augustine Pierce and L.C. Fiore
Cover photo © by Paul Grecaud under license from Bigstock.com
Design and Typesetting by Patricia A. Lynch

Published by ACTA Publications, 4848 N. Clark Street,
Chicago, IL 60640-4711, (800) 397-2282, www.actapublications.com.

Library of Congress Catalog Number: 2015948515
ISBN: 978-0-87946-553-7
Printed in the United States by Total Printing Systems
Year: 25 24 23 33 21 20 19 18 17 16 15
Printing: 8 7 6 5 4 3 2 First

♻ Text printed on 30% post-consumer recycled paper

TABLE OF CONTENTS

INTRODUCTION
by Carol DeChant 13

I. WE REMEMBER OUR HEROES

The Happiest Man on Earth: Chaplain Mychal Judge, NYFD
by Reverend Michael Duffy 23

An American Original: Mother Katharine Drexel
by Anthony Walton 33

A Hero's Last March: General William Tecumseh Sherman
author unknown 43

The "Opposing General's" Valor:
President John Fitzgerald Kennedy
by President Ronald Reagan 51

A Saint for Our Age: Dorothy Day
by Jim Forest 57

A Eulogy to Whitefeather of the Ojibway:
Larry Cloud-Morgan
by Patricia LeFevere 71

Plain-Spoken, Practical, Taking Care of Business:
Major David G. Taylor
by John Taylor 75

II. WE REMEMBER FAMILY

Aloise Steiner Buckley, R. I. P.
by William F. Buckley, Jr. 85

Remembering Pup: William F. Buckley, Jr.
by Christopher Buckley 90

Every Gift but Length of Years: John F. Kennedy, Jr.
by Senator Edward Kennedy 97

The Golfatorium: Meditation on a Mother Dying
by Thomas Lynch *103*

Coming Home to St. Pat's: Rosemary Clooney
by Nick Clooney *125*

What You Can Expect from the Son of a Bookmaker:
Wellington T. Mara
by John Mara *129*

Eulogy for a Baby Who Dies after Baptism
by his father *137*

III. WE REMEMBER OUR FRIENDS

Leaving a Legacy of Kindness: Phil Rizzuto
by Bob Klapisch *141*

Sissies Anonymous: Andre Dubus
by Tobias Wolff *145*

My Closest Friend for Sixty Years:
Remembering Walker Percy
by Shelby Foote *151*

Enemy of the Passive Voice, Who Rocked Some Jaunty Hats:
Liz Christman
by Melinda Henneberger *155*

A Friend of the Family: Mr. O'Connell Is Dead
by Dorothy Day *159*

The Cardinal's Epistle to the Jews: John Cardinal O'Connor
by Rabbi Haskel Lookstein *169*

Remembering My Friend Tim Russert
by Maria Shriver *175*

IV. WE REMEMBER OUR ARTISTS

Eulogy for Andy Warhol
by John Richardson *183*

Danny's Promise: In Memory of Danny Thomas
by Phil Donahue *187*

The Angels of Patricia Neal
by Terry Mattingly *191*

He's Comin' Through: Milton Batiste
by Jason Berry *195*

Wit and Wisdom on the Refrigerator Door:
Erma Bombeck
by D.L. Stewart and Anne Gasior *209*

An Unwieldy Radiance of Spirit: Flannery O'Connor
by Katherine Anne Porter *213*

The Invisible Artist: Sculptor Frederick Hart
by Tom Wolfe *217*

V. WE REMEMBER THOSE WHO SERVED US

Servant of Incurable Cancer Patients:
Rose Hawthorne Lathrop
by Julian Hawthorne *231*

Imperiled Men: Mourning CAG
by Andre Dubus... *243*

The Great Heart of Thomas P. "Tip" O'Neill
by Thomas O'Neill III *253*

The Angel of AA: Sister Mary Ignatia
by "Bill W." *259*

Thank God for the Life of Elly Chovel!
by Reverend George A. Garcia.................................. *271*

In the Irish Tradition: Daniel Patrick Moynihan
by Lawrence J. McCaffrey *275*

VI. WE REMEMBER THOSE WHO SHOWED US THE WAY

Didn't He Show Us the Way? Joseph Cardinal Bernardin
by Monsignor Kenneth Velo *289*

The Work of Democracy: César Chávez
by Mario T. Garcia. *295*

The Poster Boy for Hope: Ron Santo
by Monsignor Dan Mayall *305*

Elizabeth Ann Seton is the First Wholly American Saint!
Homily of the Holy Father Pope Paul VI *309*

Fixed, Solid, Holding a True Position:
Rev. Robert F. Griffin, CSC
by Luis R. Gamez *315*

One Witness, Pointing: Mary K. Meyer
by Father Mike Coleman *321*

From Slave to Priest: Father Augustine Tolton
by Deacon Harold Burke-Sivers *327*

VII. WE REMEMBER WITH POETRY

Game Called: Babe Ruth Is Gone
by Grantland Rice *335*

Quid Pro Quo: On Losing a Child
by Paul Mariani *337*

His Tools, for My Father
by Michael Fleming *341*

To Mother Marianne
by Robert Louis Stevenson *345*

To Kościuszko
by John Keats *349*

Atonement: Joyce Kilmer, R.I.P.
by Aline Kilmer *353*

To Philip
by Daniel Berrigan, SJ *355*

The Innocents: Mary Surratt and Others
by Al Rocheleau *357*

VIII. WE REMEMBER THE UNKNOWN CHILD

Restoring Dignity to Abandoned Children:
Rest in His Arms.. *365*

NOTES *369*

CREDITS AND PERMISSIONS *381*

DISCUSSION QUESTIONS FOR BOOK CLUBS *387*

ACKNOWLEDGMENTS *389*

ABOUT THE AUTHOR *391*

Strangers, lovers, friends, neighbors, family,
in the body our oneness is displayed in diversity.

Every aisle a path, every step a sign
of the journey we walk together to the end of time.

—Thomas J. Porter
"We Remember, We Believe"

INTRODUCTION

Sharing memories in order to honor the dead goes back to the beginning of Christianity. Jesus asked us to, "Do this in remembrance of me." Not in remembrance of dogma, nor a list of thou-shalt-nots, but to remember a person who *pitched his tent among us* (the literal translation of John's awe-filled words that Christ—*made his dwelling among us.*) So we remember the life of Jesus, commemorate his death, and see him among us now, often "in all his dreadful disguises," as Mother Teresa put it.

But why do we commemorate lesser mortals? Why do we watch funerals of princesses and pop stars on TV? Why do we gather together and recall the lives of our own recently deceased loved ones?

Perhaps because our sense of who we are is linked to other people, especially to those we have loved and—with Catholics in particular—to those we admire. We cherish stories about the saints, and some of us regularly commune with an even greater "cloud of witnesses" which includes sinners (ordinary folks) as well. We may pray to the heavens, but many of us also "talk" silently with departed spouses, grandparents, and dear friends. Our communion of saints is a bond of love, yearning and consolation encompassing those not (and never to be) canonized.

"Cradle" Catholics are taught from an early age to regularly examine their conscience and to set a good example of behavior for children, as well as for others in a sometimes hostile culture. This lifelong examen can lead to the habit of looking for our own models. It's no coincidence so many Catholics are bestselling authors of memoir: Frank McCourt, Mary Karr, Tobias Wolff, Mary Gordon, Edward Kennedy, Tony Hendra, Doris Kearnes Goodwin, John Powers. Such writing forms our classic spiritual literature, from Saint

Augustine and all the doctors of the Church down through the ages.
Fourteen of the deceased Catholics in this collection wrote memoirs.

Commemorations in this book span the American experience. The
earliest subjects, St. Elizabeth Ann Seton and Thaddeus Kościuiszko,
were born before the Declaration of Independence was signed. This
collection includes veterans of major American wars and of peace
advocates. The deceased include six who were awarded the Presidential Medal of Freedom, two recipients of the Congressional Gold
Medal, and three inductees into the National Women's Hall of Fame.

Catholic-American ethnic cultures are also reflected here: African, Cajun, Italian, Swiss, Irish, German, Polish, Lebanese, Aus-
trian, Mexican, Cuban, Slovak/Russian, English, French, Scottish,
Native American. All of these deceased were fully American, either
by birth or naturalization. They include pioneers in social justice,
healthcare, and the arts, as well as founders of distinctly American
religious orders designed to serve all of the people in the land they
had adopted or been born into. "The charity of the good knows no
creed and is confined to no one place," said St. Marianne Cope as
she tended lepers in the Kingdom of Hawaii in the nineteenth century. As with many in this book, her vision was far ahead of her time.
Several of these women were also far ahead of the Church in their
time.

Ah yes, the women. Striving for gender balance was my greatest
challenge. Women have not been eulogized in American history as
men have, not because they haven't made equally significant contributions, but because they have not been equally recognized. This neglect is not only because men wrote our history, but also because of

the humility of these female leaders. "What little good we can do in this world to help and comfort the suffering, we wish to do it quietly and so far as possible unnoticed and unknown," St. Marianne Cope wrote. Indeed, during her life of service, it's possible she was noticed only by the lepers of Molokai'i.

Another self-effacing pioneer, Sister Mary Ignatia (the one co-founder of Alcoholics Anonymous you've never heard of), turned all attention toward her order and the hospital staff whenever anyone tried to thank her for pioneering in-hospital medical treatment for alcoholics. This humility so impressed her two male cofounders that they credited her for inspiring the "Anonymous" aspect of the AA organization.

Catholicism has always provided models of women doing vital work outside the home. The path-forging spirituality of female doctors of the Church have instructed us in faith (Thérèse of Lisieux, Catherine of Siena, and Teresa of Avila); countless other women established orphanages and social programs as part of a lifetime devoted to serving the poor (St. Clare, St. Frances Cabrini, Mother Teresa); even Joan of Arc led on the battlefield. Yet most American Catholics aren't familiar with the work of American women who pioneered hospice; the treatment of cancer and alcoholism; and founded a nationwide educational system, through university, to benefit freed slaves and Native Americans eight decades before the civil rights movement. The names of St. Elizabeth Seton and St. Katharine Drexel may have become better-known since their canonizations in 1975 and 2000, respectively, but their contributions to this country are rarely well-known.

The accomplishments of these women shows them to be rare visionaries. Consider the speaker from a prominent family who made an impassioned plea at the 1893 World's Columbian Exposition in Chicago. Her opening remarks were to an audience of females who then lacked the right to vote:

Oh, woman, the hour has struck when you are to arise and defend your rights, your abilities for competition with men in intellectual and professional endurance, the hour when you are to prove that purity and generosity are for the nation as well as the home.

The speaker, Rose Hawthorne Lathrop, daughter of writer Nathaniel Hawthorne, went on to found an order of nuns. Their years of hands-on service to terminally ill cancer patients, with none of the nuns contracting the disease, proved to the medical community that cancer was not contagious.

An extraordinarily high percentage of the women in this book—and every one of those who were single or widowed—didn't begin what was to become their significant life's work until they were approaching or past the average age of death for their time. All were late bloomers who continued to work many more years into advanced old age. This phenomenon has an awe-inspiring consistency.

Consider those born into the nineteenth century: Rose Lathrop, Marianne Cope, Dorothy Day, Katharine Drexel, and Sister Ignatia. In their era, a woman's life expectancy was between 40.5 and 44.5 years. Rose Lathrop was forty-four when she moved to a New York tenement to care for the dying, initiating what became known as hospice; she was forty-nine when she founded her order of nuns. Marianne Cope was forty-five when she answered a call to go to Hawaii to care for lepers. Dorothy Day was about thirty-seven when she began the Catholic Worker Movement, and Katharine Drexel was thirty-three when she simultaneously established her religious order and a vast nationwide school system for minorities. At age thirty-nine, Sister Ignatia, "the angel of Alcoholics Anonymous," began working with the other two cofounders of AA after her twenty-year career as a musician.

Going back to the eighteenth century, the late bloomer is St. Elizabeth Seton. She founded her order at age thirty-five, in colonial America, when the average life expectancy was twenty-five years. Although that average reflects the high death rate of children, colonists who survived to adulthood were stalked by epidemics of smallpox, influenza, tuberculosis, and malaria. "Indian" massacres also took many lives.

This trend continues into the twenty-first century. Mary K. Meyer began running a settlement house in Kansas at age forty-seven, after a career in business. Elizabeth Christman began her college preparation as a teacher in her fifties; she earned her Ph.D and became an associate professor in her sixties; then she had a long career and died at age ninety-six.

The lesson of these odds-defying, late-blooming women is clear: it is never too late to find your calling, to develop your talents, and to pursue your dream. Women who recreate themselves with a grace-filled spirit can change the face of the earth.

A section in this book is devoted to poems. Elegiac poetry exists in every language, but many more Americans read and wrote poetry in earlier times than we do now. During World War I, Alexander Woollcott visited the grave in France of his New York Times colleague Joyce Kilmer, who had been killed in battle. Woollcott feared the poet Kilmer might have been out of place in his famed "Fighting 69th" Regiment. But that was not the case, as he wrote his editor in 1918:

> [T]hey all knew his verse. I never got over my surprise at finding that all soldiers read verse and most of them write it. Most of them carry a little notebook in which they set down their own couplets.... I found any number of men who had only to fish about in their tattered blouses to bring out the copy of a poem Kilmer wrote in memory of some of their number who were killed ....

After the newspaper announced Kilmer's death, it was flooded with poetic tributes written by readers, and many were published. The day has long passed when newspapers publish verse written by readers, but people still write elegies. Perhaps composing a poem helps make sense of sorrow and honors the deceased when ordinary language seems insufficient. Several of the prose eulogies in this collection also end with a poem, as if the speaker needed help to finish pondering a loved one's life, and decided, appropriately, to let the poet have the last word.

Honored here are fathers, mothers, brothers, sisters, spouses, children, teammates, coaches, friends, colleagues, competitors, shipmates, and mentors. Although a handful of the deceased have been canonized, and many were recognized as great leaders, this collection also reminds us that the world is full of unsung people who lived righteously. The lifelong benefits derived from mothers and fathers who raised their children well; from a loving spouse; from a sibling who always had their back; from the teacher who recognized their gift—such people are heroes to those whose lives they have enriched.

Who inspired such people is a very Catholic concern, and these American lives reflect a development of influences over time. Francis of Assisi and Thomas á Kempis were most often cited by those who lived in the late-eighteenth century. Many also mentioned Thérèse Lisieux and Catherine of Siena. European role models gave way to an American role model once Dorothy Day began writing about her Catholic Worker Movement. Day became—and remains—the single most frequently cited inspiration among these American Catholics since the mid-twentieth century.

The Gospel of Matthew was another guiding light. Mary K. Meyer took to heart its mandate to visit the prisoner and feed the hungry in her career as a peace advocate and homeless shelter director. Former Speaker of the House Tip O'Neill considered the Beatitudes (Matthew 5:1-13) "the greatest political speech ever written." Others cited Dr. Martin Luther King, Jr. and Gandhi as role models, and Robert F. Kennedy influenced lives as diverse as César Chávez and singer Rosemary Clooney.

The oldest *In Memoriam* tributes are offered in the language of their time. I present these pieces without substituting contemporary usage for archaic words, spelling or punctuation. Reflecting their individual creators, tributes appear here as they did then.

When I began compiling these remembrances, I assumed their central message would be some form of "Well done, thy good and faithful servant." But I found they encompass a wider territory. Often, the task is to draw meaning out of an unthinkable loss and to comfort those left behind after the death of a child, or, in one case, a suicide.

These remind us that the world we inhabit differs from televised funerals with celebrity eulogists. Where we live—and die—eulogy is not a performance art: It is a gift, often necessarily an act of self-sacrifice. In everyday life, most people name public speaking as their greatest fear, even above dying. This means, as columnist Peggy Noonan once pointed out, if asked to choose between standing at the lectern and lying in the coffin at a funeral, most people would opt to be the dead body. Speaking at a memorial service about someone we cared for, while also mourning that loss, is a sacrificial act for most of us and not without its accompanying terrors.

All of this brings us back to why we want and even need to do this. The common theme in eulogies suggests an answer: it seems to be "What this Catholic life has taught me." Although only one of the deceased in this collection was a teacher by profession, the inescapable conclusion here is that we are all teachers—like it or not. And that we can be all perpetual students as well, as long as we are paying attention. There is something hopeful in that, and in all the Christian death rituals. The last rites, the wake, the funeral, the Mass cards, the food—and especially shared reminiscences about a loved one—make grief more bearable. They mean that we are not alone: It is in community, at a time of loss, that healing begins.

Unless we've been there and done that, it would seem counterintuitive that eulogies so often involve laughter. What makes us smile as we read them usually filled a church with the loud laughter of mourners. Such shared delight in the midst of grief can only occur in community. It affirms the bond of those who loved and lost someone and is deeply reassuring. Solitary grieving cannot accommodate laughter.

The shared memories can also heal, as they broaden or confirm our own experience with the deceased. At a time when memories are all we will have left of someone dear to us, eulogies allow us to add to those memories. This experience can also give us great appreciation for the storyteller. We form as vivid an impression of many of the eulogists in this collection as we do of their subjects.

We also inevitably reflect upon our own life when we do this, wondering how we will be remembered. We review the cycle of life, loss, and the end of suffering, and may consider how it is we want to go on living. Because such tributes are *about* the deceased but *for* the living, they can help us find the strength to go back to our life, and to live it more deliberately.

The dead don't need to be told what their life has meant to us. We who are still here need to tell it and to share it.

Carol DeChant
Sarasota, FL
July 4, 2015

I. WE REMEMBER
Our Heroes

THE HAPPIEST MAN ON EARTH:
CHAPLAIN MYCHAL JUDGE, NYFD

by Father Michael Duffy
September 15, 2001
St. Francis of Assisi Church, New York, NY

The first recorded death of the September 11, 2001, terrorist attacks on the United States was that of peace-loving Franciscan Friar Mychal Judge. Chaplain of the New York City Fire Department, Father Judge was killed while ministering to those firefighters who were first on the scene. Ultimately, some four-hundred-and-seventeen firefighters, paramedics, and police officers lost their lives in the Twin Towers.

This eulogy was given just four days later to a city still in shock, before the full extent of the devastation was known.

After all that has been written about Father Mychal Judge in the newspapers, after all that has been spoken about him on television, the compliments, the accolades, the great tribute that was given to him last night at the wake service, I stand in front of you and honestly feel that the homilist at Mother Teresa's funeral had it easier than I do.

We Franciscans have very many traditions. You, who know us, know that some are odd, some are good. I don't know what category this one fills.

One of our traditions is that we're all given a sheet of paper. The title on the top says, "On the Occasion of Your Death." Notice, it doesn't say, "In case you die." We all know that it's not a matter of *if*, it's a matter of *when*. But on that sheet of paper lists categories that each one of us is to fill out: where we want our funeral celebrated, what readings we'd like, what music we'd like, where we'd like to be buried.

Mychal Judge filled out, next to the word "homilist," my name: Mike Duffy. I didn't know this until Wednesday morning. I was shaken and shocked...for one thing, as you know from this gathering, Mychal Judge knew thousands of people. He seemed to know everybody in the world. And if he didn't then, they know him now, I'm sure. Certainly he had friends that were more intellectual than I, certainly more holy than I, people more well-known. And so I sat with that thought, "Why me?" And I came down to the conclusion that I was simply and solely his friend...and I'm honored to be called that.

I always tell my volunteers in Philadelphia that through life, you're lucky if you have four or five people whom you can truly call a friend. And you can share any thought you have, enjoy their company, be parted and separated, come back together again and pick up right where you left off. They'll forgive your faults and affirm your virtues. Mychal Judge was one of those people for me. And I believe and hope I was for him.

We as a nation have been through a terrible four days, and it doesn't look like it's ending. Pope John Paul called Tuesday a "dark day in the history of humanity." He said it was a terrible affront to human dignity. In our collective emotions, in our collective consciousness, all went through the same thing on Tuesday morning.

I was driving a van in Philadelphia, picking up food for our soup kitchen, when I began to hear the news, one after another after another. You all share that with me. We all felt the same. It was at two o'clock in the afternoon that I came back to the soup kitchen, feeling very heavy with the day's events. At four-thirty, I received a call from Father Ron Pecci. We were serving a meal to the homeless. And he said, "It's happened." I said, "What?" And he said, "Mychal Judge is dead."

At that moment, my already-strained emotions did spiritually what the World Trade towers had done physically just hours before.

And I felt my whole spirit crumble to the ground and turn into a pile of rubble at the bottom of my heart. I sat down on the stairs to the cellar, with the phone still to my ear, and we cried for fifteen minutes.

Later, in my room, a very holy friar whom I have the privilege to live with gently slipped a piece of paper in front of me and whispered, "This was written thousands of years ago in the midst of a national tragedy. It's a quote from the book of Lamentations: 'The favors of the Lord are not exhausted. His mercies are not spent. Every morning, they are renewed. Great is his faithfulness. I will always trust in him.'"

I read that quote and I pondered and listened. I thought of other passages in the Gospel that said evil will not triumph. That in the darkest hour when Jesus lay dying on the cross, that suffering led to the resurrection.

I read and thought that the light is better than darkness, hope better than despair. And in thinking of my faith, and the faith of Mychal Judge, and all he taught me, and from scripture, I began to lift up my head and once again see the stars.

And so today I have the courage to stand in front of you and celebrate Mychal's life. For it is his life that speaks, not his death. It is his courage that he showed on Tuesday that speaks, not my fear. And it is his hope and belief in the goodness of all people that speaks, not my despair. And so I am here to talk about my friend.

Because so much has been written about him, I'm sure you know his history. He was a New Yorker through and through. As you know, he was born in Brooklyn. Some of you may not know this, but he was a twin—Dympna is his sister. He was born May 11, she was born May 13. Even in birth, Mychal had to have a story. He just did nothing normally, no.

He grew up in Brooklyn playing stickball and riding his bike like all the little kids then. Then he put some shoe polish and rags in a bag, rode his bicycle over here, and in front of the Flatiron building shined shoes for extra money. But very early on in his life, when he was a teenager—and this is a little unusual—because of the faith that his mother and his sisters passed on to him, because of his love for God and Jesus, he thought he would like to be a Franciscan for the rest of his life. And so, as a teenager, he joined the friars. And he never left. He never left because his spirit was truly, purely Franciscan: simple, joyful, life-loving, and laughter. He was ordained in 1961 and spent many years as a parish priest in New Jersey: East Rutherford, Rochelle Park, West Milford. Spent some time at Siena College. One year, I believe, in Boston.

And then he came back to his beloved New York. I came to know him ten years after he was ordained. This is ironic: My thirtieth anniversary of ordination was Tuesday, September 11. This always was a happy day for me, and I think from now, it's going to be mixed.

My first assignment was wonderful: I was sent to East Rutherford, New Jersey, and Mychal was there doing parochial work. In the seminary we learned a lot of theory, but you really have to get out with people to know how to deal and how to really minister. So, I arrived there with my eyes wide open and my ears wide open. And my model turned out to be Mychal Judge. He was, without knowing it, my mentor, and I was his pupil. I watched how he dealt with people. He really was a people person. While the rest of us were running around organizing altar boys and choirs and liturgies and decoration, he was in his office listening. His heart was open. His ears were open, and especially he listened to people with problems.

He carried around with him an appointment book. He had appointments to see people four and five weeks in advance. He would come to the rec room at night at one-thirty, having just finished his last appointment, because when he related to a person, they felt like he was their best friend. When he was talking with you, you were the only person on the face of the earth. And he loved people, and that showed, and that makes all the difference. You can serve people, but unless you love them, it's not really ministry. In fact, a description that St. Bonaventure wrote of St. Francis once, I think, is very apt for Mychal: St. Bonaventure said that St. Francis had a bent for compassion. Certainly Mychal Judge did.

The other thing about Mychal Judge is he loved to be where the action was. If he heard a fire engine or a police car, any news, he'd be off. He loved to be where there was a crisis, so he could insert God in what was going on. That was his way of doing things.

I remember once I came back to the friary and the secretary told me, "There's a hostage situation in Carlstadt, and Mychal Judge is up there." I got in the car and drove there: A man on the second floor with a gun pointed to his wife's head and the baby in her arms. He threatened to kill her. There were several people around, lights, policemen, and a fire truck. And where was Mychal Judge? Up on the ladder in his habit, on the top of the ladder, talking to the man through the window of the second floor. I nearly died, because in one hand he had his habit out like this, because he didn't want to trip.

So, he was hanging on the ladder with one hand. He wasn't very dexterous, anyway. His head was bobbing like, "Well, you know, John, maybe we can work this out. This really isn't the way to do it. Why don't you come downstairs, and we'll have a cup of coffee and talk this thing over?"

I thought, "He's going to fall off the ladder. There's going to be gunplay." Not one ounce of fear did he show. He was telling him, "You know, you're a good man, John. You don't need to do this." I don't know what happened, but he put the gun down, and the wife and the baby's lives were saved. Of course, there were cameras there. Wherever there was a photographer within a mile, you could be sure the lens was pointed at Mychal Judge. In fact, we used to accuse him of paying *The Bergen Record*'s reporter to follow him around.

Another aspect, a lesson that I learned from him, his way of life, is his simplicity. He lived simply. He didn't have many clothes. They were always pressed, of course, and clean, but he didn't have much. No clutter in his very simple room.

He would say to me once in a while, "Michael Duffy"—he always called me by my full name—"Michael Duffy you know what I need?" And I would get excited because it was hard to buy him a present.

I said, "No, what?"

"You know what I really need?"

"No, what Mike?"

"Absolutely nothing. I don't need a thing in the world. I am the happiest man on the face of the earth." And then he would go on for ten minutes, telling me how blessed he felt. "I have beautiful sisters. I have nieces and nephews. I have my health. I'm a Franciscan priest. I love my work. I love my ministry." And he would go on, and always conclude by looking up to heaven and saying, "Why am I so blessed? I don't deserve it. Why am I so blessed?" But that's how he felt all his life.

Another characteristic of Mychal Judge: he loved to bless people, and I mean physically. Even if they didn't ask. A little old lady would come up to him and he'd talk to her, you know, as if she was the only person on the face of the earth. Then he'd say, "Let me give you a blessing." He put his big, thick Irish hands and pressed her head till I thought the poor woman would be crushed, and he'd look up to heaven, and he'd ask God to bless her, give her health and give her peace and so forth.

A young couple would come up to him and say, "We just found out we're going to have a baby."

"Oh, that's wonderful! That's great!" He'd put his hand on the woman's stomach and call to God to bless the unborn child.

When I used to take teenagers on bus trips, he'd jump in the bus, lead the teenagers in prayer, and then bless them all for a safe and a happy time. If a husband and wife were in crisis, he would go up to them, take both their hands at the same time, and put them right next to his and whisper a blessing that the crisis would be over.

He loved to bring Christ to people. He was the bridge between people and God, and he loved to do that. And many times over the past few days, several people have come up and said, "Father Mychal did my wedding. Father Mychal baptized my child. Father Mychal came to us when we were in crisis." There are so many things that Father Mychal Judge did for people. I think there's not one registry in a rectory in this diocese that doesn't have his name in it for something, a baptism, a marriage, or whatever.

But what you may not know, it really was a two-way street. You people think he did so much for you. But you didn't see it from our side, we that lived with him. He would come home and be energized and nourished and thrilled and be full of life because of you.

He would come back and say to me, for instance, "I met this young man today. He's such a good person. He has more faith in his little finger than I do in my own body. Oh, he's such good people. Oh they're so great." Or, "I baptized a baby today." And just to see the new life, he'd be enthused. I want just to let you know, and I think he'd want me to let you know, how much you did for him. You made his life happy. You made him the kind of person that he was for all of us.

It reminds me of that very well-known Picasso sketch of two hands holding a bouquet of flowers. You know the one I mean—there's a small bouquet, it's colorful, and a hand is coming from the left side and another hand is coming from the right side. Both are holding the bouquet. The artist was clever enough to draw the hands in the exact same angle. You don't know who's receiving and who is giving. And it was the same way with Mychal. You should know how much you gave to him, and it was that love that he had for people, and that way of relating to him, that led him back to New York City and to become part of the fire department.

On Tuesday, one of our friars, Brian Carroll, was walking down Sixth Avenue and actually saw the airplane go overhead at a low altitude. And then a little further, he saw smoke coming from one of the Trade towers. He ran into the friary. He ran into Mychal Judge's room. And he said, "Mychal, I think they're going to need you. I think the World Trade tower is on fire." Mychal was in his habit. So, he jumped up, took off his habit, got his uniform on, and I have to say this, in case you really think he's perfect, he did take time to comb and spray his hair.

But just for a second, I'm sure. He ran down the stairs, and he got in his car, and with some firemen, he went to the World Trade towers. While he was down there, one of the first people he met was the mayor, Mayor Giuliani. Later, the mayor recounted how he put his hand on Mychal's shoulder and said, "Mychal, please pray for us." And Mychal turned and with that big Irish smile said, "I always do."

And then kept on running with the firefighters into the building. While he was ministering to dying firemen, administering the Sacrament of the Sick and Last Rites, Mychal Judge died. The firemen scooped him up to get him out of the rubble and carried him out of the building and wouldn't you know it? There was a photographer there. That picture appeared in *The New York Times, The New York Daily News* and *USA Today* on Wednesday, and someone told me last night that *People* magazine has that same picture in it. I bet he planned it that way.

When you step back and see how my friend Mychal died, when we finish grieving, when all this is over and we can put things in perspective, look how that man died. He was right where the action was, where he always wanted to be. He was praying, because in the ritual for anointing, we're always saying, "Jesus come, Jesus forgive, Jesus save." He was talking to God, and he was helping someone. Can you honestly think of a better way to die? I think it was beautiful.

The firemen took his body, and because they respected and loved him so much, they didn't want to leave it in the street. They quickly carried it into a church, and instead of just leaving it in the vestibule, they went up the center aisle. They put the body in front of the altar. They covered it with a sheet. And on the sheet, they placed his stole and his fire badge. And then they knelt down and they thanked God. And then they rushed back to continue their work.

And so, in my mind, I picture Mychal Judge's body in that church, realizing that the firefighters brought him back to the Father in the Father's house. And the words that come to me, "I am the Good Shepherd, and the Good Shepherd lays down his life for the sheep. Greater love than this no man hath than to lay down his life for his friends. And I call you my friends."

So I make this statement to you this morning that Mychal Judge has always been my friend. And now he is also my hero.

Mychal Judge's body was the first one released from Ground Zero. His death certificate has the number one on the top. I meditated on the fact of the thousands of people that we are going to find out who perished in that terrible holocaust. Why was Mychal Judge number one? And I think I know the reason. Mychal's goal and purpose in life at that time was to bring the firemen to the point of death, so they would be ready to meet their maker. There are between two and three hundred firemen buried there, the commissioner told us last night.

Mychal Judge could not have ministered to them all. It was physically impossible in this life but not in the next. And I think that if he were given his choice, he would prefer to have happened what actually happened. He passed through the other side of life, and now he can continue doing what he wanted to do with all his heart. And the next few weeks, we're going to have names added, name after name, of people who are being brought out of that rubble. And Mychal Judge is going to be on the other side of death to greet them instead of sending them there. And he's going to greet them with that big Irish smile. He's going to take them by the arm and the hand and say, "Welcome, I want to take you to my Father." And so, he can continue doing in death what he couldn't do in life.

And so, this morning we come to bury Mychal Judge's body but not his spirit. We come to bury his mind but not his dreams. We come to bury his voice but not his message. We come to bury his hands but not his good works. We come to bury his heart but not his love.

Never his love.

We his family, friends, and those who loved him, should return the favor that he so often did for us. We have felt his big hands at a blessing. Right now, it would be so appropriate if we called on what the liturgy tells us we are: a royal priesthood and a holy nation. And we give Mychal a blessing as he returns to the Father.

So, please stand. And raise your right hand and extend it towards my friend Mychal and repeat after me.

Mychal, may the Lord bless you. May the angels lead you to your Savior. You are a sign of his presence to us. May the Lord now embrace you and hold you in his love forever. Rest in peace. Amen.

AN AMERICAN ORIGINAL:
MOTHER KATHARINE DREXEL

by Anthony Walton
Autumn, 2004

Katharine Drexel's long life spanned twenty American presidencies. She lived through our country's bloodiest wars and Indian massacres, from the Civil War to the year that America sent its first military advisors into Vietnam. Eulogist Anthony Walton, an African-American studies specialist and writer in residence at Bowdoin College in Brunswick, Maine, rightly sees her as an "American original" who greatly impacted her country, although she transcended its politics and every known style of leadership. He wrote this memorial tribute after she was canonized.

By the time she was twenty-one, Katharine had made her debut into society, refused a marriage proposal, and was writing her former pastor, Bishop James O'Connor, about her vocation. His new diocese included the Northeast Territory, Dakota, and parts of Montana, Missouri, and Wyoming. His letters told of the terrible Custer massacre and of America's betrayal of the Indians.

The order of nuns she founded in 1891, at age thirty-three, added to their pledge of poverty, chastity, and obedience a vow unique in American and Catholic history: "To be the mother and servant of the Indian and Negro races according to the rule of the Sisters of the Blessed Sacrament; and not to undertake any work which would lead to the neglect or abandonment of the Indian or Colored races." She dedicated her vast fortune and her life to that work.

Katharine's father had set up a trust in order to protect his daughters from fortune hunters. Their fourteen-million dollar inheritance was divided into three equal portions; the daughters were to receive the income. It is impossible to give an exact modern equivalent on such an amount from 1885, the year he died, but it is safe to say that each daughter would *have had an income of more than 100 million in today's dollars. Katharine outlived both of her childless sisters, inherited their income, and gave it all to her work.*

And what amazing work it was: establishing a vast charitable empire that built and staffed schools and churches across America, operated by more than five hundred nuns of her order at the time of her death. She served as CEO, COO, and CFO, negotiating with architects, lawyers, contractors, tribes, and community and diocesan officials, while overseeing the education and faith formation of her own expanding congregation of nuns.

She usually built schools in remote bayou, desert, and rural areas, where the need was greatest. She worked in primitive conditions and travelled by horse, stage coach, and train. She survived typhoid with pneumonia, although some of her nuns died from the rigors of such service.

As early as 1903, eleven of her nuns were educated Navajo women, ready to carry on her work. And by showing what African-Americans could do given the opportunity, she influenced many Catholic schools to accept them long before integration was nationally mandated.

She didn't live to see the passage of the 1964 Civil Rights Act or the U. S. Indian Claims Commission's efforts toward the government's reparation for its wrongs against minorities. But Mother Drexel had begun the task of reparations eighty years before. She and the women who joined her had done much to save America from its great shame.

Any appreciation of Mother Drexel ends with the question: Who was this woman, so far removed from every notion of what a woman of her time could be or do? Two traits offer a clue. The many letters she left behind reveal a witty woman whose lively sense of humor often targeted herself, and one whose friends and associates invariably cited the joy that she radiated and brought to her mission. That joy is said to survive among the sisters of the Blessed Sacrament, the "fruit of the Spirit" described in Scripture as a notable grace in difficult times.

Her eulogist understands that focusing on the astonishing fortune she gave away can be misleading when assessing St. Katharine's service. For she gave something even more valuable to African- and Native-Americans: She gave dignity and hope, and ultimately, she gave herself.

~~~

The *Oxford Dictionary of Saints* describes Katharine Drexel as a "long-lived American lady...often forgotten...who devoted her life and considerable fortune to American Indians and African Americans." Drexel was by turns heroic, complicated, and an absolute U. S. original—a woman who was both saintly in the traditional ways of spiritual and religious conviction, and entirely effective within the legal, social and political realities of her time and place. But she seems virtually anonymous in U. S. history and in the day-to-day experience of the American Catholic Church. This may in fact have been her wish, but she is someone everyone in the United States, not just Catholics, should recognize, admire and understand. Our society has yet to resolve the issues to which she chose to dedicate her life and resources, and there is much to learn from her actions and achievements.

Katharine Drexel was born on November 26, 1858, to Francis and Hannah Langstroth Drexel, members of the extraordinarily wealthy Drexel family of Philadelphia. Francis Drexel and his brother Anthony were globally prominent investment bankers and business partners of Junius and J. P. Morgan, the most powerful financiers of the nineteenth century. The Drexels were involved with the financing of the construction of the railroads, shipping canals and other key components of the U. S. industrial revolution. Katharine was the second daughter and, after the death of her mother when she was five weeks old, was raised by a kind and devout stepmother, Emma Bouvier. The Drexels lived in palatial comfort, at the pinnacle of high society. But they were also known for their extensive charity and philanthropy: The second Mrs. Drexel yearly gave away what today would be more than eleven million dollars, regularly passed out food and clothing to the city's poor directly from the family mansion, and supported many other charities anonymously, activities that had a lasting effect on the values and world-view of her stepdaughter. As a child Katharine secretly gave away money and was relieved that her father encouraged rather than chastised her when he found out.

At age fourteen, the young heiress considered joining a convent. She was discouraged by her parents, who wanted her to marry and have children, and by her priest and spiritual adviser, Bishop James O'Connor, who believed that a young woman so accustomed to wealth and freedom would have trouble adjusting to convent life. Katharine herself had doubts—enduring trials of spirit which she set forth in a series of eloquent, unsparingly honest journals and letters. Among her reasons for questioning her fitness, she listed, "I hate community life.... I'd hate never to be alone. I do not know how I could bear the privations of poverty of the religious life. I have never been deprived of luxuries."

When Katharine was twenty-one years old, Emma Bouvier Drexel developed cancer, and in the three years before her death endured excruciating pain. Rather than leading Katharine to question her faith, nursing Mrs. Drexel and witnessing the intense physical hardship seems to have deepened it. Katharine became convinced that suffering was an inescapable part of the human condition and decided that any truth which transcended suffering could be found only through devotion to God. Following Emma's death, while on a trip out west with her father, Katharine was profoundly disturbed by the appalling conditions she witnessed on the government's poorly administered Indian reservations. When she inherited money upon her father's death in 1885, she began donating large sums toward bettering the situation of Native Americans. She had become deeply concerned as well with the plight of the recently freed African Americans, particularly in the Deep South.

Through these interests her spiritual calling grew to outweigh her self-doubts. She would write, "I didn't think of becoming a religious until years after I'd become interested in missionary work on the Indian reservations. It was long after I'd helped build schools for Indians and Negroes, and endeavored to get priests and nuns to do the work of religious training in those schools. It suddenly seemed one night that something inside of me was saying, 'Why do you keep sending other people to do this great work for you? Why don't you do it yourself?'"

In 1891, the same year her uncle Anthony founded the Drexel Institute of Art, Science and Industry (now Drexel University), Katharine Drexel took her final religious vows in an order she founded. She called the order the Sisters of the Blessed Sacrament for Indians and Colored People. Though she strongly felt the need for a new order of nuns specifically devoted to African American and Native American populations, she questioned her own fitness for the role of Mother Superior: "The responsibility of such a call almost crushes me," she wrote to Bishop O'Connor, "because I am so infinitely poor in the virtues necessary." However, with O'Connor's encouragement and his faith—after many years of struggle—in the strength of her calling, she agreed to head her new order.

Today we most likely interpret the actions of someone who dedicates herself to the cause of the betterment of racial minorities as a kind of social worker. We might even disparage such a person as naive, motivated by political pieties and the guilt of privilege. Such simplifications fall away in the case of Drexel, who was, first and foremost, a young woman completely immersed in her relationship with God. She wanted to go as far as she could into that relationship (her initial wish as a young adult had been to join a contemplative and cloistered, rather than active, order), and her missionary and social work grew from a desire to share with others what she had found in her spiritual development.

This is a different motivation from that which is commonly seen in our society's pursuit of social concerns. Understanding that difference is crucial when studying her life. In Drexel's view, it was not enough to provide money and material relief. As she understood things, there was to be no peace in life without God, and she believed that the disregarded African and Native American populations could not be fully emancipated and equal members of society until they knew religion—until they had fully experienced for themselves God's love and liberation, just as she had. And to know religion, she reasoned, they had to be *educated.*

Drexel as a revolutionary—but a quiet one. She and her initial group of fifteen nuns founded an Indian school in Santa Fe, New Mexico, in 1893, and founded several others in the years that followed. She faced bitter opposition from within and outside the Catholic church. Inside the church of that time, as Father Joseph Martino—the priest assigned by the Vatican to write the *positio* arguing for her canonization—noted, "Most Catholic priests abhorred working with Blacks because of racial prejudice." Martino summarizes at length a letter written to the Holy See by a Belgian missionary to the American South in the early 1900s, stating that "Black girls were denied admission to convents, and there were also girls who had been expelled from religious communities, even years after, once it was discovered that they were actually Black."

Opposition from the outside was even more intense. The main center for the Sisters of the Blessed Sacrament in Bensalem, Pennsylvania, received a bomb threat when it was under construction. One of the buildings of a school in Rock Castle, Virginia, was destroyed by arson in 1899; in Texas, in 1922, the Ku Klux Klan threatened to burn down another of Drexel's schools. Countless similar threats were received and summarily ignored as the Sisters of the Blessed Sacrament persisted in their work.

Operating in the segregated South, Mother Katharine never called directly for the overthrow of the Jim Crow legal system. Instead she followed a hard-headed and pragmatic strategy that was probably the only one, in that social era and context, which had a possibility of working: "Render unto Caesar that which is Caesar's." Nominally living within the laws of the jurisdictions where they found themselves, the sisters insisted, in the work and practices of the order, on the equal worth of every individual. It was customary in Catholic churches in the South to make blacks stand or sit in roped-off areas at the rear. Following Drexel's orders, the churches connected to the Sisters of the Blessed Sacrament offered two rows of pews running from front to back, one for the blacks and one for whites, side by side. This small step in the direction of equality gave segregationist authorities no statutory grounds for closing the churches down. When confronted with intense resistance in certain locales to the opening of schools for African Americans, the sisters quietly put in practice another of Christ's maxims, "Be as wise as serpents and as gentle as doves." They utilized shell corporations and other legal maneuvering to purchase land anonymously and circumvent opposition.

The simultaneous delicacy of spirit and iron force of will evident in Drexel's life and works are stunning. From its modest beginnings of a small number of schools and missions, the Sisters of the Blessed Sacrament were able to train teachers from the disadvantaged groups who then went out to found new schools and teach others. Drexel's insight in setting in motion a process of teachers creating teachers and community leaders in an ever-expanding pool of educated men and women amounts to a kind of genius. It is one of the most long-lasting and solid foundations that has been built in the attempt to provide assistance to African and Native Americans. The order was ultimately responsible for founding one-hundred forty-five missions, twelve schools for Native Americans, and fifty schools for African Americans.

Katharine Drexel, who died in 1955 at age 96, did not wish to be considered for canonization. Canonization requires significant amounts of money for research and documentation, and she, according to *Making Saints* by Kenneth L. Woodward...believed "the money required for the process would be better spent on helping Indians and blacks." Her cause, however, had such enormous support, including from many of those who had been educated at her schools, that the process was set in motion. Canonization requires extensive documentation of miracles performed through prayer to the individual in question; in Drexel's case, two deaf individuals regained their hearing in ways inexplicable to doctors. But by far the great miracle, as Pope John Paul II emphasized in his homily at her canonization Mass in 2000, lay in what she accomplished during her life.

Xavier University in New Orleans stands as perhaps the most notable testament to the force of Katharine Drexel's vision.

Xavier was founded in 1915 through an initial grant of $750,000 from Drexel. The only historically black and Catholic college in the United States, Xavier was—according to nuns of her order—one of the projects closest to Drexel's heart. Xavier began with a small collection of buildings on the grounds of what had previously been a high school; today it has grown to house more than 3,800 students. *The New York Times' Selective Guide to Colleges* describes Xavier as "a school where achievement has been the rule and beating the odds against success a routine occurrence."

Xavier currently places more African Americans into medical schools than any other college in the nation. It awards more degrees than does any other college to African Americans in biology and the life sciences, in the physical sciences, and in physics. Its prominent graduates have included Alvin Boutte, class of 1951, founder and CEO of Indecorp Hotels; Louis Castenall, class of '68, dean of the University of Cincinnati's College of Education, praised by *The New York Times* and *The Washington Post* for his innovations in teacher education; and Alexis Herman, class of '69, the first black U. S. secretary of labor. With its stated mission of preparing students "to assume roles of leadership and service in society," Xavier has graduated countless others who have led in smaller but deeply significant ways in their communities, among them physician Regina Benjamin, class of '79, who returned to her home region of Bayou La Batre, Alabama, to found a health clinic dedicated to serving people who lacked the money to afford health care. She financed the clinic herself for over a decade by moonlighting in the ERs of local hospitals.

Drexel's emphasis on the central importance of equal education holds key lessons for a society that was—as Pope John Paul II stated at her canonization Mass—still torn apart in many ways by issues of race. The ripple effects of Drexel's work can never precisely be measured or calculated, but it is hard to imagine that even she could have predicted these effects. Then again, given the central mystery of a life of faith in any age, particularly ours, perhaps it is not so hard. She once wrote of her mission, "I looked up in wonder at God's wonderful ways and thought, 'How little we imagine what may be the result of listening and acting on a desire He puts into the heart. He will bless it, if we try to act upon it.'"

She made one request at Xavier University's dedication ceremony: that her own name not be mentioned. She watched, unmentioned and unremarked, from a seat at the back of the auditorium.

A HERO'S LAST MARCH:
GENERAL WILLIAM TECUMSEH SHERMAN

author unknown
February 19, 1891

General William Tecumseh Sherman's son, Thomas, a Jesuit priest, features prominently in this elegiac newspaper coverage of the General's death. The funeral was delayed five days so that Thomas could make the Atlantic crossing home from England. During this time, friends came to view the open casket in the Sherman house in New York. Every incident of these days was covered in the press.

Newspapers at the time, and some subsequent biographers, have disputed Sherman's desire to receive last rites. The General's complicated Catholic history was no secret: Sherman had been a foster child in the home of Thomas Ewing, whose wife and children were Catholic. Two priests officiated Sherman's marriage to a Ewing daughter. Although it was a notable event—President Zachary Taylor, his Cabinet, and Senators Henry Clay and Daniel Webster were among the guests—it was a home wedding because it was a "mixed marriage." Although he had been baptized in the Ewing home as a boy, neither Sherman nor his beloved foster father—at that time—was a practicing Catholic. (When he was elderly, Thomas Ewing requested to be baptized and receive the sacraments.)

Of the couple's eight children, two of their four sons died young. In his memoir, Sherman writes of his devastation at losing his oldest son Willy: "that child upon whose future I based all the ambition I ever had." When the nine-year-old boy died, Sherman wrote from the battlefield to Willy's younger brother Thomas: "You must take Poor Willy's place, to take care of your sisters, and to fill my place when I am gone."

Years later Thomas wrote friends, "I go [to the seminary]…in direct opposition to his best wishes on my behalf, for he had…other hopes and expectations in my regard." He admitted to being "painfully aware that I have grieved and disappointed my father."

Sherman eventually became a widower, with grown daughters who lived beyond his means. He wrote friends lamenting that Thomas was not there to help him support their expensive habits. Evidence exists in the Sherman family papers at Notre Dame University, however, that in spite of their differences, Sherman maintained an affectionate correspondence with Thomas throughout his life. Two of the daughters eventually married, and the youngest child and last son, Philemon, became a lawyer and helped support the maiden sisters.

After their father died, the Sherman children protested newspaper reports which suggested they had sacraments administered to a father too frail to object. An interview that ran alongside this tribute to the General allowed Father Thomas to reply: "My father was baptized in the Catholic Church, married in the Catholic Church, and attended the Catholic Church until the outbreak of the Civil War. Since that time my father has not been a communicant, but he always said to me: 'If there is any true religion it is the Catholic religion.' A week ago to-day my father received absolution and extreme unction at the hands of Father Taylor. My father was unconscious at the time, but this fact has no important bearing, for the Sacrament could be administered to any person whose mind could be interpreted as desirous of receiving it."

A Sherman biographer adds that the last rites were administered one morning before Father Thomas arrived, and that the General rallied later that day, got out of bed, and talked briefly, saying that "Faithful and Honorable" was what he wanted on his tombstone.

This tribute is recorded as it appeared in the 1891 Philadelphia Inquirer, preserving some now-archaic words, spelling and punctuation. Omitted are final paragraphs detailing the route of the funeral procession through the New York streets and the lengthy list of dignitaries accompanying the coffin. Two of these were Catholic archbishops; another two were priests.

An honorary pallbearer was Confederate General Joseph E. Johnston, who had surrendered his forces to Sherman in North Carolina after Lee had surrendered to Grant. The papers did not know at the time that Johnston, then eighty-two, was advised to put on his hat to protect himself from the cold February weather during the funeral procession. Johnston *refused, saying, "If I were in his place and he were standing here in mine, he would not put on his hat." Ten days later, Johnston died of pneumonia.*

A HERO'S LAST MARCH

A MAGNIFICENT TRIBUTE
TO THE MEMORY OF THE DEAD GENERAL

The Rev. Father Thomas E. Sherman Reads the Church
Service Over His Father's Body—Booming Guns and Toiling
Bells Greet the Sad Cortege as It Passes Through the Streets

SPECIAL TO THE PHILADELPHIA INQUIRER
New York, Feb. 19

His work is done,
But while the races of mankind endure
Let his great example stand
Colossal, seen of every land,
And keep the soldier firm, the statesman pure,
Till, in all lands and through all human story,
The path of duty be the way to glory.

The sword is sheathed. The man whose life lent honor to a nation is borne to-day to his last home. But he, being dead, yet speaketh. For he lives in his deeds, and his deeds can never die in history. He was one of those who saved a nation, and the memory of him shall keep it safe and pure. The hearts of all his country men are sad this day—sad, and yet proud; they are bowed in grief, for Sherman is no more; they are high with pride, for Sherman has been.

The boys in blue and the boys in gray take hands to-day. Over this patriot hero's bier they stand in national fraternity, and pride and

reverence—those who stormed Fort McAllister; those who trained
the rebel guns; those who swept with Sherman to the sea, and those
who fled before his flowing battalions.

There is no man of them living who does not feel a heart pang
to-day. The dull tramp of the funeral march echoes in every breast.

The head of the English army—the old Duke of Cambridge—
said a few months ago that this century had given birth to three
great generals. And these three—one of them is an old, bent, slight
man, whom the curious look upon in Berlin (von Moltke). The other
two were Grant and Sherman. Each in his own way is great. It may
be they were equally great. He had the faculty of winning the love
of those he led; there is no soldier living who would not have given
up his life for "Uncle Billy." This was shown whenever the general
appeared in public.

Republics have been taunted with ingratitude. To-day the
greatest Republic of time refutes the libel. Over the grave of a man
that it has always loved and honored a nation weeps to-day, and in
a short time it shall rear a monument worthy of itself and worthy of
the warrior. But forever the best monument shall be in the hearts of
the people, for he was of the people and for the people.

Not since the great demonstration which attended the placing
of General Grant's body in the tomb in Riverside Park has there
been seen in this city such impressive ceremonies as those attending
the funeral of General William T. Sherman to-day. The pageant was
less imposing than that which attended Gen. Grant to the grave,
and there was less military pomp and, sad to say there were fewer of
the great figures of war heroes about Sherman's bier than were gathered about the bier of Gen. Grant. About the little vault at Riverside when the Seventh Regiment fired its solemn volleys there stood
Sherman, Hancock, Sheridan and Logan. All these have followed
their great leader into the dark unknown.

Not one of the strong overmastering spirits with which the
memory of the civil war is identified was present in the mourning
procession to-day which bore all this is mortal of General Sherman away from New York forever. They are gone—all gone. Sher-

man himself was the last. But of all his old comrades in arms who have gone before him not one left more genuine sorrow behind than did Sherman. Above all the admiration for the successful soldier and brilliant general there was in the hearts of all the people a sadness akin to that which comes with a personal grief. Sherman's lovable manly personality had endeared itself to the hearts of thousands who had never even seen him.

THE GENERAL'S SON ARRIVES.

The rays of the sun flooded the street in front of the Sherman house at 75 West Seventy-first street, this morning, with cheerful light. The crisp air rendered each sound so distinct that every one spoke in subdued tones and the noise of an occasional carriage or delivery wagon sounded unusually loud.

Small groups of children approached to gaze for a minute at the house and then went back to their play. Half a dozen giant policemen stood on the sidewalk in front of the house and warned visitors to make no noise. The warning was almost unnecessary, for even the least intelligent visitors seemed to be unusually impressed with the near presence of death.

The windows of nearly all the houses in the street displayed the Stars and Stripes. A broad band of black crape on the bottom of each banner lent a sad aspect to the dancing colors.

Father Thomas Sherman arrived at the house at 1.50 o'clock this morning, the exact hour at which his father died on Saturday afternoon. He did not at once visit the room where the remains lay, but rested for a little time. Father Sherman was received at the house by his brother, Mr. P. T. Sherman, Mrs. Thackera and Miss Rachel Sherman. He did not view the remains of his father until 7.30 this morning.

At that time he went alone into the room where the dead warrior lay. The cover had not been replaced on the coffin, and the features could be seen through the glass casing. He was very calm. On his way over he had concealed his identity from the rest of the passengers. He is a singularly retiring man and was anxious to avoid the notice he would have attracted had he been known.

The Majestic on its passage did not meet with any of the vessels from this country which had been instructed to signal the latest news in regard to the general's condition. It was not until Friday that Father Sherman received the first intelligence from a Providence pilot.

CALLERS AT THE HOUSE.

At 11 o'clock Secretary of Agriculture Rusk and Secretary of War Proctor drove up, and were received at the door by Lieutenant Thackera. They were taken to the drawing room, where they viewed the remains of the dead soldier.

A telegram was sent to President Harrison at the Fifth Avenue Hotel this morning, informing him that the casket, which was to be kept open until 12 o'clock for the accommodation of such officers as might wish to see the general's face, would be closed promptly at that hour, and asking him if it would be possible for him to reach the house before noon.

The President replied that he did not wish to see the remains. It was his desire to remember the departed warrior as he had last seen him.

At 11.20 o'clock Secretary Blaine and General Ewing walked up Seventy-first street arm in arm. They entered the house, and Mr. Blaine was immediately taken into the drawing room to view the remains.

THE FUNERAL SERVICES.

Arrangements for the funeral were made early this morning. The fifth choir boys from St. Francis Xavier's Church entered the house at 12 o'clock. They wore no vestments. The services were conducted by Father Thomas Sherman, beginning a few minutes after 12 o'clock.

He read a few passages from the Scriptures, concluding with that portion of the burial service, "I am the resurrection and the life." The services were simple. The choir boys, under the leadership of B. A. Kline, of St. Francis Xavier's Church, sang these selections: Miserere, which was sung by the Pope's choir on last Good Friday; "Life Thine Eyes," from Mendelssohn's "Elijah"; "O, Rest in the Lord," also from "Elijah," and the chant "Pio Jesu."

Only the immediate members of the family were present at the services. The services were finished at 12.30 o'clock.

At 1 o'clock approached large crowds poured through Seventy-first street from Ninth avenue and filed slowly down Eighth avenue along the Park, where they were lined out on the sidewalks by the police. Eighth avenue, as far down as Fifty-ninth street, was lined with curious spectators on both sides of the street, and the crowds were increasing in numbers every moment.

The street for several blocks around were crowded by large throngs of civilians, soldiers and militia. Grand Army veterans in various degrees of full and fatigue dress stood around the sidewalks and overflowed into the adjacent avenues. Mounted aides dashed through the streets and avenues at full speed. The caisson which was to bear the casket was driven up to the door at 12.20 o'clock. It was heavily draped in black cashmere, and drawn by four coal-black horses. The caisson, in keeping with every other detail of the funeral arrangements, was unpretentious, being merely a covered vehicle on which the coffin was to rest exposed. The charger, equipped with the general's accoutrements, followed close behind and remained stationed in front of the house until the line should form.

Sergeant Jordan and two men of Captain Wilson's Second Battery, N. G. S. N. Y., had charge of the caisson. Private E. C. Webb led the horse. President Harrison arrived at the house at 1.50 o'clock. General Sherman's body was placed on the caisson at 2.05 o'clock.

THE "OPPOSING GENERAL'S" VALOR: PRESIDENT JOHN FITZGERALD KENNEDY

by President Ronald Reagan
June 24, 1985

President Ronald Reagan had survived an attempt on his own life when he paid homage to John Fitzgerald Kennedy, the first and only Catholic to be elected President of the United States, who was assassinated in 1963. There were no eulogies at John F. Kennedy's funeral; this generous tribute from another president, from the opposing party, served as a fitting memorial years later.

Columnist Peggy Noonan, then a Reagan speechwriter, later described the special meaning this tribute had for President and Mrs. Reagan. It was delivered at the home of Senator Edward M. Kennedy in McLean, Virginia, at a fundraising reception for the John F. Kennedy Library Foundation in Boston, Massachusetts. The new Kennedy Library was the only presidential library that didn't have an endowment, and the Reagans felt the library was a vital part of American history. The tribute was important in its own right, Noonan says, in that the Reagans were fond of the Kennedys. "We were close," Nancy Reagan later said, "and it didn't make any difference...that one was a Republican and one a Democrat."

After the speech, President Kennedy's widow Jackie Onassis lauded President Reagan's portrayal of his predecessor: "That was Jack!" The next morning, Senator Ted Kennedy wrote President Reagan a letter: "Your presence was...a magnificent tribute to my brother. The country is well served by your eloquent graceful leadership....My prayers and thanks for you as you lead us through these difficult times."

I was very pleased a few months ago when Caroline and John came to see me and to ask for our support in helping the library. I thought afterwards what fine young people they are and what a fine testament they are to their mother and father.

It was obvious to me that they cared deeply about their father and his memory. But I was also struck by how much they care about history. They felt strongly that all of us must take care to preserve it, protect it, and hand it on.

They're right, of course. History has its claims, and there's nothing so invigorating as the truth. In this case, a good deal of truth resides in a strikingly sculpted library that contains the accumulated documents, recollections, diaries, and oral histories of the New Frontier. But I must confess that ever since Caroline and John came by, I've found myself thinking not so much about the John F. Kennedy Library as about the man himself and what his life meant to our country and our times, particularly to the history of this century.

It always seemed to me that he was a man of the most interesting contradictions, very American contradictions. We know from his many friends and colleagues, we know in part from the testimony available at the library, that he was self-deprecating yet proud, ironic yet easily moved, highly literary yet utterly at home with the common speech of the ordinary man. He was a writer who could expound with ease on the moral forces that shaped John Calhoun's political philosophy. On the other hand, he possessed a most delicate and refined appreciation for Boston's political wards and the characters who inhabited it. He could cuss a blue streak—but then, he'd been a sailor.

He loved history and approached it as both romantic and realist. He could quote Stephen Vincent Benet on General Lee's army: "The aide de camp knew certain lines of Greek and other such unnecessary things that are good for peace, but are not deemed so serviceable for war..."

And he could sum up a current statesman with an earthy epithet that would leave his audience weak with laughter. One sensed that he loved mankind as it was, in spite of itself, and that he had little patience with those who would perfect what was not really meant to be perfect.

As a leader, as a President, he seemed to have a good, hard unillusioned understanding of man and his political choices. He had written a book as a very young man about why the world slept as Hitler marched on. And he understood the tension between good and evil in the history of man; understood, indeed, that much of the history of man can be seen in the constant working out of that tension. He knew that the United States had adversaries, real adversaries, and they weren't about to be put off by soft reason and good intentions. He tried always to be strong with them and shrewd. He wanted our defense system to be unsurpassed. He cared that his country could be safe.

He was a patriot who summoned patriotism from the heart of a sated country. It is a matter of pride to me that so many men and women who were inspired by his bracing vision and moved by his call to "ask not," serve now in the White House doing the business of government. Which is not to say I supported John Kennedy when he ran for President; I didn't. I was for the other fellow, but you know, it's true, when the battle's over and the ground is cooled, well, it's then that you see the opposing general's valor.

He would have understood. He was fiercely, happily partisan. And his political fights were tough—no quarter asked, none given. But he gave as good as he got. And you could see that he loved the battle.

Everything we saw him do seemed to betray a huge enjoyment of life. He seemed to grasp from the beginning that life is one fast-moving train, and you have to jump aboard and hold on to your hat and relish the sweep of the wind as it rushes by. You have to enjoy the journey; it's unthankful not to.

I think that's how his country remembers him, in his joy—and it was a joy he knew how to communicate. He knew that life is rich with possibilities, and he believed in opportunity, growth, and action.

And when he died, when that comet disappeared over the continent, a whole nation grieved and would not forget. A tailor in New

York put up a sign on the door: *Closed because of a death in the family.* The sadness was not confined to us. "They cried the rain down that night," said a journalist in Europe. They put his picture up in huts in Brazil and tents in the Congo, in offices in Dublin and Warsaw. That was some of what he did for his country, for when they honored him they were honoring someone essentially, quintessentially, completely American. When they honored John Kennedy they honored the Nation whose virtues, genius, and contradictions he so fully reflected.

Many men are great, but few capture the imagination and the spirit of the times. The ones who do are unforgettable. Four administrations have passed since John Kennedy's death; five Presidents have occupied the Oval Office; and I feel sure that each of them thought of John Kennedy now and then and his thousand days in the White House.

And sometimes I want to say to those who are still in school and who sometimes think that history is a dry thing that lives in a book: Nothing is ever lost in that great house; some music plays on.

I've even been told that late at night when the clouds are still and the moon is high, you can just about hear the sound of certain memories brushing by. You can almost hear, if you listen close, the whir of a wheelchair rolling by and the sound of a voice calling out, "And another thing, Eleanor!" Turn down a hall and you hear the brisk strut of a fellow saying, "Bully! Absolutely ripping!" Walk softly, now, and you're drawn to the soft notes of a piano and a brilliant gathering in the East Room and a crowd surrounds a bright young President who is full of hope and laughter.

I don't know if this is true, but it's a story I've been told. And it's not a bad one because it reminds us that history is a living thing that never dies. A life given in service to one's country is a living thing that never dies—a life given in service, yes.

History is not only made by people; it is people. And so, history is, as young John Kennedy demonstrated, as heroic as you want it to be, as heroic as you are.

And that's where I'll end my remarks on this lovely evening, except to add that I know the John F. Kennedy Library is the only

Presidential library without a full endowment. Nancy and I salute you, Caroline and John, in your efforts to permanently endow the library. You have our support and admiration for what you're doing.

Thank you, and God bless you all.

A SAINT FOR OUR AGE: DOROTHY DAY

by Jim Forest
October, 1997

Jim Forest's portrayal of Dorothy Day sheds additional light on the eulogy she gave to honor the irascible Mr. O'Connell (see page 171). Forest paints a vivid picture of Day as a controversial, prayerful woman who constantly struggled with her own temper and impatience, "a radical without a party line" dedicated to a Christ-centered hospitality.

Sounds like a saint to him.

Forest co-authored Love is the Measure, *a biography of Dorothy Day.*

Can you think of a word that describes a person who devoted much of her life to being with people many of us cross the street to avoid? Who for half a century did her best to make sure they didn't go hungry or freeze on winter nights? Who went to Mass every day until her legs couldn't take her that far, at which point communion was brought to her? Who prayed every day for friend and enemy alike and whose prayers, some are convinced, had miraculous results? Who went to confession every week? Who was devoted to the rosary? Who wore hand-me-down clothes and lived in cold-water flats? Whose main goal in life was to follow Christ and to see him in the people around her?

A saint.

Can you think of a word that describes a person who refused to pay taxes, didn't salute the flag, never voted, went to prison every now and then for protests against war and social injustice? Who spoke in a plain and often rude way about our way of life? Who complained that the Church wasn't paying enough attention to its own teaching and compared some of its bishops to sharks?

A troublemaker.

Dorothy Day, saint and troublemaker.

Mostly saints lived in the distant past, that is, before we were born, and have been presented to us with all blemishes removed. We are not surprised to learn that St. Wonderbread of the North Pole, daughter of pious parents, had her first vision when she was four, joined the Order of the Holy Pallbearers at the age of eleven, founded forty-seven convents, received the stigmata when she was fifty-five, and that when she died twenty years later, not only was her cell filled with divine light but the nuns attending her clearly heard the angelic choir.

What has been left out about the actual St. Wonderbread is that she ran away from home, had a voice that could split rocks and a temper that could melt them back together again, experienced more dark nights of the soul than celestial visions, was accused of heresy by her bishop, narrowly escaped being burned at the stake, and, though she lives long enough to be vindicated, felt like a failure on her deathbed. But all this was edited out after she died—facts like that might tarnish her halo.

If Dorothy Day is ever canonized, the record of who she was, what she was like and what she did is too complete and accessible for her to be hidden in wedding cake icing. She will be the patron saint not only of homeless people and those who try to care for them but also of people who lose their temper.

Dorothy Day was not without rough edges.

To someone who told her she was too hot-headed, she replied, "I hold more temper in one minute than you will hold in your entire life." To a college student who asked a sarcastic question about her recipe for soup, she responded, "You cut the vegetables until your fingers bleed." To a journalist who told her it was the first time he had interviewed a saint, she replied, "Don't call me a saint—I don't want to be dismissed that easily."

I was twenty years old the first time I saw her. She was ancient, that is to say sixty-two years old—seven years older than I am today. This means for thirty-five years she has been scolding and encouraging me on a daily basis. The mere fact of her having died seventeen years ago doesn't seem to get in the way.

I met her at the Catholic Worker Farm on Staten Island in the days when the island still had rural areas, its only link to the rest of New York City being the ferry. She was sitting with several other people at the battered table where the community had its meals. Before her was a pot of tea, a few cups, none of them matching, and a pile of letters. The Catholic Worker received a good deal of mail every day, much of it for Dorothy. She often read the letters aloud, telling a story or two about the people who had written them.

This was the Dorothy Day University in full swing, though I didn't know it at the time. She wrote countless letters and notes in response every year, but some letters she gave to others to answer either because a personal reply wasn't needed or because she wanted to connect the correspondent with someone on staff. A good part of Dorothy's life was spent reading and writing letters—even her monthly columns were usually nothing more than long letters. If ever she is canonized, she will be the patron saint of letter writers.

People sometimes think of her as the personification of the simple life, but in reality her days tended to be busy, complicated and stressful. Often she was away traveling—visiting other Catholic Worker communities, speaking at colleges, seminaries, local parishes, getting around by bus or a used car on its last spark plug.

Before an audience, she had a direct, unpremeditated, story-centered way of speaking—no notes, no rhetorical polish, a manner that communicated a certain shyness but at the same time wisdom, conviction, faith and courage. She wasn't the kind of speaker who makes those she is addressing feel stupid or without possibilities.

Her basic message was stunningly simple: we are called by God to love one another as He loves us. (These days many of us go to great lengths to avoid saying He in such a sentence, but Dorothy steadily resisted a sexually neutral vocabulary.)

If God was one key word, hospitality was another. She repeated again and again a saying from the early Church, "Every home should have a Christ room in it, so that hospitality may be practiced." Hospitality, she explained, is simply practicing God's mercy with those around us.

Christ is in the stranger, in the person who has nowhere to go and no one to welcome him. "Those who cannot see the face of Christ in the poor are atheists indeed," she often said. Hardly a day passed in her adult life when she didn't speak about the works of mercy. For her these weren't simply obligations which the Lord imposed on his followers. As she said, "We are here to celebrate Him through these works of mercy."

A day never passed without Dorothy speaking of the works of mercy: feeding the hungry, giving drink to the thirsty, clothing the naked, giving shelter to the homeless, caring for the sick, visiting prisoners, burying the dead, admonishing the sinner, instructing the ignorant, counseling the doubtful, comforting the sorrowful, bearing wrongs patiently, forgiving all injuries, praying for the living and the dead. She helped us understand a merciful life has so many levels: there is hunger not only for food but also for faith, not only for a place at the table but also for a real welcome, not only for assistance but also for listening, not only for kind words but also for truthful words. There is not only hospitality of the door but also hospitality of the face and heart.

Hospitality of the heart transforms the way to see people and how we respond to them. Their needs become primary. Tom Cornell tells the story of a donor coming into the New York house one morning and giving Dorothy a diamond ring. Dorothy thanked her for the donation and put it in her pocket without batting an eye. Later a certain demented lady came in, one of the more irritating regulars at the CW house, one of those people who make you wonder if you were cut out for life in a house of hospitality. I can't recall her ever saying "Thank you," or looking like she was on the edge of saying it. She had a voice that could strip paint off the wall. Dorothy took the diamond ring out of her pocket and gave it to this lady.

Someone on the staff said to Dorothy, "Wouldn't it have been better if we took the ring to the diamond exchange, sold it, and paid that woman's rent for a year?" Dorothy replied that the woman had her dignity and could do what she liked with the ring. She could sell it for rent money or take a trip to the Bahamas. Or she could enjoy wearing a diamond ring on her hand like the woman who gave it away. "Do you suppose," Dorothy asked, "that God created diamonds only for the rich?"

For all her traveling, most of Dorothy's life was spent in New York City. Before her conversion, in 1924, when she was twenty-eight years old, she had bought a small beach house on Staten Island that remained part of her life until she was too weak to make the trip any more. It was a simple structure with a few plain rooms and a cast iron stove. Walking on the beach or to the post office, rosary in hand, she prayed her way through an out-of-wedlock pregnancy, prayed her way through the Baltimore Catechism, prayed her way to her daughter Tamar's baptism in a nearby Catholic parish, prayed her way through the collapse of a common-law marriage and to her own baptism, prayed her way through the incomprehension of her atheist friends who regarded all religion as snake oil. Years later it was mainly in the beach house that she found the peace and quiet to write her autobiography, *The Long Loneliness*.

The main part of her New York life was in Manhattan with the urban part of the Catholic Worker community. In the early sixties, St. Joseph's House of Hospitality was on Chrystie Street—a decrepit three-story building a block from the Bowery, in those days the city's grimmest avenue. As there wasn't enough room inside, the down-and-out were often lined up at the door waiting either for food or clothing—men mainly, people often grouped under the heading "bums." Bums had been a major part of Dorothy's life since leaving college in Illinois to come to New York. She rented a room on the Lower East Side and, at age eighteen, became a reporter for New York's socialist daily newspaper, *The Call*.

Dorothy's office at the Catholic Worker, just inside the front door, was hardly big enough for her desk. Here she and I would sometimes discuss—occasionally argue—about what should be in the next issue of the paper. It wasn't the easiest place for conversation. The ground floor was where the food was prepared and meals served, each meal in shifts as there were only a few bench-style tables. From morning till night, it tended to be noisy. Sitting at her desk one afternoon, talking about the next issue, we could hardly hear each other. Dorothy got up, opened her office door and yelled, "Holy silence!" For a few minutes it was almost quiet.

On the second floor, site of the two clothing rooms, one for men, one for women, there was an area used for daily prayer—lauds, vespers, compline—as well as recitation of the rosary every afternoon. None of this was obligatory, but part of the community being a mixture of "staff" (as those of us who came as volunteers were called) and "family" (people who had once come in for clothing or a bowl of soup and gradually became part of the household).

It wasn't a comfortable life. At the time I joined, Dorothy had a sixth-floor walk-up apartment in a tenement on Spring Street. For $25 a month she got two small rooms, a bathtub next to the kitchen sink, and a bathroom the size of a broom closet.

This may sound uninviting, but Dorothy regarded the neighborhood as luxury enough. With an Italian bakery across the street, the smell of bread in the oven was often in the air, and there was always the intoxicating perfume of Italian cooking. The San Gennaro Festival was celebrated annually around the corner—for a week, that part of Manhattan became a village in sight of Naples.

The day finally came when climbing those five flights of stairs became too much for her aging knees, so we moved her to a similar apartment only one flight up on Ridge Street—also $25 a month, but in a seedier neighborhood. The place was in appalling condition. Stuart Sandberg and I went down to clean and paint the two rooms, dragging box after box of old linoleum and other debris down to the street, including what seemed to us a hideous painting of the Holy Family—Mary, Joseph and Jesus rendered in a few bright colors against a battleship gray background on a piece of plywood. We shook our heads, deposited it in the trash along the curb, and went back to work. Not long after Dorothy arrived carrying the painting. "Look what I found! The Holy Family! It's a providential sign, a blessing." She put it on the mantle of the apartment's bricked-up fireplace. Dorothy had a gift for finding beauty where others tended to see rubbish.

If she was one of the freest persons alive, she was also one of the most disciplined. This was most noticeable in her religious life. Whether traveling or home, it was a rare day when Dorothy didn't go to Mass, while on Saturday evenings she went to confession. Sacramental life was the rockbed of her existence. She never obliged anyone to follow her example. When I think of her, the first image that comes to mind is Dorothy on her knees praying before the Blessed Sacrament either in the chapel at the farm or in one of several urban parish churches near the Catholic Worker. One day, looking into the Bible and Missal she had left behind when summoned for a phone call, I found long lists of people, living and dead, who she prayed for daily.

Occasionally she spoke of her "prayings": "We feed the hungry, yes. We try to shelter the homeless and give them clothes, but there is strong faith at work; we pray. If an outsider who comes to visit us doesn't pay attention to our prayings and what that means, then he'll miss the whole point."

She was attentive to fast days and fast seasons. It was in that connection she told me a story about prayer. For many years, she said, she had been a heavy smoker. Her day began with lighting up a cigarette. Her big sacrifice every Lent was giving up smoking, but having to get by without a cigarette made her increasingly irritable as the days passed, until the rest of the community was praying she would light up a smoke.

One year, as Lent approached, the priest who ordinarily heard her confessions urged her not to give up cigarettes that year but instead to pray daily. "Dear God, help me stop smoking." She used that prayer for several years without it having any impact on her addiction. Then one morning she woke up, reached for a cigarette, and realized she didn't want it—and never smoked another.

Dorothy was never "too polite" to speak about God. Nothing we achieved was ever our doing, it was only God's mercy passing through us. Our own love wasn't our love. If we experienced love for another person, whether wife or child or friend or enemy, it was God's love. "If I have accomplished anything in my life," she said late in her life, "it is because I wasn't embarrassed to talk about God."

People sometimes tell me how lucky I am to have been a part of the same community that Dorothy Day belonged to. They picture a group of more or less saintly people having a wonderful time doing good works. In reality Catholic Worker community life in Manhattan in the early sixties had much in common with purgatory. The "staff" was made up of people with very different backgrounds, interests, temperaments and convictions. We ranged from the gregarious to the permanently furious.

There was a recluse named Keith living in a back room on the third floor who maintained the mailing list—a big job, as *The Catholic Worker* had nearly a hundred-thousand subscribers.

He was rarely seen and never said a word; communication with him was by notes. Another member of the staff was the angry daughter of a millionaire newspaper publisher; the last I heard, she had become a leader of a Marxist sect.

But not everyone was all thorns. There was lean, gentle, long-suffering Charlie Butterworth, a lawyer who had graduated from Harvard but whose pacifism had led him to the Catholic Worker.

Arthur J. Lacey, with his matchstick body, was chiefly responsible for the men's clothing room; he called himself "haberdasher to the Bowery."

There was the always-teasing Stanley Vishnewski, who said most of us belonged "not to the Catholic Worker movement but to the Catholic Shirker movement."

Agreement within the staff was as rare as visits by the President of the United States. The most bitter dispute I experienced had to do with how best to use the small amount of eggs, butter and other treats that sometimes were given to us—use them for "the line" (people we often didn't know by name who lined up for meals) or the "family," as had been the custom? Though we worked side by side, saw each other daily, and prayed together, staff tension had become too acute for staff meetings. Dorothy or Charlie Butterworth handed out jobs and once you had a job, it was yours until you stopped doing it. The final authority was Dorothy Day, not a responsibility she enjoyed, but no one else could make a final decision that would be respected by the entire staff.

When Dorothy returned from a cross-country speaking trip she told the two people running the kitchen that the butter and eggs should go to the family, which led to their resigning from kitchen work and soon after leaving the community trailing black smoke, convinced that Dorothy Day wasn't living up to the writings of Dorothy Day.

One of the miracles of Dorothy's life is that she remained part of a conflict-torn community for nearly half a century. Still more remarkable, she remained a person of hope and gratitude to the end. (She occasionally spoke of "the duty of hope.")

Dorothy was and remains a controversial lady. There was hardly anything she did which didn't attract criticism. Even hospitality scandalizes some people. We were blamed for making people worse, not better, because we were doing nothing to "reform them." A social worker asked Dorothy one day how long the down-and-out were permitted to stay. "We let them stay forever," Dorothy answered. "They live with us, they die with us, and we give them a Christian burial. We pray for them after they are dead. Once they are taken in, they become members of the family. Or rather, they always were members of the family. They are our brothers and sisters in Christ."

What got her in the most hot water was her sharp social criticism. She pointed out that patriotism was a more powerful force in most people's lives than the Gospel. While she hated every kind of tyranny and repression, she was fierce in her criticism of capitalism and consumerism. She said America had a tendency to treat people like Kleenex—"use them, and throw them away."

"Our problems stem," she said, "from our acceptance of this filthy, rotten system."

She had no kind words for war or anything having to do with it—war was simply murder wrapped in flags. She was convinced Jesus had disarmed all his followers when he said to Peter, "Put away your sword, for whoever lives by the sword will perish by the sword." A way of life based on love, including love of enemies, left no room for killing. You couldn't practice the works of mercy with one hand and the works of vengeance with the other.

No stranger to prison, she was first locked up as a young woman protesting with Suffragettes in front of the White House during World War I and was last jailed in her seventies for picketing with farm workers. She took pride in the young men in the Catholic Worker who went to prison rather than be drafted—"a good way to visit the prisoner," she pointed out. Yet she also welcomed back others who had left Catholic Worker communities to fight in the Second World War. They might disagree about the best way to fight Nazism, but—as she often said— there is no "party line" in the Catholic Worker movement.

Dorothy was sometimes criticized for being too devout a Catholic. How could she be so radical about social matters and so conservative about her Church? While she occasionally deplored statements or actions by members of the hierarchy, she was by no means an opponent of the bishops or someone campaigning for structural changes in the Church. What was needed, she said, wasn't new doctrine but our living the existing doctrine. True, some pastors seemed barely Christian, but one had to aim for their conversion, an event that would not be hastened by berating them but rather by helping them see what their vocation requires. The way to do that was to set an example.

"I didn't become a Catholic in order to purify the Church," Dorothy once said to Bob Coles. "I knew someone, years ago, who kept telling me that if [the Catholic Workers] could purify the Church, then she would convert. I thought she was teasing me when she first said that, but after a while I realized she meant what she was saying. Finally, I told her I wasn't trying to reform the Church or take sides on all the issues the Church was involved in; I was trying to be a loyal servant of the Church Jesus had founded. She thought I was being facetious. She reminded me that I had been critical of capitalism and America, so why not Catholicism and Rome?....My answer was that I had no reason to criticize Catholicism as a religion or Rome as the place where the Vatican is located....As for Catholics all over the world, including members of the Church, they are no better than lots of their worst critics, and maybe some of us Catholics are worse than our worst critics."

Pleased as she was when home Masses were allowed and the Liturgy translated into English, she didn't take kindly to smudging the border between the sacred and the mundane. When a priest close to the community used a coffee cup for a chalice at a Mass celebrated in the soup kitchen on First Street, she afterward took the cup, kissed it, and buried it in the back yard. It was no longer suited for coffee—it had held the Blood of Christ. I learned more about the Eucharist that day than I had from any book or sermon. It was a learning experience for the priest as well—thereafter he used a chalice.

Dorothy's sensitivity for the sacred helps explain her love, rare at the time, of the Orthodox Church, famous—or infamous—for its reluctance to modernize, rationalize, speed up or simplify its liturgical life. She longed for the reunion of the Church. She occasionally took me to the small meetings of a group in New York City, The Third Hour it was called, that brought together Catholic and Orthodox Christians, as well as at least one Anglican, the poet W. H. Auden. It was Dorothy who brought me to visit the Russian Orthodox cathedral up on East 97th Street where she introduced me to the Russian priest serving there, Father Matvei Stadniuk, now dean of the Epiphany Cathedral in Moscow. In 1988, it was Father Matvei who launched the first project of Christian volunteer hospital service in what was still Soviet Russia, and it was he, not I, who recalled our first meeting twenty-six years earlier, but only when I had given him a copy of my biography of Dorothy. "Dorothy Day? Did you know her?" And then he looked more closely at my face and said, "I knew you when you were a young man, when Dorothy brought you to our Church."

I'm not sure what had given Dorothy such a warmth for Orthodox Christianity in general and the Russian Orthodox Church
in particular, but one of the factors was certainly her love of the
books of Dostoevsky, and most of all his novel, *The Brothers Karam-
azov*. Perhaps the most important chapter for Dorothy concerns a
conversation between a wealthy woman and an elderly monk, Father Zosima. The woman asks him how she can really know that
God exists. Fr. Zosima tells her than no explanation or argument
can achieve this, only the practice of "active love." He assures her
that there is no other way to know the reality of God. The woman
confesses that sometimes she dreams about a life of loving service
to others—she thinks perhaps she will become a nun, live in holy
poverty and serve the poor in the humblest way. It seems to her such
a wonderful thought that it makes tears come to her eyes. But then
it crosses her mind how ungrateful some of the people she is serving will be. Some will complain that the soup she is serving isn't hot
enough, the bread isn't fresh enough, the bed is too hard, the covers
are too thin. She confesses she couldn't bear such ingratitude—and
so her dreams about serving others vanish, and once again she finds
herself wondering if there really is a God. To this, Fr. Zosima re-
sponds with the words, "Love in practice is a hard and dreadful thing
compared to love in dreams." Words Dorothy often repeated. I think
of the Orthodox monk Father Zosima as somehow a co-founder of
all the Catholic worker houses of hospitality.

It is in the same book that Dostoevsky relates the story of a
woman who was almost saved by an onion. She had been a person
of absolute selfishness and so, when she died, she went to hell. After
all, she had chosen hell every day of her life. Even after her death,
her guardian angel wanted to save her and so approached the Savior,
saying a mistake had been made. "Don't you remember? Olga once
gave an onion to a beggar." It was left unsaid that the onion had
started to rot, and also that it wasn't so much given as thrown at the
beggar. The Savior said, "You are right. I bless you to pull her out of
hell with an onion." So the angel flew into the twilight of hell—all
those people at once so close to each other and so far apart—and

there was the selfish woman, glaring at her neighbors. The angel offered her the onion and began to lift her out of hell with it. Others around her saw what was happening, saw the angel's strength, and saw their chance. They grabbed hold of the woman's legs and so were being lifted with her, a ribbon of people being rescued by one onion. Only the woman had never wanted company. She began kicking with her legs, yelling at her uninvited guests. "Only for me! Only for me!" These three words are hell itself. The onion became rotten and the woman and all the others attached to her fell back into the disconnection of hell.

"Hell is not to love anymore," Dorothy said so many times, quoting another author she loved, Georges Bernanos.

Dorothy Day's main achievement is that she taught us the "Little Way" of love, which it so happens involves cutting up a great many onions. The path to heaven, it seems, is marked by open doors and the smell of onions. "All the way to heaven is heaven," she so often said, quoting St. Catherine of Siena, "because He said, 'I am the Way.'"

It was chiefly through the writings of St. Thérèse of Lisieux that Dorothy had been drawn to the "Little Way." No term, in her mind, better described the ideal Christian way of doing things. As she once put it, "Paper work, cleaning the house, dealing with the innumerable visitors who come all through the day, answering the phone, keeping patience and acting intelligently, which is to find some meaning in all that happens—these things, too, are the works of peace, and often seem like a very little way."

I'm sometimes asked, "Dorothy Day gives a fine example for people who don't have a family to take care of and mortgages to pay, but what about the rest of us?"

The rest of us includes my wife and me. I don't have enough fingers on one hand to count our children, and the first of the month is mortgage payment day. But every time I open the door to guests, it's partly thanks to Dorothy Day. Every time I think about things in the bright light of the Gospel rather than in the gray light of money or the dim light of politics, her example had has its influence. Every time I try to overcome meanness or selfishness rising up in myself, it is partly thanks to the example of Dorothy Day. Every time I defeat the impulse to buy something I can get along without, Dorothy Day's examples of voluntary poverty have had renewed impact. Every time I try to see Christ's presence in the face of a stranger, there again I owe a debt to Dorothy Day.

No one else has made me think so much about the words we hear at the Last Judgment: "What you did to the least person, you did to me." What I know of Christ, the Church, sacramental life, the Bible, and truth-telling, I know in large measure thanks to her, while whatever I have done that was cowardly, opportunistic or cruel, is despite her.

It isn't that Dorothy Day is the point of reference. Christ is. But I can't think of anyone I've known whose Christ-centered life did so much to help make me a more Christ-centered person.

It's a century since Dorothy Day was born and nearly twenty years since she died, but she continues to touch our lives, not only as a person we remember with gratitude, but also as a saint—if by the word "saint" we mean a person who helps us see what it means to follow Christ.

"It is the living from day to day," she once said, "taking no thought for the morrow, seeing Christ in all who come to us, and trying literally to follow the Gospel that resulted in this work."

EULOGY TO WHITEFEATHER OF THE OJIBWAY: LARRY CLOUD-MORGAN

by Patricia LeFevere
1999

Patricia LeFevere points out that Larry Cloud-Morgan was buried with his peace pipe.

The Whitefeather Peace Community continues his work. Their mission statement:

> *Whitefeather Peace Community was founded in Portland, Oregon, in 2005, in the spirit of nonviolence, in the spirit of Dorothy Day, in the spirit of Larry Cloud-Morgan— Whitefeather of the Ojibway—and in the spirit of resistance to war, militarism, and injustice. We are a vegetarian, non-smoking, alcohol-free activist community. When possible, we open our doors and offer overnight hospitality to traveling nonviolent resisters. We offer Roundtables in the Catholic Worker tradition—a meal followed by focused discussion. We help organize nonviolent resistance to war, injustice, and militarism. We are hoping for your involvement.*

I'm told they buried Larry Cloud-Morgan in his ribbon shirt, beaded medallion and new beaded moccasins, even though he'd lost a foot and some toes to diabetes. The mourners wrapped him in his Four Direction Pendleton blanket holding his carved walking stick.

Those attending Cloud-Morgan's wake at the St. Paul-

Minneapolis Archdiocesan Office of Indian Ministry reported that his peace pipe lay next to his right arm. In addition, his casket held an Indian doll, a china plate with a picture of a horse, various medicine bundles and a stuffed black bear cub, representing the mother bear and cubs that so delighted him at his Ball Club Reservation cabin in Northern Minnesota.

When I first met Cloud-Morgan in November, 1984, in the Jackson County jail in Kansas City, Missouri, it was just days after he and Oblate Fathers Paul and Carl Kabot, along with Helen Woodson, had symbolically spilled their blood and hammered on a missile silo in Missouri.

For someone destined to spend the next few years in federal prisons, Cloud-Morgan appeared as at home in jail as I found him years later at a summer picnic or Sunday Mass in Minneapolis.

The hundreds who bade farewell in June to this social justice activist, poet, playwright, artist, liturgist, translator, peacemaker and spiritual leader did so with ceremony and a Native American Catholic ritual, scripted and choreographed by Cloud-Morgan. The mourners included white, red and black Americans, street people, a U. S. senator, an Orthodox rabbi, and clergy from every denomination who serve the Indian community.

In his days at Marquette University in Milwaukee and later at St. John's University in Collegeville, Minnesota, Cloud-Morgan was encouraged to become a priest, an invitation he rejected, friends said, because he felt it would take him away from his Native American people and make him an official spokesman on "Indian" affairs.

He asked to be laid in a casket without a cover on it. He wanted it placed in the middle of the room on a bed of cedar. Chairs were arranged around it to form a natural talking circle so that no one could ignore the others and all would be in community.

The circle of diverse friends was symbolic of Cloud-Morgan's life, said mourner Catherine Mamer of Minneapolis, who had known him through fifteen years of social activism and spiritual ministering to the poor. Mamer had also appeared in his plays, attended his sweatlodge and was one of the group of friends and family surrounding his hospital bed when he died June 10 at age sixty-one.

Father James Notebaart, director of Indian Ministry in the archdiocese, officiated at Cloud-Morgan's wake and transported his body to the funeral in Cass Lake, Minnesota, stopping en route at Larry's favorite Dairy Queen. Notebaart, a friend for ten years, is fluent in Ojibway, the language that Cloud-Morgan spoke in his home and helped preserve on recorded tapes at Harvard.

The priest recalled Cloud-Morgan earlier this decade as he led a grass-roots reform movement against corruption and nepotism at his own White Earth Reservation. His protests led to the indictment and ouster of tribal officers.

He also led demonstrations on behalf of tribal fishing rights, and he opposed Indian casinos. "Larry had a soft presence; he was not an activist in an accusatory way, not one with invective. He stood by what he believed. He stayed by the fire at White Earth, talking to the people, praying with them," Notebaart said.

This son of a pietistic Catholic father and an Episcopalian mother—who had her mouth taped shut by nuns for speaking Ojibway in public—grew up loving Joan of Arc. The adolescent French warrior was Cloud-Morgan's first heroine, and he read her story, the first book he'd ever received, over and over again to his dog, said scholar Chris Vecsey.

Many other Catholic heroes followed: Thomas Merton, the Berrigan brothers and Matthew Fox, his roommate at St. John's. Vecsey, who directs humanities at Colgate University, has included Cloud-Morgan in Volumes 2 and 3 of his trilogy on the history of Native American Catholicism from 1492 to the present.

Vecsey told the *National Catholic Reporter* that Cloud-Morgan will live on in Native American and Catholic history. "Larry looked beyond his own community to the universe. He stands apart by his devotion to other movements and his activist spirituality," he said. Vecsey regretted that his translation of the Catholic liturgy into Ojibway remains incomplete.

McNally found Cloud-Morgan's greatest gift to be his ability to be present in the moment with people. He had equal rapport with

a Harvard anthropologist or an abused woman, with a wealthy host-
ess or her Hispanic maid, McNally noted. It was just such a band
of admirers who placed the items in his coffin, told stories and sang
hymns for Cloud-Morgan's journey to his ancestors in *Ishpeming*
(Ojibway for heaven).

PLAIN-SPOKEN, PRACTICAL, TAKING CARE OF BUSINESS: MAJOR DAVID G. TAYLOR

by John Taylor
October, 2006

This book contains forty-nine Catholic eulogies and this catholic one. The Apostle's Creed reveals that a "small c" doesn't make it lesser: It makes it broader.

Major David G. Taylor was a Baptist; his widow and son are Catholic. Because he lost his life while serving Americans of every faith—and none—and because his brother's eulogy exemplifies the Christ all Christians share, it deserves to be included in this section on heroes.

The story of this eulogy proves that solace can come from unexpected and distant quarters. Eulogizer John Taylor, who teaches on a U.S. Naval base in Japan, frequently ordered food from GermanDeli.com to send to his brother David, who was stationed in Baghdad, Iraq. The brothers' parents live near a U.S. Naval base in London, England, where their mother, Kay, also teaches at the Department of Defense School. Military families such as the Taylors, who live and serve on different continents, know that closeness does not depend upon physical proximity.

The German Deli employees, who work in Dallas, Texas, became interested in and fond of their far-flung Taylor customers. After Major Taylor was killed in action on October 22, 2006, they posted the full text of John Taylor's eulogy on their website. One employee, Inge, provided the links for it to be published here.

Kay Taylor, whose relationships are often forged and maintained over the Internet, considers the German Deli folks "our close friends, even though we've never met. But folks like Inge at German Deli have particular insights that give balm to our souls that most people can't touch. She has a gift."

The Taylor parents have since met Inge and her coworkers. Some of the German Deli crew met them at the airport when the Taylors had a brief stopover in Dallas.

⌣

On behalf of the Taylor, Thresher, Seckar, Overman, and Goodwin families, I would like to thank you for all attending.

"This man need not be magnified in death, larger than he was in life," was the quote used at David's grandfather's funeral in 1999, borrowed from Robert Kennedy's funeral eulogy. Both David and his grandfather, whom he called "Nannie," were plain-spoken, practical, and took care of business.

David was born at Ft. Hood, Texas, thirty-seven years ago. He traveled to Ft. Knox, Kentucky—as an infant—and back to Olive Chapel when he was a year old. He and my mother stayed with our grandparents, Doris and J.C. Overman, here in Apex, North Carolina, during our father's second tour to Vietnam. We grew up in Cookeville, Tennessee, where our dad taught ROTC; we moved to Ft. Bragg, Schweinfurt, and Heidelberg, Germany—returning to Olive Chapel in the summers to enjoy life at "Nannie and Mom's."

One of my favorite early childhood memories of David occurred when we lived in Heidelberg. B. J. Dunlevey, a neighborhood bully, ordered me outside to the playground for a showdown, a fight of monumental proportions. Truth be told, I think my mouth got me in trouble. Word spread like wildfire among the apartment buildings in Mark Twain Village. B.J. was two years older and much bigger than I, if you can believe that. David took me aside before the showdown—the gunfight at the MTV Corral—and said, "John, you have to fight your own battles, but that doesn't mean I can't help you out some." He taped some German Pfenning coins to my hands, then put my hands inside gloves. I felt like I had angels on my shoulders when I marched downstairs and met B. J. on the playground. B.J.

took one look at my homemade brass knuckles and ran away. David saved the day and gave me playground bragging rights for months. These things are important to a seven-year-old kid.

This little story exemplifies our relationship. David let me make mistakes, let me live my life, but he was always there to offer advice, support, and love. I revered David and I have always held his values and choices up as a model I should follow.

This is not to say my brother was a perfect little angel. David had a talent for knowing exactly what he could and couldn't do; sometimes gleefully crossing that line. There was the time the Raleigh Police chased him and a fellow officer out of a Raleigh dance club because David took offense at the club's perceived discrimination against Army soldiers—and David then had to use his Army jungle survival training to evade capture...I remember him knocking on my door at three-thirty a.m., covered from head to toe in mud. Then there were the numerous times he scaled the very-closed and very-locked Leiman swimming pool in Germany for late-night kamikaze cannonballs off the ten meter board. David truly understood what it meant to live life to its fullest, the whole time assuring our parents he was a model Ambassador representing the U. S. abroad.

Always a leader and often bossy—can you imagine that?—David reached the rank of Eagle Scout at age thirteen. He was president of his senior class at HHS, earning two ROTC scholarships for college—and graduating with a political science major from Davidson College, where he entered the military as a Second Lieutenant in 1991.

David's life as he knew it was about to change when he met "the one"! David first met Michelle at a computer convention in St. Louis. David encountered her in the hotel courtyard where Michelle thought David arrogant, too confident, and irreverent. I'm sure we're all shocked by such an initial assessment. But he left a lasting impression on Michelle. David's always had that ability. And when she was visiting Georgia for a political protest, which mortified David, they reconnected, and she was won over by his sensitive heart. They were as different as night and day when it came to politics—but they both respected the other's views and often entertained themselves by pushing each other's buttons in playful ways.

In describing Michelle to his parents, David paid her the ultimate compliment—and described her as a "good Catholic girl." He was welcomed into the Thresher family and both loved and greatly respected Joanne and Joe. They weren't exactly in-laws as much as they were genuine family.

Much of their relationship has been conducted "long-distance"—from their days of dating to their separation due to his military responsibilities. This seemed to strengthen their relationship, and they cherished the times they were physically in the same place. Their marriage worked because they made it work, and they pressed through the obstacles that could have easily divided lesser couples.

In spite of David's playful side, he was modest and self-effacing—the only instructions David left in the event of his death while in Kosovo was that the popularized Bette Midler song, "Wind Beneath my Wings" should not be sung at his funeral. Please note this is not in the program today.

You'd have to know David to get this next part, but people who call him "friend" will agree: He lived by a code. If you want to write these down, please get out a pen and take notes.

These are David's life lessons:

1. Life isn't fair—get over it.
2. Freedom isn't free, someone has to pay the price, and it might as well be you.
3. Things often get worse before they get worse.
4. No whining.
5. Take care of your own business.
6. Sometimes you just need to find your backbone to do the right thing.
7. People who do the right thing aren't heroes, they are just doing the right thing.
8. You are probably not entitled to anything you didn't work for.

David was a soldier's soldier who would not like this part of the service. He was mostly modest—he really was—and he believed the best soldier was the soldier who fought quietly for his country—not out of any Hollywood-styled sense of patriotism, but rather because it was an inherent duty and part of his obligation as a citizen living in this country.

David and the rest of his men appreciated the cards and goodies people sent. I would routinely send him Haribo Gummibears from GermanDeli.com. One of the first things David would do when he got the packages was to bring all the men in and let them get first dibs on the treats.

He loved and cared for his men. That was one of the reasons he wanted to leave the relative safety of a headquarters unit and head to a forward base camp. He wanted to offer whatever he could to the troops out on the line. He was, very simply, a good and decent man. He was bothered that other soldiers were taking risks to get the job done, and he felt he needed to take his place amongst them and do his bit.

This fall my mother and her students wrote cards to the soldiers in David's unit.

In an email dated two days before David died, he said the following:

> *We had a staff sergeant killed and three soldiers in their vehicle seriously injured yesterday in an IED attack. It puts something of a fog over the place. My patrol guys were the first responders and they knew the guys; these men needed something like those cards you sent to remind them that the world is still out there, waiting for them to get back to it. I can't promise they'll all write back to the students, but that's only because we're leaving shortly and everyone is working nineteen-hour days to get things ready. The cards definitely were a hit. I asked a couple of them afterwards, "Did you get a card from the American school kids in England?" In every case, they were very animated in their responses. That's a great thing and shows how little it takes to lift someone's spirits.*

One of my mother's students at London Central summed up David's death by saying that, "You should be proud of him—he was trying to keep us safe. And that is the greatest honor anyone can have." Another wrote: "Your son was fighting for what everyone in Iraq is fighting for—peace, and to help other countries live in a world without violence, giving hope where there is none."

David once mentioned to me that there are those people who merely talk about America and our wonderful freedom, rights, and privileges, and then there are those who step up and put their money where their mouth is. David came from a long line of military men. Our proud and decorated father, David Sr., was an armored cavalry officer who did two tours in Vietnam. His father-in-law Joe Thresher served in Vietnam; our grandfather Kenneth Taylor was a WWII naval officer; and our other grandfather, J.C. Overman, was a staff sergeant who was critically wounded in the Battle of the Bulge. Our great-grandfather, John Overman Sr., served in WWI, and our great-uncles served in WWII.

Hearts are breaking all over the world. Rarely has a man touched so many lives. LTC John Holden, a British officer in the Queen's Royal Artillery, current serving in Basrah, Iraq, received letters and treats from my mom's students just as David's soldiers did. LTC Holden wrote: "Only the brave, who have stood the line, can comment on what has been done out here. And the glimmer of democracy and liberty in this once biblical land is a wonderful thing to behold. There are many who would say we are failing—but they are the doubters and the weak. Your son had courage and was one who believed in the true value of freedom."

David really wasn't afraid in the traditional sense—he was aware, careful, and sensitive to danger. He referred to the enemy just as "the bad guys" and felt sorry that they had poor guidance and a flawed sense of what constitutes humanity.

It is ironic that David died in the biblical land between the Tigris and Euphrates rivers, which is believed to be the site of the Garden of Eden. He was killed by the very people he came to help.

David desperately loved his wife Michelle, and baby Jake. Everyone agreed that the happiest time was when Michelle and Jake entered his life. He loved me very much. And was a good son to his parents. David loved and was attentive to his grandparents, and "Mom" Doris Overman, held a special place in his heart. He likewise loved and embraced the Thresher and Seckar family.

On a balmy Sunday afternoon, David sent his loved ones email messages assuring them that he was O.K. and told his beloved Michelle that he loved her, noting that he had the best wife, son and even a ribbon-winning dog Max. He then got in his Humvee with several of his troops. David was killed instantaneously when an IED exploded. He did not take the Iraqi insurgents' misguided extremism personally; he simply believed that evil had to be challenged and somebody had to take the lead.

Finally, there are only two defining forces who have ever offered to die for you. One is Jesus Christ and the other is the American G.I. One died for your soul; the other for your freedom.

May we never forget either.

II. WE REMEMBER
Family

ALOISE STEINER BUCKLEY, R. I. P.

by William F. Buckley, Jr.
April 19, 1985

and

REMEMBERING PUP:
WILLIAM F. BUCKLEY, JR.

by Christopher Buckley
March, 2008

The following two eulogies involve three generations of a well-known American family.

Aloise Steiner Buckley was an American of Swiss-German ancestry who married an Irish-American oil baron in 1917. Her son, William F. Buckley, Jr., portrays her as the hands-on matriarch of a happy, Catholic home bustling with ten children.

William became the most famous of those Buckley children, first as a writer and later as the witty, erudite host of PBS-TV's "Firing Line" from 1966-1999. In 1951, his first book, God and Man at Yale, *criticized his alma mater for its pretense of academic freedom and for failing to uphold its professed Christian ideals. The Ivy League was not impressed. Harvard's president wrote, "It seems strange for any Roman Catholic to undertake to speak for the Yale religious tradition." That book, still in print, is credited with launching America's intellectual conservative movement and influencing presidential candidacies ever since. William F. Buckley, Jr. went on to write fifty books and to found the* National Review *magazine, in which this eulogy appeared.*

Aloise, her son William, and his only child, Christopher, reveal an evolution of social views in America over three generations. William's

eulogy tells of chiding his southern-born mother to square her segrega-
tionist views with her faith. (He does not remind his audience of his own
early opposition to civil rights legislation, which he had come to regret.)
In other matters, William remained an old-school, Latin-Mass Catholic
and—along with his wife Pat—a lifelong chain-smoker.

Christopher is also a writer. His best-known novel (also a film),
Thank You for Smoking, *satirizes America's tobacco industry. After his*
mother's death from emphysema, his elderly, emphysemic father, William,
advocated a ban on tobacco before also succumbing to the disease.

In 2008, Christopher posted his essay, "Sorry Dad, I'm Voting for
Obama," online at TheDailyBeast.com. The eulogy of his father was posted
at the site a year later, in commemoration of William F. Buckley, Jr.'s
death. Christopher's own preface accompanies it.

Christopher's most recent book, Losing Mum and Pup, *is a family*
memoir.

ALOISE STEINER BUCKLEY, R. I. P.

by William F. Buckley, Jr.
April 19, 1985

She bore ten children, nine of whom have written for this journal [*National Review*] or worked for it, or both, and that earns
her, I think, this half-acre of space normally devoted to those
whose contributions are in the public mode. Hers were not. If ever
she wrote a letter to a newspaper, we don't remember it, and if she
wrote to a congressman or senator, it was probably to say that she
wished him well, notwithstanding his mistaken votes, and would
pray for him as she did regularly for her country. If she had lived one
more day, she'd have reached her ninetieth birthday. Perhaps somewhere else one woman has walked through so many years charming
so many people by her warmth and diffidence and humor and faith.
I wish I might have known her.

ASB was born in New Orleans, her ancestors having come from Switzerland some time before the Civil War. She attended Sophie Newcomb College but left after her second year in order to become a nurse, her intention being to go spiritedly to the front, Over there, Over there. But when the young aspiring nurses were given a test to ascertain whether they could cope with the sight of blood and mayhem, she fainted, and was disqualified. A year later she married a prominent thirty-six-year-old Texas-born attorney who lived and practiced in Mexico City, with which she had ties because her aunt lived there.

She never lived again in New Orleans, her husband taking her, after his exile from Mexico (for backing an unsuccessful revolution that sought to restore religious liberty), to Europe, where his business led him. They had bought a house in Sharon, Connecticut, and in due course returned there. The great house where she brought us up still stands, condominiums now. But the call of the South was strong, and in the mid-thirties they restored an antebellum house in Camden, South Carolina. There she was wonderfully content, making others happy by her vivacity, her delicate beauty, her habit of seeing the best in everyone, the humorous spark in her eye. She never lost a Southern innocence in which her sisters even more conspicuously shared. One of her daughters was delighted on overhearing an exchange between her and her freshly widowed sister who had for fifty years been married to a New Orleans doctor and was this morning, seated on the porch, completing a medical questionnaire, checking this query, ex-xing the other. She turned to Mother and asked, "Darling, as girls did we have gonorrhea?"

Her cosmopolitanism was unmistakably Made-in-America. She spoke fluent French and Spanish with undiluted inaccuracy. My father, who loved her more even than he loved to tease her, and whose knowledge of Spanish was flawless, once remarked that in forty years she had never once placed a masculine article in front of a masculine noun, or a feminine article in front of a feminine noun, except on one occasion when she accidentally stumbled on the correct sequence, whereupon she stopped—unheard of in her case, so fluently did she aggress against the language—and corrected herself by changing the article: the result being that she spoke, in Spanish, of the latest encyclical of Pius XII, the Potato of Rome ("Pio XII, la Papa de Roma"). She would smile and laugh compassionately, as though the joke had been at someone else's expense, and perhaps play a little with her pearls, just above the piece of lace she always wore in the V of the soft dresses that covered her diminutive frame.

There were rules she lived by, chief among them those she understood God to have specified, though she outdid Him in her accent on good cheer. And although Father was the unchallenged source of authority at home, she was unchallengeably in charge of arrangements in a house crowded with ten children and as many tutors, servants, and assistants. In the very late thirties her children ranged in age from one to twenty-one, and an inbuilt sense of appropriate parietal arrangements governed the hour at which each of us should be back from wherever we were—away at the movies, or at a dance, or hearing Frank Sinatra sing in Pawling. The convention was inflexible. On returning, each of us would push, on one of the house's intercoms, the button that said, "ASB." The conversation, whether at ten when she was still awake, or at two when she had been two hours asleep, was always the same: "It's me, Mother." "Good night, darling." If—as hardly ever happened—it became truly late, and her mind had not recorded the repatriation of all ten of us, she would rise, and walk to the room of the missing child. If there, she would return to sleep, and remonstrate the next day on the forgotten telephone call. If not there, she would wait up, and demand an explanation.

Her anxiety to do the will of God was more than ritual. I wrote her once early in 1963. Much of our youth had been spent in South Carolina, and the cultural coordinates of our household were Southern. But the times required that we look Southern conventions like Jim Crow hard in the face, and so I asked her how she could reconcile Christian fraternity with the separation of the races, a convention as natural in the south for a hundred years after the Civil War as women's suffrage became natural after their emancipation, and she wrote, "My darling Bill: This is not an answer to your letter, for I cannot answer it too quickly. It came this morning, and, of course, I went as soon as possible to the Blessed Sacrament in our quiet, beautiful little church here. And, dear Bill, I prayed so hard for humility and for wisdom and for guidance from the Holy Spirit. I know He will help me to answer your questions as He thinks they should be answered. I must pray longer before I do this."

A few years earlier she had raised her glass on my father's seventy-fifth birthday to say, "Darling, here's to fifteen more years together, and then we'll both go." But my father died three years later. Her grief was profound, and she emerged from it through the solvent of prayer, her belief in submission to a divine order, and her irrepressible delight in her family and friends. A few years later her daughter Maureen died at age thirty-one, and she struggled to fight her desolation, though not with complete success. Her oldest daughter, Aloise, died three years later. And then, three months ago, her son John.

She was by then in a comfortable retirement home, totally absentminded; she knew us all, but was vague about when last she had seen us, or where, and was given to making references, every now and then, to her husband ("Will") and the trip they planned next week to Paris, or Mexico.

But she sensed what had happened, and instructed her nurse (she was endearingly under the impression that she owned the establishment in which she had a suite) to drive her to the cemetery, and there, unknown to us until later than afternoon, she saw from her car, at the edge of an assembly of cars, her oldest son lowered into the earth. He had been visiting her every day, often taking her to a local restaurant for lunch, and her grief was, by her standards, convulsive; but she did not break her record—she never broke it— which was never, ever to complain, because, she explained, she could never repay God the favors He had done her, no matter what tribulations she might need to suffer.

Ten years ago, my wife and I arrived in Sharon from New York much later than we had expected, and Mother had given up waiting for us, so we went directly up to the guest room. There was a little slip of blue paper on the bed lamp, another on the door to the bathroom, a third on the mirror. They were love notes, on her 3 X 5 notepaper inscribed "Mrs. William F. Buckley." Little valentines of welcome, as though we were back from circling the globe. There was no sensation to match the timbre of her pleasure on hearing from you when you called her on the telephone, or the vibration of her embrace when she laid eyes on you. Some things truly are unique.

Five days before she died, one week having gone by without her having said anything—though she clutched the hands of her children and grandchildren as they came to visit, came to say good-bye—the nurse brought her from the bathroom to the armchair and—inflexible rule—put on her lipstick, and the touch of rouge, and the pearls. Suddenly, and for the first time since the terminal descent had begun a fortnight earlier, she reached out for her mirror. With effort she raised it in front of her face, and then said, a teasing smile on her face as she turned to the nurse, "Isn't it amazing that anyone so old can be so beautiful?" The answer, clearly, was, Yes, it was amazing that anyone could be so beautiful.

REMEMBERING PUP:
WILLIAM F. BUCKLEY, JR.

by Christopher Buckley
March, 2008

My father, William F. Buckley, Jr., died a year ago this week, and I thought to mark the occasion in this space, normally devoted to making raspberries at the cosmos and endorsing Democrats for high office.

I've found myself reaching for the phone so many times since last February 27, not just to hear his voice, but to ask him what—on earth—he would have made of (in no particular order): Sarah

Palin, the future of the GOP, John Thaine's $35,000 commode, these trillion-dollar "stimulus" programs, Senator Roland Burris, Caroline Kennedy's about-face, Judd Gregg's about-face, the on-going rationalization of the U. S. Banking industry and President Obama as he deals with one of the worst in-boxes in U. S. history.

It's tricky, trying to channel your father's ghost. Hamlet tried it. I think I won't. But I miss WFB's takes on everything that's going on. Often, I'd find myself flailing aimlessly or circularly about some issue trying to sort it out in my own head. Then I'd ring him and he'd nail it for me in two or three neat sentences that left me laughing and shaking my head, for the thousandth time, in amazement. Even if I suspected he might be wrong, he was always elegantly wrong.

He died at his desk in Stamford, Connecticut, while working on a book. He'd been ill for many months, worn down by emphysema. His wife of 57 years had died ten months earlier, and he missed her desperately. A DVD had been made of her memorial service, with a PowerPoint slide show I'd assembled of dozens of photos of her through the years. He watched it again and again, tears streaming down his face. I understand now, the business of long-time mates not outliving each other by long.

My father was a man of devout, unflinching, sometimes exasperating Catholic faith. He believed absolutely in heaven and hell. I lost (or misplaced) my faith, but I find myself on this anniversary hoping that I'm wrong, and that he's there, correcting God's grammar. I have on my desk an editorial cartoon showing him arriving at the Pearly Gates, St. Peter whispering to an angel, "I'm going to need a bigger dictionary."

I got the phone call at 9:30 in the morning—I'd been doing my income taxes; death and taxes, all in the same day. I'd been mentally preparing for this day for months, and yet when it finally happened it came embedded in a shock wave. I actually found myself thinking, Maybe I'll just go on doing the taxes. That way no one will notice it's happened. After taking a few deep breaths, I made my calls and sent out the first emails.

The New York Times had his obituary up on its website within an hour and a half. His death was announced from the White House, and a few minutes after that, The President of the United States called to express his condolences. I had always known my father was a great man—great, that is, in the literal sense of the word. He changed the era he lived in. The reaction to his death, from far corners of the world, confirmed this for me, not that it mattered. To the world he was William F. Buckley, Jr. To me he was "Pup."

I buried him in Sharon, Connecticut, where he grew up and where he had been, by his own admission, happiest, between the ages of five and seven. A month later, his funeral Mass was held at Saint Patrick's Cathedral in New York, in front of a full house of 2,200 souls.

Jews observe a formal period of one year's mourning for a parent, called an avelut. We aren't Jewish, but I get, and like, the idea even though I don't suppose the mourning ever really ends, until one's own time comes. In the meantime, *ave atque vale*. The eulogy I gave at St. Pat's I reproduce here below.

We talked abut this day, He and I, a few years ago. He said to me, "If I'm still famous, try to convince the Cardinal to do the service at St. Patrick's. If I'm not, just tuck me away in Stamford."

Well, Pup, I guess you're still famous.

Pope Benedict will be saying Mass here in two weeks. I was told that the music at this Mass for my father would in effect be the dress rehearsal for the Pope's. I think that would have pleased him, though doubtless he'd have preferred it to be the other way around.

On the day he retired from "Firing Line" after a 33-year long run, "Nightline" (no relation) did a show to mark the occasion. At the end, Ted Koppel said, "Bill, we have one minute left. Would you care to sum up your 33 years in television?" To which my father replied, "No."

Taking his cue, I won't attempt to sum him up in my few minutes here. A great deal has been written and said about him in the month since he died, at his desk, in his study in Stamford. After I absorbed the news, I sat down to compose an email. My inner English major asserted itself and I found myself quoting (misquoting, slightly) a line from Hamlet,

> *He was a man, Horatio, take him for all in all,*
> *I shall not look upon his like again.*

One of my first memories of him was of driving up to Sharon, Connecticut, for Thanksgiving. It would have been about 1957. He had on the seat between us an enormous reel-to-reel tape recorder. For a conservative, my old man was always on the cutting edge of the latest gadgetry—despite the fact that at his death, he was almost certainly the only human being left on the planet who still used Word Star.

It was a recording of *Macbeth*. My five-year-old brain couldn't make much sense of it. I asked him finally, "What's eating the queen?" He explained about the out-out-damned-spot business. I replied, "Why doesn't she try Palmolive?" So began my tutelage with the world's coolest mentor.

I placed inside his casket a few items to see him across the River Styx: his favorite rosary, the TV remote control—private joke—a jar of peanut butter, and my mother's ashes. I can hear her saying, "Bill—what is that dis-*gusting* substance leaking all over me?" No pharaoh went off to the afterlife better equipped than he does.

The last time I was with him in Sharon was last October. It was a fundraiser for the local library, billed as "A Bevy of Buckleys"—my father, Uncle Jimmy, Aunt Pitts, Aunt Carol, me—reading from the aggregate Buckley oeuvre—a word I first heard from his lips many years ago, along with other exotic, multi-lingual bon mots: *mutatis mutandis; pari passu; quod licet Jove, non licet bovi.*

An article had appeared in the local paper a few days before, alerting the community to this gala event. As I perused the clipping, my eyes alighted on the sentence: "The Buckleys are a well-known American family, William F. Buckley being arguably the best known."

I concealed my amusement, and handed to Pup the clipping and waited for the reaction I knew would come. Sure enough, within seconds, he looked up with what I would describe as only faintly-bemused indignation and said, "*Ar-guably?*"

He was—inarguably—a great man. This is, from a son's perspective, a mixed blessing, because it means having to share him with the wide world. It was often a very mixed blessing when you were out sailing with him. Great men always have too much canvas up. And great men set out from port in conditions that keep lesser men—such as myself—safe and snug on shore.

One October day in 1997, I arrived from Washington in Stamford for a long-planned overnight sail. As the train pulled into the station, I looked out and saw people hanging onto lampposts at ninety-degree angles, trying not to be blown away by the northeast gale that was raging. Indeed, it resembled a scene from, *The Wizard of Oz*. When the train doors opened, I was blown back into the carriage by the fifty mile-an-hour wind. I managed to crawl out onto the platform, practically on all fours, whereupon my father greeted me with a chipper, "We'll have a brisk sail."

I looked at him incredulously and said, "We're going out in *this?*"

Indeed we did go out in it. We always went out in it. Some of my earliest memories are of my mother, shrieking at him as the water broke over the cockpit and the boat pitched furiously in boiled seas, "Bill—*Bill!* Why are you trying to kill us?"

But the cries of timorous souls never fazed him. He had been going out in it for years, ever since he published his first book, *God and Man at Yale*. Nor did he need a sailboat to roil the waters. His Royal typewriter—and later Word Star—would suffice.

How many words flowed from those keyboards. I went up to Yale recently to inspect his archive of papers. They total 550 linear feet. To put it in perspective, the spire of St. Patrick's rises 300 feet above us. By some scholarly estimates, he may have written more letters than any other American in history. Add to that prodigal output: six thousand columns; 1,500 "Firing Lines"; countless articles; over fifty books. He was working on one the day he died.

Jose Marti famously said that a man must do three things in life: write a book, plant a tree, have a son. I don't know that my father ever planted a tree. Surely whole forests, whole eco-systems were put to the axe on his account. But he did plant a lot of seeds and many of them, grown to fruition, are here today. Quite a harvest, that.

It's not easy coming up with an epitaph for such a man. I was tempted by something Mark Twain once said, "Homer's dead, Shakespeare's dead, and I myself am not feeling at all well."

Years ago, he gave an interview to Playboy magazine. Asked why he did this, he couldn't resist saying, "In order to communicate with my sixteen-year-old son." At the end of the interview, he was asked what he would like for an epitaph and he replied, "I know that my Redeemer liveth." Only Pup could manage to work the book of Job into a Hugh Hefner publication.

I finally settled on one, and I'll say the words over his grave at sunset today in Sharon, as we lay him to rest. They're from a poem he knew well, each line of which, indeed, seemed to have been written just for him:

> *Under the wide and starry sky*
> *Dig the grave and let me lie.*
> *Glad did I live, and gladly die.*
> *And I lay me down with a will.*
>
> *This be the verse you grave for me:*
> *Here he lies where he longed to be.*
> *Home is the sailor, home from sea,*
> *And the hunter home from the hill.*

EVERY GIFT BUT LENGTH OF YEARS: JOHN F. KENNEDY, JR.

by Senator Edward Kennedy
July 23, 1999
Church of St. Thomas More, New York, NY

Senator Edward "Ted" Kennedy has had to give more eulogies following the tragic deaths of his loved ones than anyone in this book—perhaps more than anyone in our time. His long and distinguished career led Time *in 2006 to name him one of "America's Ten Best Senators" for collaborating with Republican colleagues to pass legislation affecting "the lives of virtually every man, woman, and child in the country."*

Yet the primary image many Americans have of Ted Kennedy is of him in the pulpit rather than in the senate chamber, as eulogizer rather than legislator. It is a role no one wants, and a task few could grace as he well as he did for so many decades.

Ted Kennedy was a surrogate father to the thirteen children of his two assassinated brothers, John F. Kennedy and Robert Kennedy. This eulogy was for John Jr., killed in a plane crash with his wife Carolyn and her sister Lauren.

Thank you, President and Mrs. Clinton and Chelsea, for being here today. You've shown extraordinary kindness through the course of this week.

Once, when they asked John what he would do if he went into politics and was elected president, he said, "I guess the first thing is call up Uncle Teddy and gloat." I loved that. It was so like his father.

From the first day of his life, John seemed to belong not only to our family, but to the American family. The whole world knew his name before he did. A famous photograph showed John racing across the lawn as his father landed in the White House helicopter and swept up John in his arms. When my brother saw that photo, he exclaimed, "Every mother in the United States is saying, 'Isn't it wonderful to see that love between a son and his father, the way that John races to be with his father.' Little do they know, that son would have raced right by his father to get to that helicopter."

But John was so much more than those long ago images emblazoned in our minds. He was a boy who grew into a man with a zest for life and a love of adventure. He was a pied piper who brought us all along. He was blessed with a father and mother who never thought anything mattered more than their children.

When they left the White House, Jackie's soft and gentle voice and unbreakable strength of spirit guided him surely and securely to the future. He had a legacy, and he learned to treasure it. He was part of a legend, and he learned to live with it. Above all, Jackie gave him a place to be himself, to grow up, to laugh and cry, to dream and strive on his own.

John learned that lesson well. He had amazing grace. He accepted who he was, but he cared more about what he could and should become. He saw things that could be lost in the glare of the spotlight. And he could laugh at the absurdity of too much pomp and circumstance.

He loved to travel across the city by subway, bicycle, and roller blade. He lived as if he were unrecognizable, although he was known by everyone he encountered. He always introduced himself, rather than take anything for granted. He drove his own car and flew his own plane, which is how he wanted it. He was the king of his domain.

He thought politics should be an integral part of our popular culture, and that popular culture should be an integral part of politics. He transformed that belief into the creation of *George* [magazine]. John shaped and honed a fresh, often irreverent journal. His new political magazine attracted a new generation, many of whom had never read about politics before.

John also brought to *George* a wit that was quick and sure. The premier issue of *George* caused a stir, with a cover photograph of Cindy Crawford dressed as George Washington with a bare belly button. The "Reliable Source" in *The Washington Post* printed a mock cover of *George* showing not Cindy Crawford, but me dressed as George Washington, with my belly button exposed. I suggested to John that perhaps I should have been the model for the first cover of his magazine. Without missing a beat, John told me that he stood by his original decision.

John brought this same playful wit to other aspects of his life. He campaigned for me during my 1994 election and always caused a stir when he arrived in Massachusetts. Before one of his trips to Boston, John told the campaign he was bringing along a companion, but would need only one hotel room. Interested, but discreet, a senior campaign worker picked John up at the airport and prepared to handle any media barrage that might accompany John's arrival with his mystery companion. John landed with the companion all right: an enormous German shepherd dog named Sam he had just rescued from the pound.

He loved to talk about the expression on the campaign worker's face and the reaction of the clerk at the Charles Hotel when John and Sam checked in. I think now not only of these wonderful adventures, but of the kind of person John was. He was the son who quietly gave extraordinary time and ideas to the Institute of Politics at Harvard that bears his father's name. He brought to the Institute his distinctive insight that politics could have a broader appeal, that it was not just about elections, but about the larger forces that shape our whole society.

John was also the son who was once protected by his mother. He went on to become her pride—and then her protector in her final days. He was the Kennedy who loved us all, but who especially cherished his sister Caroline, celebrated her brilliance, and took strength and joy from their lifelong mutual admiration society. And for a thousand days, he was a husband who adored the wife who became his perfect soul mate. John's father taught us all to reach for the moon and the stars. John did that in all he did—and he found his shining star when he married Carolyn Bessette.

How often our family will think of the two of them, cuddling affectionately on a boat, surrounded by family—aunts; uncles; Caroline and Ed and their children, Rose, Tatiana, and Jack; Kennedy cousins; Radziwill cousins; Shriver cousins; Smith cousins; Lawford cousins—as we sailed Nantucket Sound. Then we would come home, and before dinner, on the lawn where his father had played, John would lead a spirited game of touch football. And his beautiful young wife, the new pride of the Kennedys, would cheer for John's team and delight her nieces and nephews with her somersaults.

We loved Carolyn. She and her sister Lauren were young extraordinary women of high accomplishment—and their own limitless possibilities. We mourn their loss and honor their lives. The Bessette and Freeman families will always be part of ours.

John was a serious man who brightened our lives with his smile and his grace. He was a son of privilege who founded a program called Reaching Up to train better caregivers for the mentally disabled. He joined Wall Street executives on the Robin Hood Foundation to help the city's impoverished children. And he did it all so quietly, without ever calling attention to himself. John was one of Jackie's two miracles. He was still becoming the person he would be, and doing it by the beat of his own drummer. He had only just begun. There was in him a great promise of things to come.

The Irish Ambassador recited a poem to John's father and mother soon after John was born. I can hear it again now, at this different and difficult moment:

> *We wish to the new child,*
> *A heart that can be beguiled,*
> *By a flower,*
> *That the wind lifts,*
> *As it passes.*
> *If the storms break for him,*

May the trees shake for him,
So that his time be doubled,
And at the end of all loving and love
May the Man above,
Give him a crown.

We thank the millions who have rained blossoms down on John's memory. He and his bride have gone to be with his mother and father, where there will never be an end to love. He was lost on that troubled night, but we will always wake for him, so that his time, which was not doubled, but cut in half, will live forever in our memory, and in our beguiled and broken hearts. We dared to think, in that other Irish phrase, that this John Kennedy would live to comb gray hair, with his beloved Carolyn by his side. But like his father, he had every gift but length of years. We, who have loved him from the day he was born, and watched the remarkable man he became, now bid him farewell.

God bless you, John and Carolyn. We love you and we always will.

THE GOLFATORIUM:
MEDITATIONS ON A MOTHER DYING

by Thomas Lynch
1996

In the following eulogy, poet and undertaker Thomas Lynch gives us permission to enjoy the unbridled humor that can erupt during our own fearful encounters with death. If you have ever provided care to the dying and felt your chronically exhausted self skating on the edge of instability, inadequacy, and even insanity, only to have dark humor boil up, you will find relief in Lynch's off-the-wall wit. The emotional chaos of watching a loved one die—which can lead to a bizarre hilarity in the midst of grief—may seem shameful to someone who hasn't been there. Lynch has been there.

Here, Lynch alternates his fears about his mother's refusal to treat a fatal cancer with a wacky business plan for a combination golf course/ mortuary, turning it all into a meditation on suffering and redemption. It takes courage for a man to put this outrageous notion out there for others to read, especially if he makes his living as a small-town funeral director, as Lynch does.

Lynch learns that Ecclesiastes is not precisely on the money about everything having its season: Sometimes the time to mourn and the time to laugh are one and the same. That's one way to get through a terrible loss, at least, as you come to appreciate the old king's sobering truth that, "In much wisdom is much grief; and he that increaseth knowledge increaseth sorrow" (Ecclesiastes 1:18).

Write, read, sing, sigh, keep silence, pray,
bear thy crosses manfully; eternal life
is worthy of all these, and greater combats.

—Thomas à Kempis

It came to me high over California. I was flying across the country to read poems in L. A. I had gigs at the Huntington Library,
UCLA, San Bernardino, and Pomona College. And between en-
gagements, four days free to wander at will in Southern California.
It was a beautiful blue end of September, the year I quit drinking and
my mother died. Crisp and cloudless, from my window seat the nation's geography lay below me. The spacious skies, the fruited plane,
the purple mountains' majesty.

I was counting my blessings.

To have such a day for my first transcontinental flight, to have
someone else paying for the ticket and the expenses and to be prof-
fering stipends I'd gladly pay taxes on, to say that I was the poet and
I had the poems that People in California were paying to hear—
these were good gifts.

My mother was dying back in Michigan, of cancer. She had
told the oncologists, "Enough, enough." They had discontinued the
chemotherapy. I was running from the implications.

I was scared to death.

From Detroit we first flew over Lake Michigan then the grainy
Midwest and Plains states, then the mountains and valleys of the
Great West, and finally the desert west of Vegas and Reno until, in
the distance, I could make out the western edges of the San Bernardino Mountains. The Mojave was all dry brown below until, just
before the topography began to change from desert to mountain, I
saw an irregular rectangle of verdant green. It was the unspeakable
green of Co. Kerry or Virgin Gorda purposely transposed to the
desert and foothills. I could only hazard a guess at its size—a couple
hundred acres I reckoned, though I had no idea what altitude we
were flying at. Had we already begun our final descent? The captain

had turned on the seat belt sign. All of our seat backs and tray tables were forward.

"Must be a golf course," is what I said to myself. I could see geometrically calculated plantings of trees and irregular winding pathways. "Or a cemetery. Hell!" I remember thinking, "This is California, it could be both!"

And then it came to me, the vision. It *could* be both!

I've been working in secret ever since.

It is no especial genius that leads me to the truth that folks in their right minds don't like funerals. I don't think we need a special election or one of those CNN polls on this. Most folks would rather shop dry goods or foodstuffs than caskets and burial vaults. Given the choice, most would choose root canal work over the funeral home. Even that portion of the executive physical where the doctor says, "This may be a little uncomfortable," beats embalming ninety-nine times out of every hundred in the public races. Random samplings of consumer preference almost never turn up "Weeping and mourning" as things we want to do on our vacations. Do you think a funeral director could be elected president? Mine was and is and, godhelpus, ever will be The Dismal Trade. We might be trusted (the last ones to let you down my father used to say) or admired (I don't know how you do it!) or tolerated (well, somebody has to do it) and even loved, though our lovers are often a little suspect (how can you stand to have him touch you after...?). But rare is that man or woman who looks forward to funerals with anything even approaching gladness, save perhaps those infrequent but cheerful obsequies for IRS agents or telemarketers or a former spouse's bumptious attorney.

What's worse, all the advertising in the world won't ever make it an expandable market. Mention of our ample parking, clearance prices on bronze and copper, easy credit terms, readiness to serve twenty-four hours a day, does little to quicken in any consumer an appetite for funerals in the way that, say, our taste for fast food can be incited to riot by talk of "two all beef patties, special sauce, lettuce, cheese, pickles, onion on a sesame seed bun." How many of us don't salivate, Pavlovian, when someone hums the tune that says, "You deserve a break today?" A drop in the prime rate will send shoppers out in search of the "big ticket" items—homes, cars, and pleasure craft— but never funerals. Chesty teenagers with good muscle tone can sell us more Marlboros than we need, more cruises, more computers, more exercise equipment; more and better, and fewer and better and new and improved and faster and cheaper and sexier and bigger and smaller; but the one funeral per customer rule has held for millennia, and we don't really need a study to show us that for most folks even the one and only is one too many.

Thus we regard funerals and the ones who direct them with the same grim ambivalence as those who deliver us of hemorrhoids and boils and bowel impactions—*Thanks*, we wince or grin at the offer, *but no thanks!*

There are some exceptions to this quite ponderable truth.

As always, the anomalies prove the rule.

Poets, for example, will almost always regard any opportunity to dress up and hold forth in elegiac style as permissible improvement on their usual solitude. If free drink and a buffet featuring Swedish meatballs are figured in the bargain, so much the better. A reviewer of mine quite rightly calls poets the taxidermists of literature, wanting to freeze things in time, always inventing dead aunts and uncles to eulogize in verse. He is right about this. A good laugh, a good cry, a good bowel movement are all the same fellow to those who otherwise spend their days rummaging in the word horde for something to say, or raiding the warehouses of experience for something worth saying something about. And memorable speech like memorable verse calls out for its inscription into stone. Poets know that funerals and gravesides

put them in the neighborhood of the memorable. The ears are cocked
for answers to the eternal adverbs, the overwhelming questions. "And
may these characters remain," we plead with Yeats, in this permanent
phrase, "When all is ruin once again."

And there are elements of the reverend clergy who have come
to the enlightenment that, better than baptisms or marriages, funerals press the noses of the faithful against the windows of their faith.
Vision and insight are often coincidental with demise. Death is the
moment when the chips are down. That moment of truth when the
truth that we die makes relevant the claims of our prophets and
apostles. Faith is not required to sing in the choir, for bake sales or
building drives; to usher or deacon or elder or priest. Faith is for
the time of our dying and the time of the dying of the ones we love.
Those parsons and pastors who are most successful—those who have
learned to "minister"—are those who allow their faithful flocks to
grieve like humans while believing like Jews or Christians or Mus-
lims or Buddhists or variants of these compatible themes. They affirm the need to weep and dance, to blaspheme and embrace the
tenets of our faith, to upbraid our gods and to thank them.

Uncles find nickels behind our ears. Magicians pull rabbits
from out of hats. Any good talker can preach pie in the sky or break
out the warm fuzzies when the time is right. But only by faith do the
dead arise and walk among us or speak to us in our soul's dark nights.

So rabbi and preacher, pooh-bah and high priest do well to understand the deadly pretext of their vocation. But for our mortality
there's no need for churches, mosques, temples, or synagogues. Those
clerics who regard funerals as so much fuss and bother, a waste of
time better spent in prayer, a waste of money better spent on stained
glass or bell towers, should not wonder for whom the bell tolls. They
may have heard the call but they've missed the point. The afterlife
begins to make the most sense *after life*—when someone we love
is dead on the premises. The *bon vivant* alone in his hot tub needs
heaven like another belly button. Faith is for the heartbroken, the
embittered, the doubting, and the dead. And funerals are the venues
at which such folks gather. Some among the clergy have learned to

like it. Thus they present themselves at funerals with a good cheer and an unambiguous sympathy that would seem like duplicity in anyone other than a person of faith. I count among the great blessings of my calling that I have known men and women of such bold faith, such powerful witness, that they stand upright between the dead and the living and say, "Behold I tell you a mystery..."

There are those, too, who are ethnically predisposed in favor of funerals, who recognize among the black drapes and dirges an emotionally potent and spiritually stimulating intersection of the living and the dead. In death and its rituals, they see the leveled playing field so elusive in life. Whether we bury our dead in Wilbert Vaults, leave them in trees to be eaten by birds, burn them or beam them into space; whether choir or cantor, piper or jazz band, casket or coffin or winding sheet, ours is the species that keeps track of our dead and knows that we are always outnumbered by them. Thus immigrant Irish, Jews of the Diaspora, Black North Americans, refugees and exiles and prisoners of all persuasions, demonstrate, under the scrutiny of demographers and sociologists, a high tolerance, almost an appetite, for the rites and ceremonies connected to death.

Furthermore, this approval seems predicated on one or more of the following variables; the food, the drink, the music, the shame and guilt, the kisses of aunts and distant cousins, the exultation, the outfits, the heart's hunger for all homecomings.

The other exception to the general abhorrence of funerals is, of course, types of my own stripe whose lives and livelihoods depend on them. What sounds downright oxymoronic to most of the subspecies—a good funeral—is, among undertakers, a typical idiom.

And though I'll grant some are pulled into the undertaking by big cars and black suits and rumors of riches, the attrition rate is high among those who do not like what they are doing. Unless the novice mortician finds satisfaction in helping others at a time of need, or "serving the living by caring for the dead" as one of our slogans goes, he or she will never stick it. Unless, of course, they make a pile of money early on. But most of us who can afford to send our kids to the orthodontist but not to boarding school, who are tied to our brick and mortar and cash-flow worries, who live with the business phone next to our beds, whose dinners and intimacies are always being interrupted by the needs of others, would not do so unless there were satisfactions beyond the fee schedule. Most of the known world could not be paid enough to embalm a neighbor on Christmas or stand with an old widower at his wife's open casket or talk with a leukemic mother about her fears for her children about to be motherless. The ones who last in this work are the ones who believe what they do is not only good for the business and the bottom line, but good, after everything, for the species.

A man that I work with named Wesley Rice once spent all of one day and all night carefully piecing together the parts of a girl's cranium. She'd been murdered by a madman with a baseball bat after he'd abducted and raped her. The morning of the day it all happened she'd left for school dressed for picture day—a schoolgirl dressed to the nines, waving at her mother, ready for the photographer. The picture was never taken. She was abducted from the bus stop and found a day later in a stand of trees just off the road in a township south of here. After he'd raped her and strangled her and stabbed her, he beat her head with a baseball bat, which was found beside the child's body. The details were reported dispassionately in the local media along with the speculations as to which of the wounds was the fatal one—the choking, the knife, or the baseball bat. No doubt these speculations were the focus of the double postmortem the medical examiner performed on her body before signing the death certificate *Multiple Injuries*. Most embalmers, faced with what Wesley Rice was faced with after he'd opened the pouch from the morgue, would have simply said "closed casket," treated the remains enough to control the odor, zipped the pouch, and gone home for cocktails. It would have been easier. The pay was the same. Instead, he started working. Eighteen hours later the girls' mother, who had pleaded to see her, saw her. She was dead, to be sure, and damaged; but her face was hers again, not the madman's version. The hair was hers, not his. The body was hers, not his. Wesley Rice had not raised her from the dead nor hidden the hard facts, but he had retrieved her death from the one who had killed her. He had closed her eyes, her mouth. He'd washed her wounds, sutured her lacerations, pieced her beaten skull together, stitched the incisions from the autopsy, cleaned the dirt from under her fingernails, scrubbed the fingerprint ink from her fingertips, washed her hair, dressed her in jeans and a blue turtleneck, and laid her in a casket beside which her mother stood for two days and sobbed as if something had been pulled from her by force. It was the same when her pastor stood with her and told her "God weeps with you." And the same when they buried the body in the ground. It was then and always will be awful, horrible, unappeasably sad. The outrage, the horror, the heartbreak belonged, not to the murderer or the media or the morgue, each of whom had staked their claims to it. It belonged to the girl and to her mother. Wesley had given them the body back. "Barbaric" is what Jessica Mitford called this "fussing over the dead body." I say the monster with the baseball bat was barbaric. What Wesley Rice did was a kindness. And, to the extent that it is easier to grieve the loss that we see, rather than the one we imagine or read about in papers or hear of on the evening news, it was what we undertakers call a good funeral.

It served the living by caring for the dead.

But save this handful of the marginalized—poets and preachers, foreigners and undertakers—few people not under a doctor's care and prescribed powerful medications, really "appreciate" funerals. Safe to say that part of the American Experience, no less the British, or the Japanese or Chinese, has been to turn a blind eye to the "good" in "goodbye," the "sane" in "sadness," the "fun" in "funerals."

Thus, the concept of merging the highest and best uses of land, which came to me high over California, seemed an idea whose time had come. The ancient and ongoing duty of the land to receive the dead aligned with the burgeoning craze in the golf business led, by a post-modern devolution, to my vision of a place where one could commemorate their Uncle Larry and work on their short game at the same time—two hundred acres devoted to memories and memorable holes; where tears wept over a missed birdie commingled with those wept over a parent's grave. A Golfatorium! It would solve, once and for all, the question of Sundays—what to do before or after or instead of church. The formerly harried husband who always had to promise he'd do the windows "next weekend" in order to get a few holes in during good weather, could now confidently grab his golf shoes and Big Berthas and tell his wife he was going to visit his "family plot." He might let slip some mention of "grief work" or "unfinished business" or "adult-child issues still unresolved." Or say that he was "having dreams" or was feeling "vulnerable." What good wife would keep her mate from such important therapy? What harm if the cure includes a quick nine or eighteen or twenty-seven holes if the weather holds?

So began the dialogue between myselves: the naysayer and the true believer—there's one in every one of us. I read my poems in L.A., chatted up the literary set, waxed pithy and beleaguered at the book signings and wine and cheese receptions. But all along I was preoccupied by thoughts of the Golfatorium and my mother dying. When, after the reading at the Huntington Library, I asked the director where would she go if she had four days free in Southern California, she told me "Santa Barbara" and so I went.

There are roughly ten acres in every par four. Eighteen of those and you have a golf course. Add twenty acres for practice greens, club house, pool and patio, and parking and two hundred acres is what you need. Now divide the usable acres, the hundred and eighty, by the number of burials per acre—one thousand—subtract the greens, the water hazards, and the sand traps, and you still have room for nearly eight thousand burials on the front nine and the same on the back. Let's say, easy, fifteen thousand adult burials for every eighteen holes. Now add back the cremated ashes scattered in sand traps, the old marines and swabbies tossed overboard in the water hazards and the Italians entombed in the walls of the club house and it doesn't take a genius to come to the conclusion that there's gold in them there hills!

You can laugh all you want, but do the math. Say it costs you ten thousand an acre and as much again in development costs—you know, to turn some beanfield into Roseland Park Golfatorium or Arbordale or Peachtree. I regard as a good omen the interchangeability of the names of golf courses and burial grounds: Glen Eden and Grand Lawn, like Oakland Hills or Pebble Beach could be either one, so why not both? By and large we're talking landscape here. So two million for property and two million for development, the club house, the greens, the watering system. Four million in up-front costs. Now you install an army of telemarketers-slash-memorial counselors to call people during the middle of dinner and sell them lots at an "introductory price" of, say, five hundred a grave—a bargain by any standard—and cha-ching you're talking seven point five million. Add in the pre-arranged cremations at a hundred a piece and another hundred for scattering in the memorial sand traps and you've doubled your money before anyone has bought a tee time or paid a greens fee or bought golf balls or those overpriced hats and accessories from your pro shop. Nor have you sold off the home lots around the edges to those types that want to live on a fairway in Forest Lawn. Building sights at fifty thousand a pop. Clipping coupons is what you'd be. Rich beyond any imagination. And that's not even figuring how much folks would pay to be buried, say, in the same fairway as John Daly or Arnold Palmer. Or to have Jack Nicklaus try to blast out of your sand trap. And think of the gimmicks—free burial for a hole in one, select tee times for the pre-need market. And the package deals: a condo on the eighteenth hole, six graves on the par-three on the front nine. Dinner reservations every Friday night, tennis lessons for the missus, maybe a video package of you and your best foursome for use at your memorial service, to aid in everyone's remembrance of the way you were, your name and dates on the wall of the nineteenth hole where your golf buddies could get a little liquored up and weepy all in your memory. All for one low price, paid in a way that maximized your frequent flyer miles.

The impulse to consolidate and conglomerate, to pitch the big tent of goods and services is at the heart of many of this century's success stories. No longer the butcher, the baker, the candlestick maker, we go to supermarkets where we can buy meats, breads, motor oils, pay our light bill, rent a video, and do our banking, all in one stop. Likewise the corner gas station sells tampons and toothpaste (of course, no one comes out to check your oil, nor can the insomniac behind the glass wall fix your brakes or change your wiper blades). Our churches are no longer little chapels in the pines but crystal cathedrals of human services. Under one roof we get day care and crisis intervention, bible study and columbaria. The great TV ministries of the eighties—the Bakkers and Swaggarts and Falwells—were theme parks and universities and hospital complexes that flung the tax-free safety net of God over as much real estate as could be bought.

Perhaps the tendency, manifest in many of today's megachurches, to entertain rather than to inspire, to wow rather than to worship, proceeds from the intelligence, gained generations back, that the big top needed for the tent revival and the three-ring circus was one and the same. Some of these televangelists went to jail, some ran for president, and some rode off into the sunset of oblivion. But they seemed to be selling what the traffic would bear. A kind of one-stop shopping for the soul, where healing, forgiveness, a time-share in the Carolinas, musical ministry, water arks, and pilgrimages to the Holy Land can all be put on one's Visa or MasterCard.

In the same way the Internet is nothing if not an emergent bazaar, a global mall from which one can shop the shelves of a bookstore in Galway, order a pizza or some dim sum, talk dirty to strangers bored with their marriages, and check the demographics of Botswana all without budging from—this would have sounded daft twenty years ago—the "home office."

Thus the paradigm of dual-purpose, high-utility multi-tasking applications had taken hold of the market and my imagination.

This had happened to me once before.

Years back before the cremation market really—I can't help this one—heated up, I dreamed a new scheme called "Cremorialization." It was based on the observation that those families who elected to cremate their dead, much as those who buried theirs, felt a need to memorialize them. But unlike earth burial where the memorial took the form of stone—informative but silent and otherwise useless—those who reduced their dead to ashes and bone fragments seemed to be cheered by the thought that something good might come of something bad, something useful might proceed from what they saw as otherwise useless. Such notions have root in what has been called the Protestant ethic that honors work and utility. The dead, they seemed to be saying, ought to get off their dead ashes and be good for something beyond the simple act of remembrance.

This is the crowd who can always be counted on to say "such a shame" or "what a waste" when they see a room full of flowers at one end of which is a dead human body. The same flowers surrounding a live human body hosting a tea for the visiting professor are, for the most part, "perfectly lovely." Or when the body amid the gladioli is one recovering from triplets, say, or triple bypass surgery, the flowers are reckoned to be "how very thoughtful." But flowers surrounding a casket and corpse are wasteful and shameful—the money better spent on "a good cause." This notion, combined with cremation, which renders the human corpse easily portable—ten to twelve pounds on average—and easily soluble with new age polymers and resins, brought me to the brainstorm years ago of the dead rising from their ashes, doing their part again—Cremorialization. Rather than dumbly occupying an urn, what old hunter wouldn't prefer his ashes to be used to make duck decoys or clay pigeons? The dead fisherman could become a crank-bait or plastic worms, perhaps given, with appropriate ceremony, to a favorite grandson. The minister's wife, ever the quiet and dignified helpmate, could be resurrected as a new tea service for the parsonage, her name etched tastefully into the saucers. Bowlers could be mixed into see-through bowling balls, or bowling pins, or those bags of rosin they are always tossing. Ballroom dancers could be ocarinas, cat lovers could be memorial kitty litter. The possible applications were endless. The ashes of gamblers could become dice and playing chips, car buffs turned into gear shift knobs or hood ornaments or whole families of them into matching hubcaps. After years spent in the kitchen, what gourmand could resist the chance to become a memorial egg-timer, their ashes slipping through the fulcrum in a metaphor of time. Bookends and knickknacks could be made of the otherwise boring and useless dead. And just as the departed would be made more valuable by becoming something, what they became would be more valuable by placing the word "memorial" in front of it.

We always kept the ashes in a closet—those that weren't picked up by the family or buried or placed in a niche. After ten years I noticed we'd accumulated several dozen unclaimed boxes of ashes. It seemed as if nobody wanted them. I wondered about the limits of liability. What if there were a fire. I tried to imagine the lawsuit—old family members turning up for "damages." There are, of course, damages that can be done even to a box of ashes. We'd call every year around Christmastime to see if the families of these abandoned ashes had come to any decision about what should be done, but more often than not we'd be left holding the box. One Christmas, my younger brother, Eddie, said we should declare it The Closet of Memories and establish a monthly holding fee, say twenty-five dollars, to be assessed retroactively unless the ashes were picked up in thirty days. Letters were sent out. Calls made. Old cousins and stepchildren came out of the woodwork. Widows long-since remarried returned. The Closet of Memories was near empty by Easter. Eddie called it a miracle.

What I called it was amazing—the ways we relate to a box of ashes—the remains. And all that winter and spring I'd watch as people called to claim their tiny dead, how exactly it was they "handled" it. Some grinned broadly and talked of the weather, taking up the ashes as one would something from the hardware store or baggage claim, tossing it into the trunk of their car like corn flakes or bird seed. Some received the package—a black plastic box or brown cardboard box with a name and dates on it—as one would old porcelain or First Communion, as if one's hands weren't worthy or able or clean enough to touch it. One elderly woman came to claim the ashes of her younger sister. The younger sister's children could not be bothered, though their aunt valiantly made excuses for them. She carried her sister's ashes to the car. Opened the trunk then closed it up again. Opened the back door of her blue sedan then closed that, too. She finally walked around to the front passenger seat, placed the parcel carefully there, paused momentarily then put the seat belt around it before getting in and driving away. For several it was a wound reopened. And they were clearly perturbed that we should "hassle" them to take some action or else pay a fee. "What do I want with her ashes?" one woman asked, clearly mindless of the possibility that, however little her dead mother's ashes meant to her, they might mean even less to me.

The only mother who mattered was my own. And she was dying of a cancer that reoccurred a year and a half after the surgery that the doctors assured her had "got it all." They had removed a lung.

We'd all put away our worst fears and grabbed the ring the surgeons tossed that said "everything was going to be all right." They were wrong. A cough that started at Thanksgiving and was still there at Valentine's Day sent her to the doctor's at my sister Julie's insistence. The doctors saw "an irregularity" in the x-rays and suggested a season of radiation treatments. I supposed this irregularity must be different than the one for which laxatives and diuretics are prescribed. But by June, her body made dry and purple from the radiation, it still had not occurred to me that she would be dying. Even in August, her voice near a whisper, a pain in her shoulder that never left, I clung to the user-friendly, emotionally neutral lexicon of the oncologist, who kept our focus on the progress of the "irregularity" (read: tumor) instead of the woman dying before our eyes, whose pain they called "discomfort"; whose moral terror they called "anxiety"; whose body not only stopped being her friend, it had become her enemy.

I never pursued Cremorialization. The bankers and bean counters couldn't be swayed. One said I was probably ahead of my time. He was right. Strange ads turn up in the trade journals now that promise to turn the cremains into objects of art, which bear a uniform resemblance to those marble eggs that were all the rage a few years ago. Oh, once I dumped a fellow's ashes into a clear whiskey bottle that his wife had wired to work as a desk lamp. "He always said I really turned him on," she said and still signs her Christmas cards, Bev and Mel. Likewise the widow of a man I fished with brought back his ashes after she remarried and asked me to scatter them on the Pere Marquette—the river where we'd fished the salmon run for years. She'd put them in a thermos bottle, one of those big pricey Stanley ones, and said it would be less conspicuous in the canoe than the urn I'd sold her. "Camouflage" she called it and smiled the smile of loss well-grieved. But once I got him downstream to one of our favorite holes, I couldn't let him go that way. I buried him thermos bottle and all, under a birch tree up from the riverbank. I piled stones there and wrote his name and dates on paper, which I put in a fly-box and hid among the stones. I wanted a place that stood still to remember him at in case his son and daughter, hardly more than toddlers when he died, ever took up fishing or came asking about him.

The world is full of odd alliances. Cable companies buy phone companies, softwares buy hardwares. Before you know it we're talking to the TV. Other combinations are no less a stretch: the "motor home," "Medicide." By comparison, a cemetery-golf course combo—a Golfatorium—seems, fetched only as far as, you will excuse, a nine iron.

Furthermore, cemeteries have always been widely and mistakenly regarded as land wasted on the dead. A frequent argument one hears in favor of cremation relies on the notion, an outright fiction, that we are running out of land. But no one complains about the proliferation of golf courses. We've had three open in Milford the last year alone. And no one in public office or private conversation has said that folks should take up contract bridge or ping pong or other less land-needy, acreage-intensive pastimes and dedicate the land, instead, to low-cost housing or co-op organic gardens. No, the development of a golf course is good news to the real estate and construction trades, reason for rejoicing among the hoteliers, restaurateurs, clothiers, and adjoining industries who have found that our species is quite willing to spend money on pleasure when the pleasure is theirs. Land dedicated to the memorialization of the dead is always suspect in a way that land used for the recreation of the living seldom is. There seems to be, in my lifetime, an inverse relationship between the size of the TV screen and the space we allow for the dead in our lives and landscapes. With the pyramids maybe representing one end of the continuum, and the memorial pendant—in which ashes of your late and greatly reduced spouse are kept dangling tastefully from anklet or bracelet or necklace or keychain—representing the other, we seem to give ground grudgingly to the departed. We've flattened the tombstones, shortened the services, opted for more and more cremation to keep from running out of land better used for amusement parks, off-street parking, go-cart tracks, and golf courses. A graveyard gains favor when we combine it with a nature walk or historical tour, as if the nature and history of our mortality were not lesson enough on any given day. We keep looking for community events to have in them—band concerts, birdwatchings—meanwhile, the community events they are supposed to involve, namely funerals and burials, have become more and more private spectacles. It is not enough for it to be only the repository of our dead and the memories we keep of them, or safe harbor for the often noisome and untidy feelings grief includes; comfort and serenity are not enough. We want our parks, our memorial parks, to entertain us a little, to have some use beyond the obvious. Less, we seem to be telling the dead, is more; while for the living, enough is never quite enough.

So the combination of golf and good grieving seems a natural, each divisible by the requirement for large tracts of green grass, a concentration of holes, and the need for someone to carry the bags—caddies or pallbearers.

There will, of course, be practical arguments—when are you going to actually "do" the burials? Can people play through a graveside service? What is the protocol? Is there a dress code? What about headstones, decoration day, perpetual care? And what, godhelpus, about handicaps? What will the hearse look like? Must we all begin to dress like Gary Player?

When my mother was dying I hated God. Some days when I think of her, dead at sixty-five, I think of how my father said, "These were supposed to be the Golden Years." She bore and birthed and raised nine children because the teachings or the technologies of her generation did not offer reliable "choice." The daughter of a music teacher, she understood everything but "rhythm." It is the strength in numbers I'm the beneficiary of now. The God of my anger was the God she knew—the fellow with the beard and archangels and the abandonment issues. The practical joker with a mean streak, pulling the chair out from under us, squirting us with the boutonniere, shaking our hands with the lightning-bolt joy buzzer and then wondering why we don't "get it"; can't we "take a joke"?

My mother, a Bing Crosby and Ingrid Bergman Catholic, had her heaven furnished with familiar pieces: her own parents, her sister, friends of her youth. Her vision was precise, down to the doilies.

So checking into the Miramar—an old oceanfront hotel south

of Santa Barbara, with blue roof tiles over white clapboard, I wanted
to hide, for four days only, from the facts of the matter. I remember
waking to the sound of pelicans, gulls, and cormorants diving into the
blue water, the listless lapping of the waves. The Pacific was pacific.
I needed peace. I sat on the deck overlooking the beach. Taut bodies
jogged by in primary colors or walked with their designer dogs in the
morning light. No one was dying in Santa Barbara. I began to make
notes about the golf-course-cemetery combo. Would calling it "St.
Andrews" be too bold? Would people pay more to be buried on the
greens? Would a bad divot be desecration? What about headstones?
They'd have to go. But what to replace them with? Memorial balls?
These and other questions like them quarreled like children for my
attention. I ordered coffee. A grilled cheese sandwich. I avoided the
temptation to float in the water. The undulant ocean glistened with
metaphor. To sit and watch the sea was good. Everything was going
to be all right. By sunset I was transfixed by the beauty. I'd worked
out the details of my plan—the location, the capitalization, the ad
campaign, the board of directors. Why shouldn't our cemeteries be
used for fun and fitness? Pleasure and pain were insoluble. Laughing and crying are the same release. I didn't know which I should do
next, laugh or weep.

My mother believed in redemptive suffering. The paradigm for
this was the crucifixion of Christ, an emblem of which she kept in
most rooms of the house. This was the bad day against which all
others were measured. She was a student of the fifteenth-century
mystic Thomas à Kempis, whose *Imitation of Christ* she read daily.
"Offer it up for the suffering souls," is what she would say when we'd
commence our carping over some lapse in creature comforts. I think
it was a Catholic variation on the Protestant work ethic. If you're
going to be miserable, her logic held, you may as well be miserable
for a good cause.

Who were these suffering souls? I'd ask myself.

Likewise, people of the Irish persuasion have a special knack
or affliction for searching out the blessing in every badness. "Happy
is the grave the rain falls on," they say as they stand ankle deep in

mud, burying their dead, finding the good omen in the bad weather. Thus, in a country where it rains every day, they have proclaimed the downpour a blessed thing. "Could be worse," they say in the face of disaster or "The devil you know's better than the one you don't," or, when all else fails, "Just passing through life." Invasion and famine and occupation have taught them these things. They have a mindset that tolerates, perhaps to a fault, God's little jokes on the likes of us.

So when, as a child, I'd find myself hungry or angry or lonely or tired or brutalized by one of the brothers, among my mother's several comforts was the subtle spiritual dictum to "offer it up for the suffering souls." By patient acceptance of pain I could assist in the universal business of salvation. The currency of hurt became the currency of holiness the way you'd change pounds sterling to greenback dollars. God was the celestial bank teller who kept track of the debits and credits to our accounts. Those who died in arrears went to Purgatory—a kind of bump-and-paint shop for the soul, where the dents and dings and rust of life on earth could be fixed before going on to Heaven. Hell was a Purgatory that never ended, reserved for the true deadbeats who not only didn't pay their tolls but didn't figure they owed anyone anything. Purgatory was for rehabilitation. Hell was for punishment, perpetual, eternal, cruel and unusual. The chief instrument of both locales was fire—the cleansing, if painful, flames of *purgatorio*, the fire and brimstone recompense, for pleasures ill-got and self-indulgent, of the inferno.

I think sometimes that this is why, for most of the last two millennia, the western Church has avoided cremation—because fire was punitive. When you were in trouble with God you went to hell where you burned. Perhaps this created in us feelings about fire that were largely negative. We burned the trash and buried the treasure. That is why—faced with life's first lessons in mortality—the dead kitten or bunny rabbit, or dead bird fallen from its nest on high—good parents search out shoe boxes and shovels instead of kindling wood or barbecues. It is also why we might witness burials, but cremation, like capital punishment, is hidden from us. Of course, Eastern thought has always favored fire as a purifier, as the element that reunites us with our elements and origins. Hence the great public pyres of Calcutta and Bombay, where dead bodies blacken the skies with smoke from their burning.

My mother did not believe this part. Her children needed neither punishment nor purification beyond that which she supplied. We were the children of God and her own best efforts. Salvation was a gift of God. Her gift to us was how to claim it. And when, after the Second Vatican Council, they got rid of Limbo and Purgatory, she fashioned it a kind of enlightenment. Still, life had sufferings enough to go around and she wanted us to use them well. It was part of Nature.

"All grievous things are to be endured for eternal life," is how my mother was instructed by Thomas à Kempis. Suffering was thereby imbued with meaning, purpose, value, and reason. Nature passed suffering out in big doses, random and irreverent, but faith and grace made suffering a part of the way by which we make our journey back to God. Atonement meant to be "at one." And this return, this reunion in heaven, this salvation, was the one true reason for our being, according to my mother. This opinion put her, of course, at odds with everything the culture told us about "feeling good about ourselves" or "taking care of numero uno" or the secular trophies of "happiness" and "validation" and "self-esteem." Hers was a voice crying in the suburban wilderness that we were all given crosses to bear—it was our imitation of Christ—and we should offer it up for the suffering souls.

That is how she turned it into prayer—the "irregularity," the cancer, the tumor that moved from her remaining lung up her esophagus, leapt to her spinal cord, and then made for her brain. This was what the doctors said was happening, preferring a discussion of parts failing to persons dying. But for her husband and children what was happening was that her voice was growing more and more quiet, her breath was getting shorter and shorter, her balance was lost to the advance of cancer. My mother was making it work for her, placing the pain and the fear and the grief of it into that account with God she'd kept, by which what was happening to her body became only one of several things that were happening to her. Her body, painful and tumorous, was turning on her and she was dying. I'm sure she was ready to be rid of it. She said her heart was overwhelmed with grief and excitement. Grief at the going from us—her husband of forty-three years, her sons and daughters, grandchildren born and unborn, her sister and brother, her friends. Excitement at the going "home." But as the voice inside her body hushed, her soul's voice seemed to shout out loud, almost to sing. She could see things none of us could see. She refused the morphine and remained lucid and visionary. She spoke words of comfort to each of us—at one point saying we must learn to let go, not only grudgingly but as an act of praise. I say this not because I understand it but because I witnessed it. I'm not certain that it works—only certain that it worked for her.

Once you've made the leap it's easy. Once you've seen huge tracts of greensward put to seemingly conflicting uses, the world becomes a different place. If golf courses can be graveyards, surely football fields, and soccer pitches, ball diamond and tennis courts. And what about ski slopes? What folks don't want to be buried on a mountain? Boot Hill we could call it. Listen up, the possible applications are endless. The thrill of victory, the agony of defeat. Life is like that—death is, too.

My mother's funeral was a sadness and a celebration. We wept and laughed, thanked God and cursed God, and asked God to make good on the promises our mother's faith laid claim to in her death. It was Halloween the day we buried her—the eve of All Saints, then All Souls, all suffering souls.

Eddie and I have been looking for acreage. He's a golfer. I'd rather read and write. He says he'll be the Club Pro and I can be the Brains Behind the Operation. We've worked together for years and years. Our sister Brigid does pre-need and our sister Mary has always done the books—payroll and collections and payables. The women seem to control the money. Revenge they call it for our calling it Lynch and Sons.

Whenever I have business at Holy Sepulchre, I stop in section twenty-four, where my mother and father are buried. He lived on after her for two more years. After he was buried we all decided on a tall Celtic cross in Barre granite with their instruction to "Love One Another" cut into a circle that connects the crossed beams. My father had seen crosses like this when I took him to Ireland the year after my mother died. He'd said he liked the look of them.

Stones like these make golf impossible. They stand their ground. It's hard to play through.

Those joggers with their designer dogs on leashes and stereos plugged into their ears are not allowed. A sign by the pond reads "No Fishing/Do Not Feed Ducks." The only nature trail in Holy Sepulchre is the one that takes you by the nature of our species to die and to remember.

I miss them so.

I think it's my sisters who plant the impatiens every spring at the base of the stone.

Sometimes I stand among the stones and wonder. Sometimes I laugh, sometimes I weep.

Sometimes nothing at all much happens. Life goes on. The dead are everywhere. Eddie says that's par for the course.

COMING HOME TO ST. PAT'S:
ROSEMARY CLOONEY

by Nick Clooney
July 5, 2002

Singer Rosemary Clooney's funeral in her hometown of Maysville, Kentucky, was attended by a number of celebrities, many of whom were family: Eulogist Nick, her brother, is a writer and broadcaster while his son, actor George Clooney, was a pallbearer. One of her five children by actor Jose Ferrer married singer Debby Boone.

Their old Kentucky parish was at times an oasis for the Clooney siblings during and after their parents' divorce. When Rosemary was thirteen, their mother went to California to marry a sailor, taking Nick with her. Rosemary and her sister Betty were left in Kentucky with their alcoholic father. One night, he took the household money and disappeared, leaving his daughters to fend for themselves.

Hoping to earn some money to live on, the girls sang at a radio station audition. They earned a spot on the talent show and won it. Rosemary went on to become an internationally-known pop music icon, with hit songs such as "Hey There," "Mambo Italiano," and "How Much Is That Doggie in the Window?"

She married Ferrer in 1953 and had five children in five years, at the peak of her career. She costarred with Bing Crosby in 1954's top-grossing film, White Christmas, *and by 1956 she was starring in her own weekly television series. The marriage deteriorated, however, and the strain of raising a family took its toll: She developed an addiction to tranquilizers and sleeping pills.*

Then a national tragedy led to her breakdown. In 1968, while campaigning for her friend Robert Kennedy, she was with him when he was assassinated in a Los Angeles hotel. Soon after, she collapsed while performing on stage. She checked into a treatment facility and remained in therapy for many years, supporting herself by singing at Holiday Inns and doing commercials.

Years later, she told a journalist that she had finally regained the joy of her early years of singing. She received an Emmy nomination for a guest appearance on NBC-TV's "ER"; was granted the James Smithson Bicentennial Medal in 1992 for her contribution to American music; and was honored by the Grammys with a Lifetime Achievement Award in 2002.

Another day has dawned in the little river town of Maysville, Kentucky, just one of nearly 30,000 days since settlers from the East Coast decided this would be a good place to build a few cabins, a tavern and eventually a church.

For one-third of all those days a native daughter proudly called Maysville her home town. By the time Rosemary Clooney first saw the light of day on May 23rd, 1928, Maysville had settled in as a prosperous, attractive community. Most Maysvillians thought it was just the right size. Rosemary thought so too.

No one could remember when Rosemary didn't sing. And when her sister Betty came along three years later, it seemed Betty could sing before she could talk because Rosemary wanted someone to harmonize with.

When Rosemary and I talked about it in later years, she was sure that the first time she sang before a group of people who were not family was at St. Patrick's Church. Her first personal appearance.

Today, in melancholy symmetry, it was where she made her last personal appearance. The most famous daughter of the community and, arguably, of the Commonwealth of which it is a part, never forgot her childhood here.

Not all of it was moonlight and roses, by any means. No one's childhood is. It was the time of the Depression and World War II. Our mom and dad couldn't make a go of their marriage, so Grandma Guilfoyle raised us. Money was tight, but it was the same for nearly everyone.

Rosemary, Betty and I always thought Maysville had a lot to do with any success we were able to attain. When Rosemary and Betty sang and, eventually, I began broadcasting, Maysville gave us a boost. They supported us, told us we were good, "as good as any of those other people in the radio or in the movies."

By the time the three of us found out it wasn't quite that simple, Maysville had already instilled enough confidence in us that we were able to survive whatever negative energy we might encounter in a highly competitive profession. That was a priceless gift and it would have been improper to forget it.

So any time Rosemary—or Betty or I—had a chance to tell the world about Maysville, we did so. When the time came, we told our children, too.

Rosemary's career became meteoric and she was a star of international stature, so some thought she would finally break the childhood tie. She didn't. The Kentucky roots centered her. She often kidded about it, as we all do, but it was with affection.

So there was no suspense when it came to her funeral service. It would be in the same place she was baptized, had her first communion and married Dante—St. Patrick's Church. She will be buried in St. Patrick's cemetery where her marker will remain until many years from now. Time and nature erode the granite, but never the memory.

Many have asked if there is some place where a memorial contribution might be sent. There are many worthy causes which Rosemary supported over the years; it is difficult to single one out.

However, this morning I was recalling the day Rosemary and Dante married, a happy occasion nearly five years ago at St. Patrick's. Rosemary asked if those in attendance could support St. Patrick's School Fund.

All three of us attended St. Pat's, a small private school, grades 1-12, always struggling to survive. Rosemary went there eight grades and starred in some of her first plays, including *Snow White*. She got great reviews.

My guess is that if this occasion could help St. Pat's pay the light bill for another month, it would make her smile.

"That's the secret, Nick. Smile. Even if I'm singing a sad song, I smile. People like to believe everything will turn out all right."

I'll give it a try, Rosemary. Tomorrow.

WHAT YOU CAN EXPECT
FROM THE SON OF A BOOKMAKER:
WELLINGTON T. MARA

by John K. Mara
October 28, 2005
St. Patrick's Cathedral, New York, NY

On December 27, 2009, the New York Giants played their final game at Giants Stadium. President and CEO John K. Mara watched from his customary spot in a lower-level booth at the 25-yard line. His brother, Chris, the Vice President of Player Evaluation, sat beside him. A third brother, Steve, was also seated in the booth (another brother, Frank, the Director of Promotions, was somewhere in the stadium as well). Beside Steve Mara sat an empty stool—a stool that has sat empty since the fall of 2005, when their father, Wellington Mara, who The New York Times *called "The Patriarch of the National Football League," passed away.*

The New York Giants have always been a family business. Wellington's father Tim was a bookmaker who founded the Giants in 1925. They played their first seasons in the Polo Grounds, and later, Yankee Stadium. Nine-year-old Wellington served as a ball boy in that inaugural season, and for eighty years was devoted to the well-being of his family's franchise. When Wellington was fourteen, his father divided ownership of the team between him and his brother Jack. For many years, Wellington was the chief decision maker on all football matters. In his career he served as a ball boy, secretary, scout, and eventually as a front-office executive, most recently as president and co-CEO. When he was elected to the Pro Football Hall of Fame in 1997, he and his father Tim (a charter member in 1956) became the first father and son to be inducted.

Wellington's career was a Hall of Fame career by any standard. During his tenure, the G-Men won two Super Bowls, nine conference championships, and thirteen division championships. He guided the Gi-

ants from a franchise his father founded for $500 in 1925 to a franchise worth $806 million in 2005. This would be enough for most men—enough of a career.

But Wellington was also the driving force behind the NFL's revenue sharing system, which entitles each NFL franchise to an even portion of the total television revenue generated by all thirty-two teams. This was a groundbreaking and controversial idea when he got behind it in 1962; the Giants then were the highest-grossing television market. But Wellington stated publicly that the NFL was "only as strong as its weakest link." As a result of this foresight—and his ability to put the interest of the league ahead of the interest of the team he had inherited—the NFL today offers greater parity than most professional team sports.

Father of eleven and grandfather to more than forty, Wellington Mara considered the Giants' players and staff to be part of his extended family. John, the eldest son, eulogized his father at St. Patrick's Cathedral in New York City. Attendees included Super Bowl MVP and quarterback Phil Simms and former Giants coaches Bill Parcells and Bill Belichick.

In the months leading up to his death, as he began ceding ground in his long fight against lymphoma, Wellington had not visited Giants Stadium for several weeks. He had missed training camp and every regular season game—which he hadn't done, outside of his military service, for eighty years.

On behalf of my mother and my entire family, I want to thank everyone who has come here to celebrate my father's life. Many of you came from deep distances and we are very appreciative. Thank you also to all of you who called, wrote, or visited over the past several weeks. The outpouring of love and affection displayed to my father has been overwhelming and a source of comfort to my family. Also, I want to thank Cardinal Egan for his frequent visits and comforting words; Bishop McCormick who visited my father every day and brought him communion; Frank Gifford who was a constant visitor and who has been a true friend to my family for so many years.

Thank you also to Sloan Kettering, who took such good care of my father the last six weeks. They treated him like he was their own father. When he finally decided that he wanted to go home and he was being taken out of the hospital, the nurses and the staff were all in tears. That is how close a bond they formed during that stay.

There is one person who deserves special thanks, Ronnie Barnes, who my mother refers to as her twelfth child, spent night after night and many days in my father's hospital room taking care of him night after night. "Is Ronnie coming tonight?" my father would ask. Of course, the answer was always "yes" and my father's face would light up when Ronnie's face walked into the room. We joked with Ronnie that one of the reasons he did this was because so many of the nurses kept trying to slip him their phone numbers at the hospital, but that really wasn't the reason. My father asked him one night, "Ronnie why are you so good to me?" "Because Mr. Mara you've been so good to me," Ronnie replied. Nobody took better care of him and there was no one that he trusted more. Ronnie, my family can never thank you enough.

As we made our way over here from the funeral home this morning I couldn't help but think [my father] would have been so embarrassed by all this. The police escort, the traffic being stopped, the bag pipes; he would have just shook his head and tried to hide somewhere.

As painful as it is to say goodbye to someone you love so much, to someone who has been such an important part of your life, I could not help but think, when I sat down to try and prepare this, how fortunate I am and all my brothers and sisters are to have Wellington Mara as our father. He was the finest man that we have ever known or hope to know, and he was our dad.

Many years ago his good friend Tim Rooney said something to me that I have reflected on many times since. "You realize, don't you, that your father is the best example of how we should all live our lives. You will never find anyone better to emulate." Over the years, as I have watched my father live his life, I have come to realize how true those words were and what a role model he really was.

"What can you expect from an Irishman named Wellington, whose father was a bookmaker?" A local sportswriter derisively wrote those words about thirty years ago during a time when we were going through some pretty awful seasons. My father usually didn't let criticism from the media affect him very much, but those words stung him in a very personal way.

"I'll tell you what you can expect," he said at our kickoff luncheon just a few days later. "You can expect anything he says or writes may be repeated aloud in your own home in front of your own children. You can believe that he was taught to love and respect all mankind, but to fear no man. And you could believe that his abiding ambitions were to pass on to his family the true richness of the inheritance he received from his father, the bookmaker: The knowledge and love and fear of God and, second, to give you (our fans and our coach) a Super Bowl winner."

My father's faith was his strength. It never wavered; no matter what happened in his life, no matter how sick he was. He and my mother went to Mass every day and made sure that we went on every Sunday and holy day. Long after we were married with children of our own, he would still call to remind us about an upcoming holy day of obligation. Each year at Christmas time, the confession schedule of our parish was hung on the refrigerator door with a little handwritten note: *No confession, no Santa,* he wrote. As sick as he was, he still received communion every day in the hospital. His rosary beads never left his hands.

His family, of course, was his pride and joy. He was married to my mother for more than fifty-one years, and they had as wonderful a marriage as I have ever seen. I can't even remember them raising their voices to one another. They met, of course, in church, when a woman fainted, and they both went to assist her. My father later claimed that the whole thing was staged by my mother's Aunt Lil in order to get his attention. Well, after fifty-one years of marriage, eleven children, and forty grandchildren, I would say that she got his attention. When my parents celebrated their fiftieth wedding anniversary about a year-and-a-half-ago, right here in St. Patrick's, my mother asked him if they could renew their vows. He was very reluctant at first. "The original ones haven't expired yet, have they?" he said. Of course, he went along with it, but when Cardinal Egan asked him during the ceremony, "Will you accept children lovingly from God?" the look on his face seemed to say, "Your Eminence, I think that ship sailed a long time ago."

If there was a category in the *Guinness Book of Records* for most christenings attended, or first communions, or graduations, school plays, little league games, my father would surely hold the record. He loved watching his grandchildren compete or act on stage. He always sat or stood in the background never wanting to draw attention to himself, always positive, always supportive, setting yet another example for all of us.

One of my father's greatest attributes was his loyalty. It was so much a part of his life. Whether it was his friends, former players, coaches, he was always concerned about their well-being. He considered Giants players, coaches, employees both past and present, as part of his extended family. If a member of that family was in need, he or she didn't stay that way for very long, whether it was money, a job, or just "a call from a friendly voice," as he'd like to say. There was a time years ago when he was criticized for that loyalty and for it clouding his judgment. "If that's the worst thing they can say about you," he would say, "then you must be doing something right."

I remember going on countless road trips with him over the years, and he would always make it a habit to call a former player or coach in the town that we were playing in. Many of these guys were long-forgotten by many people, but not by him. He never forgot them, and he knew how much it meant to them that he was still thinking about them.

Next to his faith and his family, the thing my father loved most was his team, the team that he spent eighty years of his life around. His father wanted him to go to law school after his graduation from Fordham in 1937. "Just give me one year with the team," he pleaded.

My grandfather agreed, and that number turned into sixty-eight. He never went to law school. He went on to spend the rest of his life, with the exception of four years that he served in the Navy during World War II, around the team and the sport he loved so much. He attended nearly every practice from minicamp right through the end of the season. It didn't matter if we were 10-2, or 2-10, he was there wearing that old floppy hat, carrying that ridiculous stool, and usually wearing a shirt or a jacket that was almost as old as he was. Each year our equipment manager would give him the new apparel for the season, and it would always wind up in the same place, stuck in the back of his closet, and out would come the same old and battered outfits. When we changed our logo several years ago back to the traditional lower case *ny*, he actually started wearing some of the shirts that he had worn the last time we had used that logo more than twenty-five years before. "I knew they would come back," he said.

He loved participating in the draft meetings. It was his favorite time of year. Day after day, he would sit there as reports were read on every prospect. No matter how remote they were, he didn't want to miss anything, and he loved interacting with our scouts. He identified with them because he had been one himself for so many years.

One of the visions I will always have of him is sitting on the equipment truck prior to Super Bowl XXXV, alone in his thoughts, a scene I had witnessed so many times over the years. No pre-game parties or festivities for him; he was where he wanted to be with his players and coaches, but off to the background so as not to interfere. During our road games, he always sat in the press box. Never one for a fancy suite or entertaining people during a game, his focus was on the game. He always maintained his composure and often tried with mixed results to calm his family down, more so his daughters than his sons. I remember one game years ago when a particular player was having a tough day and some of us became a little exacerbated with him. At one point I yelled out, "What is he doing out there?" My father put his hand on my shoulder rather firmly and said, "What he's doing is the best that he can."

My father had a special relationship with Giants fans. It amazed me that he answered nearly every letter a fan wrote to him no matter how derogatory they got. "They are our customers," he would say. "They're just demonstrating how much they care about the team, and they deserve a response." For years, it was a joke around our office that if someone wanted to have their season tickets improved, all they had to do was write my father a letter that they had some physical ailment that made it difficult to climb the stairs or see from such a distance. The tickets were always improved; the fans knew who the soft touch was.

My father was very proud of his contributions and his longtime associations with the National Football League. He believed so deeply in the principles upon which it was founded and has flourished. He served virtually on every committee imaginable, and he valued all of them. None of those committees mattered more to him than a little-known one called the NFL Alumni Dire Need Fund, which was established to take care of former players who had fallen on hard times.

There were so many lessons that my father taught us over the years, maybe none more important than in the last few weeks of his life. He never gave up his will to live. He tried so hard to get out of bed and walk. He fought until the very end, and he never complained. His faith never waned. On his last day in the hospital, when he came to the realization that the doctors could no longer treat him, he summoned me to his bedside. He could barely talk. I held his hand and he looked at me and smiled and said, "I'll be there when you get there." It was his way of telling us that he was going to be okay. He was going to a better place. He was always concerned with how his family was dealing with his condition. "I don't want to be a burden," he said just days before his death. "Go home and take care of your own families." Of course we had to be there with him. He had always been there for us, and when he took his last breath, he was surrounded by the family he loved so much and taught so well.

There's a scene from the movie *Saving Private Ryan* that is worth recounting here. A then-elderly Private Ryan visits the gravesites of some of the men who died trying to save his life. Overcome with emotion, he turns to his wife and asks her, "Have I been a good husband, a good father, a good person?" Questions I suppose we will all have to answer at some point. In the case of Wellington Mara, the answers were so clear.

Yes, you were a wonderful husband; you were the best father and grandfather that anyone could ever have; and you were the best example of how we should all live our lives. That is what we came to expect from the Irishman named Wellington, whose father was a bookmaker.

He may be gone from this world, and we certainly grieve over that. But we also rejoice over our good fortune in having had him with us for so long, for the extraordinary life he led, and for his spirit, which will live on in his children and grandchildren for generations to come. When my father's brother died forty years ago, Arthur Daley, the well-known sportswriter of *The New York Times*, wrote a column lamenting the loss of his good friend Jack Mara. My father had that column on his desk for all these years, and the last line from that column is a quote from *Hamlet*:

"Now cracks a noble heart. Goodnight sweet prince and flights of angels sing thee to thy rest."

EULOGY FOR A BABY WHO DIES AFTER BAPTISM

by his father

There could be no better preface to this eulogy than what Thomas Lynch observed in The Undertaking: Life Studies from the Dismal Trade, *his memoir about working as an undertaker in Milford, Michigan:*

> *When we bury the old, we bury the known past....Memory is the overwhelming theme, the eventual comfort. But burying infants, we bury the future, unwieldy and unknown, full of promise and possibilities, outcomes punctuated by our rosy hopes. The grief has no borders, no limits, no known ends, and the little infant graves that edge the corners and fencerows of every cemetery are never quite big enough to contain that grief. Some sadnesses are permanent. Dead babies do not give us memories. They give us dreams.*

I need to take a couple of minutes to say thank you to all of you here today. The support we have received from our neighbors, fellow parishioners, friends and co-workers has been so appreciated by our family.

We asked for and have received prayers for our family from all of you and from so many others we have come to know and love. I can say with an abiding confidence that the grace we have received as a result of your prayers has swiftly moved us from crushing grief to an attitude that, while still tinged with sorrow, is nevertheless permeated by joy.

This Faith of ours, this glorious Catholic faith, has for centuries boldly proclaimed that an infant who is baptized and then dies, as our child has, is carried directly to the waiting arms of God to enjoy the Beatific Vision and live in Paradise forever. We as Catholic parents are called by our vocation of marriage to strive above all else to work towards helping our children arrive in heaven someday. The Church assures us that our baby is now in heaven. How can we not be filled with joy?

At the same time, the Church gently encourages us to embrace sorrow. The other morning as my wife sat in her rocking chair and held our child's lifeless little body, we pulled close a small replica of the *Pietà* which depicts the Blessed Mother holding the lifeless body of her Son. God is good. He allows us to share in a small way with Mary and all of her suffering. The Church teaches us not to waste suffering but to use it as an opportunity to show our dependence on God.

One might think that it would be difficult to eulogize a baby, but let me share some of what I've been told over the past two days. I've heard people reflecting on how fragile life is and taking stock of their own life. I've heard parents express their desire to run home and hold close their own children. I've heard reassessments of how incredibly precious each and every little life is that God gives us. I've heard recognitions of how truly short life is and how suddenly it can end, which in turn resulted in personal inquiries about God, faith and eternal life.

In short, our baby's short life and sudden death has prompted some wonderful things. This, then, is our family prayer—we gladly give our baby back to God and endure the sorrowful pain if it prompts just one person to grow closer to Him.

And finally, to you my beautiful bride whose arms ache for your baby, you have sustained us through all of this unselfishly and with dignity and humility in imitation of our Blessed Mother. I know well that your heart is breaking and I love you.

"The Lord giveth and the Lord taketh away...Blessed be the name of the Lord!"

III. WE REMEMBER
Our Friends

LEAVING A LEGACY OF KINDNESS: PHIL RIZZUTO

by Bob Klapisch
August 15, 2007

In retirement, Phil Rizzuto and his wife lived in Montclair, New Jersey, and area newspapers covered his death in full. Five sportswriters wrote articles showing why the colorful shortstop was beloved by colleagues and fans, as a ballplayer and later as a broadcaster. Bob Klapisch's eulogy adds another dimension: the friendship between Rizzuto and his former teammate Yogi Berra.

They met on the playing field when Berra was seventeen years old. Later, Rizzuto became godfather to Berra's son. Klapisch describes how Berra remained a steadfast companion during Rizzuto's declining years.

When asked to express what he felt after his friend died at age eighty-nine, the usually talkative Berra had few words. What came to mind was the irony of how so many others had always misperceived and underestimated the five-foot-six-inch Rizzuto, who had loomed so large in Berra's life.

Rizzuto's plaque in Monument Park in Yankee Stadium, dedicated when the Yankees retired his number 10 in 1985, reads: "A man's size is measured by his heart."

Three times a week every week, Yogi Berra would make the drive from his home in Montclair to West Orange, where Phil Rizzuto called home. Pulling up to the gates of Green Hill, an assisted living facility, Berra knew his longtime friend and teammate had deteriorated rapidly. Rizzuto would often forget people's names, drift off in mid-sentence, and make his family yearn for the days when he was a limitless reservoir of laughs and love.

Still, Yogi's loyalty to Scooter never waned. He showed up at Green Hill without fail, walking into Rizzuto's apartment and starting up another game of bingo. There they were, two Yankee legends, Hall of Famers both, speaking in the shorthand that only major-leaguers could appreciate. Every once in awhile, like a time tunnel that had been magically activated, the old Rizzuto would awaken and fill up the room. Those were the good days; there were bad ones too, especially in the last month. Yogi told a friend the other day, "I don't think Scooter is going to make it."

Maybe that explains why Berra took the news of Rizzuto's death so philosophically; he'd been preparing for it all during those bingo games. When the little Yankee shortstop and broadcaster took his final breath late Monday, dying of pneumonia at the age of eighty-nine, Yogi was ready with a simple but poignant eulogy.

"Great guy. Great friend," Yogi told reporters at the Stadium, echoing the sentiments of anyone who ever met him. To older fans, Rizzuto was the shortstop of the Yankees' greatest golden era, when they won five consecutive championships between 1949 and 1953. On a roster full of superstars, Rizzuto was Everyman, the 5'-6", 160-pound squirt who made it possible to believe anyone could be a baseball player.

Actually, Rizzuto's legacy was about beating the odds. After a 1937 tryout with the Brooklyn Dodgers, then-manager Casey Stengel told Rizzuto to get a shoeshine box: He was too short to be a ballplayer.

After beginning his broadcasting career, Howard Cosell told Rizzuto he'd never succeed: He looked like George Burns and sounded like Groucho Marx.

And Cooperstown sent its rejection notice, too—over four decades. But in 1994 the Veterans Committee finally honored Rizzuto, putting a bright light on a fine career.

From 1941 to 1956, Rizzuto anchored the Yankee infield, winning the American League Most Valuable Player award in 1950.

He played in nine World Series and was on the winning side seven times. "Little Dago" they called him, a politically incorrect but affectionate nickname that actually honored Rizzuto. He was mini-me to Joe DiMaggio, who was known in those days as "Daig" and took Rizzuto under his wing.

In return, Rizzuto would address everyone by their last name. That, or "Huckleberry." No first names, ever, except his wife, Cora, to whom he was eternally devoted. Indeed, there was something unique about the way Rizzuto interacted with the world. Maybe it was this simple: He loved everyone, and the feeling went both ways.

"I've never seen a big-name personality treat people as kindly as Phil did," said Yankee broadcaster Michael Kay. "He was like an uncle to all of us, and that's something you can't say about announcers anymore."

Indeed, Rizzuto's career in the TV booth, which began in 1958, was nearly as distinguished as his days in Yankee pinstripes. Scooter had a way of personalizing the game that was so old-fashioned and un-hip. It was impossible to dislike him. "Holy cow" was his signature call—and he meant it. Scooter was there when Roger Maris hit his sixty-first home run in 1961, when Chris Chambliss sent the Yankees to the World Series in 1976 with a pennant-clinching home run against the Royals, and when Ron Guidry struck out eighteen Angels in 1978.

Holy cow. Who would dare say that on the air anymore? But from Rizzuto's lips, it was a measure of his honesty; he was a broadcaster without a gimmick. Scooter didn't hide his affection for the Yankees, openly rooting for them. Nor did he make a secret of his desire to be home before the last out, beating the traffic onto the George Washington Bridge by the ninth inning on his way home to Hillside.

Thing is, Scooter would tell viewers about it the next day; it was part of the ongoing dialogue about his life that made Yankee broadcasts as unpolished as they were irresistible.

"It was having a friend sitting in your living room talking about his favorite restaurant, his wife, his family, all the while he was commenting on the Yankee game," Kay said. "I don't know if that plays anymore. If Phil came into the business today, I'm not sure it would work. But everyone sure loved him."

Even his gaffes were ones for the ages. When the Yankees brought up outfielder Roberto Kelly, Rizzuto told Bill White, his partner in the booth, "I can't wait to see this new Irish kid." When Kelly, a dark-skinned Panamanian, took the field, Rizzuto deadpanned, "Funny, he doesn't look Irish to me."

We all loved him, but no one did more than Yogi, who decided to move to New Jersey at Rizzuto's urging in the Fifties. Together, they opened the Rizzuto-Berra Bowling Lanes in Clifton, where the co-owners filled a trophy case with all kinds of memorabilia. There were enough memories to last a lifetime, sort of like Scooter's career. He last appeared in the booth in 1996, just as the Yankees were beginning a second golden era in the Bronx. Then, little by little, Rizzuto started fading away from the Yankee family, appearing less frequently at the Stadium.

It was soon obvious that Rizzuto was in declining health, no longer showing up at Old-Timers' events. But through it all, Yogi was there, firing up another bingo game, accompanying his buddy through the final stages of his life. When Rizzuto finally passed on Tuesday, Yogi didn't need any long speeches. What he said was already on everyone's mind.

"They said Phil was too small to play baseball," Yogi said.

Larger than life, was more like it.

SISSIES ANONYMOUS: ANDRE DUBUS

by Tobias Wolff
2001

Once, when asked how he would describe his writing, Andre Dubus answered "Catholic." Born in Louisiana, he was educated by the Christian Brothers. After six years in the Marines, he went to the Iowa Writer's Workshop and began his career as a writer.

This eulogy refers to "the accident" that critically injured Dubus and put him in a wheelchair for the rest of his life. Through several surgeries and infections, Dubus struggled to carry on with his craft.

Among his well-known collections of short stories and essays are Meditations from a Movable Chair *and* Dancing after Hours. *His many awards include a MacArthur Foundation "Genius Grant." He died from a heart attack at age sixty-two.*

His son Andre Dubus III is also a writer. His best-known novel is House of Sand and Fog, *which was made into a film.*

Eulogizer Tobias Wolff is also a southern-born, Catholic writer. He is best known for his memoir This Boy's Life, *which was made into a movie starring Robert DeNiro and Leonardo DiCaprio. He is currently a professor in the School of Humanities and Sciences at Stanford University.*

The first time I ever laid eyes on Andre Dubus he was bearing down on me at a party. He didn't trouble to stop and introduce himself, no, he bent over my chair and in front of everyone kissed me on the mouth. I recoiled like a howitzer. "Hah!" he said. "Homosexual terror!" and laughed hugely. I was so shocked that I started laughing too. And what made him want to do such a thing?—Ah he'd liked a story of mine. There are other ways of showing appreciation, and I mostly prefer them to this way, but he somehow put me off balance and managed to keep me off balance for the next twenty years.

Andre called me Silent Death. When I picked up the phone and heard just those words, spoken in his gravelly drawl—"Silent Death"—I wanted to scream. I'd told him truly and repeatedly that my service in Vietnam had not been at all heroic or even competent, but it pleased Andre to affect disbelief, indeed to treat my very denials as proof that I had carried the war to the enemy with implacable and dire efficiency. So when I heard those words I wanted to scream but it always came out in laughter. There is generally an element of self-importance in self-deprecation, and Andre knew where to put the needle.

He could also apply the needle to himself. Andre had about him a loud blustering maleness—one of my sons, then quite young, called him Yosemite Sam—and enough binocular vision to see the sometimes cartoonish aspects of his own manner. I visited him in Haverhill one night after the accident and found him wheeling around the house in a Rambo headband and a Marine Corps t-shirt with his old Expert Rifleman's badge pinned over his heart. It was both self-parodic and serious; Andre was intensely and rightly proud of his years in the Marines, even while having a complex, illusionless sense of the limitations of military life and the unacknowledged motives that send men into it. The Marine Corps, he maintained, was basically a collection of sissies trying to prove they weren't. We sometimes talked of starting a Sissies Anonymous chapter, stocked with former jarheads and fighter pilots and paratroopers and SEALS who would, with tears and breaking voices, stand and testify to the pain of their double lives: My name is Moose Steel, and I'm a recovering sissy....

Andre had a very soft heart under that hairy chest, which didn't stop him from peeling off his shirt when the mood struck him. At a literary festival in Athens, Ohio, he was taking questions after reading one of his stories, and as was his habit he sailed off onto subjects of his own, and soon went aground on Women's Liberation. I saw it about to happen and my heart sank because though it was clear that Andre also saw the reefs looming he was happily resolved to drive upon them. He held forth for a good half hour while the men in the audience cringed at what we imagined to be the women's wrath at Andre's observation (to cite but one) that the entire result of Women's Lib was that women could now "wear suits and take the train to work and tell lies all day." And yet at the end it was the women who were laughing and laughing hard; they could recognize a bravura riff when they heard one.

Yet there was some conviction in what he said. Andre hated a bully more than anything. And so he distrusted what turns people into bullies—power. In Andre's view, the power men had hogged for themselves was no prize at all; it soured their natures, made them vain and greedy and dishonest. Wearing suits and telling lies all day was pretty much how he saw the world of business and government that women were trying to break into. Paradoxically it was his sense of women as having better or at least more interesting characters than men that led him to look skeptically on their struggle for power.

This was paternalism, of course, but of a different temper than most I've seen. It didn't proceed from any desire to protect his own position in the world. It came really from his love for women, a love they returned. There was always a company of them in attendance at the house—daughters, daughters-in-law, granddaughters, ex-wives, friends, fellow writers, former students, admiring readers paying their respects. Once a week for several years he led a workshop, gratis, for a group of girls from a local shelter. He helped women writers in every way he could. And he wrote better about women than any man of his generation, both from their point of view and from without. He wrote about mothers and daughters, women in love, women being beaten, women being raped, women being stalked, women working, women being friends with other women, women loving their husbands, and committing adultery and saving themselves and their children from bad men. Each of his women is particular and unexpected, her moral and physical nature without a shadow of male fantasy or condescension.

And yet, and yet. The desire to protect what we love can do great harm to what we love, as we see in Andre's masterful "A Father's Story," in which the pious likable narrator, Luke Ripley, arranges a cover-up for his daughter after she accidentally kills a boy with her car while out drinking. Luke does a terrible thing here, not so much in concealing his daughter's culpability as in removing her from the process of confession and acceptance of punishment that is her only road back into the human community. Luke may have saved her from legal retribution, but he has isolated her forever with her unexpiated guilt. It is an unwittingly arrogant, profoundly destructive act, and though Luke feels true compassion for the dead boy and his parents, he has no sense of what he has done to his daughter. On the contrary, he likens his love for her to God's love for him, a breathtaking flourish of pride. The story is a shrewd portrait of a man confounding his desire to save his daughter by smothering her spirit in the name of love, never once imagining that a greater love would allow her the freedom to act responsibly and redeem herself.

There is a muddle of love and self-contradiction at the heart of this great story, as in Andre's heart. For all his swagger and volume, I never saw a man so tender with his friends or for that matter with anyone who seemed in need of it. He was very brave, yet prone to question his own bravery, its true motive and effect. I can't begin to describe even the little I saw of his courage after the accident, as he lost command of the sturdy body he'd taken such delight in, and had to begin life anew; so here is a story on a more comprehensible scale.

We were leaving a bar in Bradford one snowy night and found the wheelchair exit blocked by a truck. We had the bartender ask—loudly, repeatedly—whose truck it was. No one answered. We finally gave up, and Andre's son, Andre III, and some other friends and I carried him up the steps and outside. While we were saying our good-byes in the parking lot the bartender himself came out, and, not seeing us, got some cigarettes out of that truck. It was his, the prick! He was a big guy but Andre wheeled at him in a fury, daring him to stand. The bartender ran around the lot awhile and finally made it back inside. The rest of us were giddy with the pleasure of seeing him humiliated, but Andre was embarrassed at what he'd done. Later, perhaps with this night in mind, Andre wrote: "If you confront a man from a wheelchair you're bullying him."

He was both ribald and gallant; hilariously profane, and true to his Catholic faith—toward the end of his life he was receiving communion every day. He loved earthy jokes and conversation, but never at the expense of an actual person; Andre didn't tear down other people, either in argument or gossip. He'd always been a big man. In the wheelchair he grew even bigger.

Uproarious as he was, he was also courtly and attentive. He listened closely and teared up when touched by something he'd heard or read. Physically restless, he could draw on deep pools of stillness when writing and reading. Andre was a superb reader; his essay on his own long-evolving comprehension of Hemingway's "In Another Country" is one of the very best I have ever seen on that thoroughly-scrutinized writer.

He had no want of ambition, but always rejoiced when some friend's good work got its due. And he took none of his own hard-won success for granted. He loved the ideals of the soldier—courage, comradeship, endurance, self-denial—but in the end the pictures on his wall were of Dorothy Day and Gandhi.

I miss my friend. I miss hearing that laugh explode from him like a blast from the mouth of a mine. I miss being called Silent Death. I miss the quiet and serious times, talking about our families, our work, something good we'd read and wanted the other to read. I miss hearing him read his stories and riff on the questions afterwards. I miss drinking with him and being needled by him and fishing with him and watching him deftly filet our catch with the Marine K-Bar knife he kept so deadly sharp, honing the blade on an oiled whetstone at the kitchen table with his friends and family all around, drinking, talking, laughing.

MY CLOSEST FRIEND FOR SIXTY YEARS:
REMEMBERING WALKER PERCY

by Shelby Foote, Jr.
1990

This spare and lean eulogy befits these two men: no-frills types who were both born in 1916. Shelby Foote's deep sorrow over the loss of Walker Percy, his lifelong friend, is keen, and nothing more needs—or can—be said.

*Foote and Percy both suffered life-altering bereavement at an early age. When he was five years old, Foote's father died, leading his mother to move with her only child to Greenville, Mississippi. Walker Percy moved there as a teenager following his father's suicide. Two years later, Percy's mother died, possibly also a suicide. He moved in with a bachelor uncle, who had already been influencing Foote's education, and who went on to mentor both boys. Percy became a medical doctor and later a novelist (*The Moviegoer, *his first novel, won the National Book Award); Foote became a novelist and historian.*

It wasn't until the year of Percy's death, 1990, at age seventy-four, that Foote became well-known after appearing on Ken Burns' PBS-TV documentary about the Civil War. Foote died in 2005, at age eighty-eight.

The English essayist E. H. Carr said at the close of his early-thirties critical biography of Dostoevsky: "A hundred years hence, when Dostoevsky's psychology will seem as much of a historical curiosity as his theology seems to us now, the true proportions of his work will emerge; and posterity, removed from the controversies of the early twentieth century, will once more be able to regard it as an artistic whole."

Similarly, I would state my hope that Walker Percy will be seen in time for what he was in simple and solemn fact—a novelist, not merely an explicator of various philosophers and divines, existentialist or otherwise. He was no more indebted to them, or even influenced by them, than was Proust (say) to or by Schopenhauer and Bergson. Proust absorbed them, and so did Walker absorb his preceptors. Like Flannery O'Connor, he found William Faulkner what Henry James called Maupassant, "A lion in the path." He solved this leonine problem much as Dante did on the outskirts of hell: he took a different path, around him. But their subject, his and Faulkner's—and all the rest of ours, for that matter—was the same: "the human heart in conflict with itself."

I will speak briefly. For me, the time since his death—less than half a year—is far too short to allow for any meaningful valedictory, and it probably always will be. Time, I know, will only deepen my sense of loss, my inexpressible grief at all our loss.

Sixty years is a long friendship, and it came to almost exactly that, from our meeting as boys in Greenville, Mississippi, to his death in Covington, Louisiana—incidentally on the May 10 anniversary of the death of Stonewall Jackson, which Walker had read of many times in its many versions, with the date of his own death there on the page before him.... One secret of the longevity of our friendship was that each of us knew what would make the other angry, and we were careful not to venture into such areas—except on purpose, which would open the matter to drumfire argument and laughter, time and time again, all down the years.

There are many amusing things I could tell you about his life and the way he lived it—including the report that he once declined an invitation to appear on the "Today" show because he didn't own a part of those calf-length socks which televisional propriety requires. But I am inclined to consider this account apocryphal, not only because he did in fact appear on the "Today" show (where they mortified him by calling him Dr. Walker) on the morning after he won the National Book Award, but also because, by any standards, he simply had no calves.

I can, however, give you some notion of his attitude toward life by quoting from his final letter to me, late last year. Of his wanderings in search of the latest "Cure," which he knew was quixotic at best, he wrote: "The worst thing is the traveling and hospitals. Flying around the U. S. is awful, and hospitals are no place for anyone, let alone a sick man...I'll tell you what I've discovered," he went on. "Dying, if that is what it comes to, is no big thing since I'm ready for it, and prepared for it by my Catholic faith which I believe. What is a pain is not even the pain but the nuisance. It is a tremendous bother (and expense) to everyone. Worst of all is the indignity. Who wants to go to pot before strangers, be an object of head-shaking for friends, a lot of trouble for kin?... Seriously, and now that I think of it, in this age of unbelief I am astounded at how few people facing certain indignity in chronic illness make an end of it. Few if any. I am not permitted to."

After that, we used the phone to stay in touch, except such times—including his last eight days—as I managed to ride down and see him. As writers we knew that, writing, we might get carried away and express feelings we'd rather leave unstated. We had never been sentimental about anything, and didn't want to risk ending up that way. Toward the end of April he took to his bed for good. With the help of his local doctor and friend, George Reiser, he orchestrated his dying, though—being tougher than he knew—he miscalculated its reach by more than a week. One night I called, knowing how bad things were, and his brother Leroy answered on an extension beside his bed. "How is he?" I asked and Roy said, "Wait, he wants to speak to you." Then Walker got on the phone. He sounded removed. "I've got an hour, maybe an hour and twenty minutes," he told me. "Goodbye."

I had more or less expected it, but hearing it directly from him I was unstrung. "My God, Walker," I'm afraid I said. "I'm an only child and you're the closest thing to a brother I ever had."

He wasn't having any of that. "Goodbye" he said again and handed the phone back to LeRoy.

I went down there for those last eight days, but he was much the same all through them. He wasn't concerned about my piddling grief, any more than he was concerned with giving me any piddling comfort. And he was right. There wasn't and isn't any comfort except the knowledge that his place is secure among the great American writers and that I was fortunate enough to have had him for my closest friend for all that brief and memorable span of sixty years.

ENEMY OF THE PASSIVE VOICE,
WHO ROCKED SOME JAUNTY HATS:
LIZ CHRISTMAN

by Melinda Henneberger
February 8, 2010

Some people were born to teach, and Melinda Henneberger's vivid memories of her professor reveal that Elizabeth Christman was one of them. The eulogist is editor in chief of PoliticsDaily.com, where this tribute's posting caused a stream of email response. Some was from Christman's former students whose lives she had touched, and many were from women who were inspired to follow their own mid- or late-life dreams after reading that Ms. Christman didn't begin college preparation for her career until she was in her fifties.

Many other readers shared memories of their own beloved teachers. Usually such appreciation grows over time, so that the instructor never realizes her lifelong impact on a student. Fortunately, that wasn't the case here, as Henneberger describes a post-graduation relationship that evolved into a friendship —"Though, believe me, never equals."

My writing teacher and friend Elizabeth Christman, who wore a spiffy new suit and hat on the first day of every semester and was one of the finest humans ever, died last week at age ninety-six. To be honest, I am completely bereft.

Miss Christman, professor emeritus of American studies at the University of Notre Dame, was a literary agent in New York who read *The Catcher in the Rye* when it was still in manuscript form, and once took Agatha Christie shopping for a bathing suit. But that was before she went back to school at the unheard of age of fifty-two, to pursue a doctorate and a dream—to teach young idealists how to change the world with their words.

Writer of notes and wearer of pearls, she kept a framed photo of Henry James in her kitchen and a rosary on her night stand. She taught Trollope well into her eighties, and while sensible in the extreme, also had the most contagious sense of occasion.

Although I will not succeed in communicating her awesome Liz-ness to those who did not know her, I can at least tell you what she told me: The passive voice is the enemy. There will be time enough. Reading is the most enduring of all life's pleasures. Deciding what you want is the difficult part; the rest is just hard work. No extraneous words. *Middlemarch* is the best book written in English. Writers write; you can't just tell them you won a contest! I think we should have a glass of wine, don't you? Soon you will be happy to be referred to as girls.

The only person I ever knew her to actively dislike was a college beau of mine—also her student—whom she dismissed as "too silly for you." In her later years, when her short-term memory had gone, she repeatedly confessed that—now it can be told!—she was, in fact, a Democrat. Whenever I phoned, she'd cry, "How did you ever find me here?" in assisted living—and then would laugh when I'd answer, "Hey, I'm a reporter, aren't I?"

The eldest of seven, Liz grew up in St. Louis, and after graduating from Webster College—now Webster University—in 1935, moved into a garret in her parents' house to pursue a career as a writer. In her unpublished memoir, *Twenty Septembers*, she remembers, "I fixed up a studio for myself in the attic of our home, and to it I would retreat and turn out stories and verse which I hoped would get me started commercially. My father didn't press me to get a job, though he had six other children coming up behind me to educate. He was willing to let me try this out."

She made some sales, netting $25 for a short story published in *The Catholic World* and $1.50 a line for some humorous poems that ran in *The Saturday Evening Post*. But "I didn't think of any career...

as a total lifetime undertaking," she said in her memoir. "I expected to marry, and in the days of my youth few women ever continued their careers after marriage. Writing, in fact, fitted in better with my scenario of a future as wife and mother than any other job. It was the kind of work one could do in intervals between wiping cute little noses and preparing succulent meals."

That never happened, despite two marriage proposals that I know of. And, during her New York years, "there was a man I loved long and deeply but could not marry." As a younger woman, she was "left at the altar," as she always put it, and to get over it joined the Navy as a WAVE and was posted to Washington during World War II. In New York after the war, she worked her way up from the typing pool to become a sub-agent for Harold Ober—Mr. Ober to her. Never one to hesitate on her way to making a point, she recalled a prominent writer's complaint that he'd come down with a raging case of writer's block after running a work in progress past "that horrid Miss Christman."

She received her doctorate from NYU and at last became an associate professor in her sixties, fortunately for me and every other AmStud major at Notre Dame, where she made a habit of inviting entire classes over for lasagna—and on at least one occasion, a rib-bruising marathon of the word game "Fictionary." Through I'm still not sure that writing can be taught, I never learned more from a teacher.

She was a late bloomer as a writer as well, publishing four novels, including the gloriously semi-trashy *A Nice Italian Girl*, which was made into a TV movie, and another about a woman who discovers that her husband is gay. Her greatest work, though, was the unlikely life she built for herself, brick by brick, with equal parts rigor and joy. As a Christian and as a writer, she was of the "don't tell them, show them" school; in class, she spoke of Flannery O'Connor's Catholicism rather than of her own, and I only knew she went to Mass every day because she arrived for lunch appointments straight from Sacred Heart.

Immediately after graduation, I received one of her patented notes inviting me to begin calling her Liz, and from then on we exchanged letters, calls, and visits as friends—though believe me, never equals. She was so much on my mind last week, yet I didn't call her because—ninny!—I dreaded telling her that J. D. Salinger had died.

Her sister, Mary Ellen Hyde Mooney, told me on the phone that she had been fine until just last Monday, when she announced that she was tired, went to bed, and then slipped away over the next several days, while Mary and her daughter said the rosary with her.

In her memoir, Liz ended her own story this way:

Besides teaching students, I've taught myself. The best way to learn a thing they say, is to teach it. By the constant concentration on what makes good writing, close examination of both good and bad examples, tireless reiteration to my students of such principles as "prefer the concrete to the abstract," I've improved my own writing. Even if my students haven't written many novels, I have written five. And it was teaching that got me started.

The Notre Dame campus is beautiful in September. All summer long the chirping sprinklers have kept the lawns thick and green. How charmingly these lawns are populated with sunburned young men and women in shorts, hurrying or dawdling to their classes. September in campus life is the new year, and it feels full of resolution and promise. Each September I relished this beginning more keenly realizing that there couldn't be many more for me. Having found my true calling late in life, I have nothing but gratitude for the universities that took a chance on me and the colleagues who welcomed me into their fortunate circles. Leaving these circles, I take with me the memory of charmed years.... Those golden September campuses can't fade or fray.

A FRIEND OF THE FAMILY:
MR. O'CONNELL IS DEAD

by Dorothy Day
March, 1952

This eulogy appeared in Dorothy Day's Catholic Worker Movement *newspaper more than a half-century ago. A tribute to Mr. O'Connell presented a formidable task, or would have for anyone except Dorothy Day, CWM founder. Maurice O'Connell lived at the CWM's Easton, Pennsylvania, farm for over ten years. To say that he was a difficult man understates the case, drastically. Day does not dishonor him—or her read-ers—with half-truths. She portrays the man as he was, warts and all, just as she loved him. Why? To comfort everyone who is called to love difficult people, in short, to reassure and strengthen all of us.*

We usually read and listen to eulogies to learn about a life well-lived, to be inspired by how the deceased modeled Christ. Here, it is the eulogizer who models Christ by loving a demanding, abusive, and some-times violent member of the community. In doing so, Day reveals the wisdom of the Holy Spirit's plan for us to grow in faith and truth and love, together.

Somewhere in the Psalms it says that we can look forward to three score years and ten, if we are strong, but any more years are toil and trouble. Undoubtedly they are, but I suppose most people want to hang on to this life they know, as long as possible. Not that anyone will ever be ready for death in the sense that they feel prepared to face God and the judgment. Old Maurice O'Connell, who lived with us from 1936 to 1947 at Maryfarm, Easton, PA, lived to be eighty-four. After the Catholic Worker moved to New-burgh, Maurice remained behind. When the priest from St. Bernard's Church came to anoint him a few weeks before his death, he announced jauntily that he would drop in to see him the next time he was in Easton. His appearance there was not so casual.

Yesterday, February 26, a requiem Mass was sung at ten o'clock and the body of Mr. O'Connell was laid in a grave in St. Bernard's Cemetery, behind St. Joseph's Church, on the Palisade over the Lehigh River. It was a clear spring-like day, though the ground was hard under foot.

We knelt on the cold earth around the freshly-dug grave, Eve and Victor Smith, Louis Christopher, Guy and Fifi Tobler, Winifred, Helen Montague, Fr. McGee, the pastor of St. Bernard's, the two men from Curran's funeral parlor and three of the seven Smith children, Margaret, Guy and Victor.

I thought as the coffin was being lowered into the grave, a cheap gray coffin of proper shape, but God knows what materials, the handles decorative rather than functional, that Mr. O'Connell had made a coffin for me back in 1940 or so, but that he had not made himself one. I should have brought mine and let Hans Tunneson make me another. The coffin he made for me is of proper size and varnished with the bright yellow varnish that he had used on the altar, the sacristy closet, and the benches which he had made for our chapel at Easton, PA, when Fr. Palmer and Fr. Woods first came to vacation with us back in 1937.

Mr. O'Connell put in a lot of work on that chapel. The altar, vestment closet and benches are all now in use at Maryfarm, Newburgh, and will be for many a year to come.

In addition to my coffin, which my daughter Tamar now uses to store blankets and other bedding, and the chapel furnishings, Mr. O'Connell took an old tool shed and made himself a comfortable little house in which he lived for all the last years of this life, until this last year, when he went to the Smiths and Christophers and boarded there. He had old age pension and so preserved a strong feeling of independence. He enjoyed being with the children. He helped John Fillinger remodel his chicken house, he constructed the Montague and Buley houses, all of them long rectangular affairs that could be divided into three or four rooms, small, narrow, like the emergency barracks the veterans are forced to live in now.

There was nothing beautiful or imaginative about Mr. O'Connell's building. It was utilitarian. He would not use second-hand materials, but demanded new pine boards and barrels of nails. Tarpaper covered roof and sides. That was as far as any of the buildings got, not only for lack of materials but from lack of ability or initiative. There were all kinds of poverty at Maryfarm, Easton.

He also built a little cabin for Tamar, who had saved her Christmas and birthday money for many years and had eighty-five dollars of her own. This bought enough boards at that time to put up a tiny place with double-decker beds, the coffin chest to store things, a table and chair. I had wished it larger so that it could be heated. It was so small that even the tiniest pot belly stove made it unbearably hot. But Mr. O'Connell was adamant.

"I'm making this small enough so no one but you and Tamar can sleep there."

As it was, others slept there, transients, and sometimes the men of the farm. Later a porch was put up L-shaped, and that was large enough to sleep four more people during retreats. We always had to use every inch of available space not only in the city but on the land.

We had to remind ourselves very often of how much Mr. O'Connell had done for us in the years that we lived at Easton. Of course, John Fillinger worked with him at first; Jim Montague worked on the Buley house; Gerry Griffin and Austen Hughes had put up Jim's house just before Helen came home from the hospital with her first child. The truth was, no one could work with him long, because of his violent and irascible disposition.

How to write about people—how to understand people, that is the problem. "I wrote for your comfort," St. Paul said. "I am comforted in order that I might comfort you." And so I too write as things really were, for your, my readers' comfort. For many of you have old, and sick and sinful people with you with whom you have to live, whom you have to love.

Often one is accused of not telling the truth because one tells only part of the truth. Very often you have to write about the past, because you cannot write the truth about the present. But what has occurred in the past holds good for the present. The principles remain, truth remains the same. How to write truthfully without failing in charity?

The truth was that like many old men, Mr. O'Connell was a terror. He came from Ireland so many years ago that he remembers, he says, when Canal Street was not a street but a canal. He was one of twenty-one children, and his father was an athlete and a carpenter. Maurice pictured him as a jaunty lad with his children, excelling in feats of strength, looked upon with admiring indulgence by his wife, who, according to Maurice, nursed all her children herself, baked all her bread, spun and wove, did all her housekeeping and never failed in anything. It was, indeed, a picture of the valiant woman that Maurice (accent on the last syllable to distinguish it from Morris, a Jewish name) used to draw for us when any of the women were not able to nurse their children (not to speak of other failures).

He was an old soldier, was Maurice, and had worn many a uniform, in South Africa, in India, and in this country. He had no truck with pacifists. And as for community!

According to St. Benedict, there should be a benevolent old man at the gate to receive the visitors, welcome them as other-Christs, exemplify hospitality.

Maurice's little cabin was on the road at the very entrance of the farm, and he never missed a visitor. If they were shabby he shouted at them, if well-dressed, he was more suave. He had many a tale to tell of his fellows in the community. He was not a subtle man. His thought was simple, not involved. "Thieves, drunkards and loafers, the lot of them" he would characterize those who make up what was intended to be a farming commune. And if anyone living on the farm had any skill, it was "what jail did ye learn that in?" One man who became a Catholic after living with us for a year was greeted with taunts and jeers each time he passed the cabin door. "Turncoat!

Ye'd change yer faith for a bowl of soup!"

He was ready with his fists too, and his age of course protected him. Once when he was infuriated by a woman guest who was trying to argue him into a more cooperative frame of mind, he beat his fist into a tree and broke all his knuckles. A violent and enraged man, if anyone differed from him, was Mr. O'Connell.

The first winter we began the retreat house (the roof of the barn had been repaired with second-hand lumber by Dave Hennessey, Mike Kovolak, and Jon Thornton, with whatever tools they could round up among themselves). By this time, the ninth year of Mr. O'Connell's stay with us, he had all the tools of the farm locked up in his cabin and would guard them with a shotgun. That first winter when Peter and Father Roy and the men had a dormitory in the barn, Mr. O'Connell became ill and was persuaded to be nursed in the dormitory. He was kept warm and comfortable, meals were brought to him on a tray, and he soon recovered his vigor. He decided to stay for the cold months and ensconced himself by the side of the huge pot-bellied stove, where benches, chairs and bookshelves were. Peter and Mr. O'Connell sat for hours in silence, the latter with his pipe and a book, Peter motionless, his chin sunk in a great sweater that had all but engulfed him. Mr. O'Connell was a great reader of history, but it was hard to understand him when he was trying to make a dissertation, especially when his teeth were out, as they usually were.

It was a difficult few months, especially in the morning. We sang the Mass every day, thanks to Father Roy, and Mr. O'Connell did not enjoy this at seven in the morning. He had been used to sleeping until ten or eleven. On occasion his audible grumbling was supplemented by a banging on the floor of the dormitory with his shoe. Taking him to task for this he would snarl, "I was just emptying the sand out of my shoe." It was a winter when we had to dig ourselves out to the outhouses.

When Lent came we were reading Newman's sermons during meals, and whether it was because Maurice did not like Newman as an Englishman, or a convert (he decidedly did not like converts) or whether it was because he thought the reading was directed at him, he used to stomp angrily away from the table and refuse to eat. Stanley had always gotten along well with him (he had never worked with him), but Stanley had a habit when he was reading pointed chapters from the Imitation, or Newman, of saying "This is meant for Dorothy," or "This is meant for Hans." Mr. O'Connell decided the reading was meant for him, and would put up with it no longer. He moved back to his cabin and his meals were brought to him on a tray. When spring came, he came to the kitchen and fetched them himself.

The cooking was good that winter. Either Hans or Duncan managed the kitchen, and "we never had it so good." Especially since Fr. Roy used to go down to the A&P on a Saturday night and beg their leftovers. They were very generous, especially with cold storage fish or turkeys that would not last, even in the ice box, until Monday. Part of our Sunday preparation was cleaning fish and fowl and seeing what we could do to preserve them. I shudder now when I think of the innards, so soft that all parts seemed to emerge into one! However, we had good cooks. And most of the time we had simple foods that did not need to be disguised.

It was about that time, spring and summer, when many re-treatants came, that Mr. O'Connell took to tell them all that we never gave him anything to eat, never anything to wear. The fact was that we respected his distaste for complicated dishes, and he had a regular order in at the grocer for eggs, cheese, milk, bread and mar-garine and canned soups. Not to speak of the supplies on our kitchen shelves which Maurice (or anyone else) felt free to come and help himself to. Our cooks had good training in "if anyone asks for your coat, let him have your cloak too. To him that asks give and do not turn him away, and do not ask for a return of what is borrowed."

All our friends coming for retreats, came with generous hearts of course, anxious to give to the poor, to feed the hungry and clothe the naked. Maurice had many an alms given him, and many were the packages of clothes that were addressed to him. It is wonderful that people had so charitable a spirit, I often thought, but what must they think of us, accused so constantly of this neglect. Surely they were not thinking the best of us! That is to put it positively. To put it crudely, everyone seemed quite ready to think the worst of us, to believe the worst. Or maybe they just said, "They are injudicious in that they take on more than they can handle." One can always escape from being uncharitable by being injudicious. It is a nicer word.

I find little paragraphs in my notebook at that time. "What to do about M.'s having six pairs of shoes, a dozen suits of underwear when others go without, Peter for instance. Is it right to let him get away with taking all the tool and probably selling them for drink? Where does the folly of the cross begin or end? I know that love is a matter of the will, but what about common sense?

"Fr. Roy is all for non-sense."

And Fr. Roy was right, of course. "A community of Christians is known by the love they have for one another. 'See how they love one another.'"

"Nobody can say that about us," I would groan.

"If you wish to grow in love, in supernatural love, then all natural love must be pruned as the vine is pruned. It may not look as though love were there, but have faith."

We were being pruned all right. Not only through Mr. O'Connell, but on all sides. Putting it on the most natural plane I used to think, "How sure people are of us that we believe in what we say, that all men are brothers, that we are a family that we believe in love, not in a use of force; that we would never put them out no matter how hard we are tried. If they act 'naturally' with no servility even to an extreme of showing bitterness and hatred, then one can only count that as a great victory. We believe in a *voluntary* cooperation. Our faith in these ideas must be tried through fire."

And then I would look upon Maurice with gratitude and with pity, that God should choose him to teach us such lessons. It was even as though he were a scapegoat, bearing the sins of ingratitude, hatred, venom, suspicion for all the rest of us, all of it gathered together in one hardy old man.

And, on the other hand, to go on with these subtleties, what about this business of letting the other fellow get away with it? Isn't there something awfully smug about such piety—building up your own sanctification at the expense of an increased guilt of someone else? This turning the other cheek, this inviting someone else to be a potential murderer, or thief, in order that we may grow in grace—how obnoxious! In that case I'd rather be the striker than the meek one struck.

One would all rather be a sinner than a saint at the expense of the sinner. In other words, we must be saved together.

It was Fr. Louis Farina who finally answered that question for me. And Fr. Yves de Montcheuil, who died a martyr at the hands of the Gestapo because he believed principles were worth dying for.

Fr. Farina says that the only true influence we have on people is through supernatural love. This sanctity (not an obnoxious piety) so affects others that they are saved by it. Even though we seem to increase the delinquency of others, and we have been many a time charged with it, we can do for others, through God's grace, what no law enforcement can do.

Fr. Farina extols love in all his conferences, and points out the agonies which one must pass through to attain to it. Fr. Montcheuil has a magnificent passage on freedom, that tremendous gift of God Who desires that we love Him freely and desire this love so intensely that He gave His only begotten Son for us.

Love and Freedom, they are great and noble words, but we learn about them, They grow in us in the little ways I am writing about, through community, through the heart rending and soul searing experiences we have in living together.

It is not by any form of constraint, not by "the prestige of an eloquence which tries to snatch man out of himself," not by fine writing, not by "the charms of great and enveloping friendship," that we are going to win our brothers to Christ. It is only by becoming saints ourselves. That should be easy to understand. And if we are saints, we certainly won't judge others.

According to Chestov, quoted by Fr. Danielou, "Faith is a new dimension of thought" introduced at the time of Abraham, the father of faith, "which the world did not yet know, which had no place in ordinary knowledge." Faith is part of the everlasting newness of Christianity and is something which we must be constantly exercised in.

And so I firmly believe, I have faith, that Maurice O'Connell, in addition to being a kind friend who built the furniture of our chapel and some barracks for our families, who sat and fed the birds and talked ever so kindly to the children on the sunny steps before his little house, was an instrument chosen by God to make us grow in wisdom and faith and love.

God rewarded him at the end. He received consciously the great sacrament of the Church, extreme unction, he was surrounded by little children to the end, and even at his grave, he had the prayers of kind friends, he had all any Pope or King could receive at the hands of the Church, a Christian burial, in consecrated ground. May he rest in peace.

THE CARDINAL'S EPISTLE TO THE JEWS: JOHN CARDINAL O'CONNOR

by Rabbi Haskel Lookstein
May, 2000

This eulogy of the Cardinal of the Archdiocese of New York was written by a rabbi and ran in The Jewish Week, *the largest circulation Jewish community newspaper in North America, read all over the world. Such an occasion was a long time coming.*

Following World War II, Catholics and other Christians began to examine how their teachings about Jews might have contributed to the Holocaust. But it wasn't until 1965 that Pope John XXIII jump-started a more active reconciliation by making Catholic-Jewish relationships a priority of Vatican II. There were gains and setbacks along the way, but Vatican II had begun the shift from the Church viewing its mission as one "to" the Jews (i.e., conversion) to a respectful mission "with" the Jews—of furthering the kingdom of God.

Thirteen years later, a seismic shift occurred with the election of the first Polish Pope. John Paul II had been raised in pre-war Krakow, a city with a rich Jewish cultural history. As one who had formed close friendships with Jews in his childhood, he brought a new level of understanding and appreciation to the process of moving the Church beyond a theoretical or theological relationship.

The Polish Pope advanced the process on every front: teaching, preaching, diplomacy, and visiting Jewish sacred places. But what ignited his activity was personal. He saw Jews as brothers and sisters, not as "other." The Anti-Defamation League claimed that Pope John Paul II did more to further relationships with Jews in his last twenty-seven years than had been done in the prior two-thousand years.

In the twenty-first century, Haskel Lookstein, the senior rabbi of

Congregation Kehilath Jeshurun in Manhattan, wrote a eulogy for John Cardinal O'Connor, his friend. It ends up being as simple—and as profound—as that.

The most poignant eulogy for His Eminence John Cardinal O'Connor can be found in his own words. Since his arrival in New York, he used to send to me—and, I imagine, to many others in the Jewish community—a letter before Rosh Hashanah and another one before Passover. Those letters were not perfunctory greetings; they spoke of feelings that came from the depth of the Cardinal's heart. I am reminded of some of the more recent ones as I reflect on the life's work of this extraordinary, religious personality. I have added my personal reactions in brackets.

March 29, 1999

Dear Rabbi Lookstein:

As another Passover comes, I am reminded of the steadfast faith of the Jewish people throughout all generations. It is a faith which has never diminished nor been destroyed by any enemy of the Jewish people. The reason for this is obvious to me: God promised to set Israel free and make them his own people. God has kept his promise. The Jewish people are free and continue to be a light of hope to the world.

[Two observations: the Cardinal understood what post-Zionists do not; the presence of the Jewish people in Israel is not an accident but rather an affirmation of the history of the Jews and mankind.]

This is not flattery. It is a deeply felt statement of my own faith. Without Judaism there would be no Christianity. Without Passover there would be no Easter. Without the practice of keeping Passover Judaism would suffer....As you sing and eat through the Seder you will once again be freed from bondage and given the Torah.

[The Cardinal understood that the purpose of the Exodus was not simply freedom but rather a commitment to Torah. How profoundly he comprehended the essence of Judaism.]

You will remember the years of glory and the years of pain. Much of that pain was inflicted on the Jewish people by many of my own coreligionists who rejected love and replaced it with hate. For what they did, I am most ashamed. It is my sincere hope that you will remember me as your friend....

September 8, 1999

Dear Rabbi Lookstein:

The Jewish High Holy Days come once again, reminding our world of who created it, who blesses it with life and who judges it in his merciful justice....

This Sabbath evening, as the celebration of Rush Hashanah commences, a new decade will begin. During the year of 5760 we Christians will start a new era of the year 2000, the return of another millennium in our history.

[The Cardinal elegantly distinguishes for his Jewish friends between a new Jewish decade and a new Christian millennium. It was a touching and thoughtful distinction.]

I pray that as you begin a new decade, and as we begin another millennium in our Jewish-Christian relationship, we will refresh our encounter with a new respect and even love for one another as children of God. ...I ask this Yom Kippur that you understand my own abject sorrow for any member of the

Catholic Church, high or low, including myself, who may have harmed you or your forebears in any way.

Be assured of my prayers and friendship. L'shanah tovah tikotevu!

The Cardinal need not have asked for forgiveness for himself. He was always a great friend of the Jews. I remember when, barely days after his arrival in New York, he appeared on the steps of St. Patrick's Cathedral in his ceremonial robes and came down to the curb to greet the hundreds of thousands of marchers on Solidarity Sunday. I shall never forget how he marched with us in the following years and addressed the rallies from the podium in Dag Hammarskjöld Plaza.

Last April 5, following his Passover message (quoted above), I wrote to him:

Your participation carried very special weight because of our religion and your nationality. I have no doubt that it was an important part in the successful struggle to free the Sharanskys, the Slepaks, the Ida Nudels, and all the Jews in the former Soviet Union. You have been a great friend of the Jewish people in general and you have been a wonderful friend to me as well. I am grateful for all of that but, frankly, I am even more grateful for what you represent: a man of piety and of deep religious faith and, above all, a true mensch.

And finally, April 17, 2000 (two weeks before his passing):

Dear Rabbi Lookstein:

By God's grace, I have the delightful pleasure of sending you my heartfelt greetings yet once again for a joyful celebration of Passover. It also gives me the opportunity to express my sincere thanks for the prayers you have offered for my recovery during my time of illness. No matter what the days ahead may bring, the love and support you have given me are signs of everlasting friendship and endless encouragement....

As you and your family join together at the Seder table, recalling through the Haggadah the liberation of the Jewish people and the giving of the Torah, I humbly ask that you remember me as one who wishes to be in your midst and receive blessing. Passover is a gift for the whole world.

Be assured you are in my prayers and very much in my heart.

> *Faithfully,*
> *John Cardinal O'Connor*
> *Archbishop of New York*

I didn't see the Cardinal's last letter until I returned from Israel after Passover. I immediately responded. The letter, dated May 3, is still before me on my desk. It was never sent. It was the day he died. May the soul of this righteous, loving, forgiving and repentant, religious man be forever bound up among the living.

REMEMBERING MY FRIEND TIM RUSSERT

by Maria Shriver
June 18, 2008
The John F. Kennedy Center for the Performing Arts
Washington, D.C.

Tim Russert, an NBC-TV newsman and bestselling author of Big Russ
& Me, Father & Son: Lessons of Life, *died suddenly at age fifty-eight
while taping "Meet the Press." That night, a half-hour of television was
given over to tributes by then-President George W. Bush; presidential
candidates John McCain and Barack Obama; former President Bill and
then-Senator Hillary Clinton; and others.*

*Later, a private funeral was followed by a nationally televised me-
morial service. Among the eulogists were Russert's media colleagues Tom
Brokaw, Brian Williams, Al Hunt, Mike Barnicle, and Betsy Fischer (who
accompanied Russert to the hospital after his collapse, where he was pronounced dead of a heart attack). Also paying tribute were Mario Cuomo,
former governor of New York; Doris Kearns Goodwin, author and historian; Russert's son, Luke; and Lucille Socciarelli, a Sister of Mercy who was
Russert's seventh grade teacher at St. Bonaventure School, in Buffalo, New
York. Bruce Springsteen's tribute was musical, via satellite from Europe.*

*Particularly touching memories of their friendship were shared by
Maria Shriver, a longtime friend.*

*Shriver's husband Arnold Schwarzenegger was Governor of Cali-
fornia at the time of this tribute; her mother was Eunice Kennedy (sister
of President John Kennedy); her father was Sergeant Shriver, first head
of the Peace Corps, established by executive order of President Kennedy in
1961; and the loss of her cousin John, mentioned in her eulogy, refers to
the death of John F. Kennedy Jr., in a plane crash.*

Hi, I'm Maria Shriver, and I'm a friend of Tim's.

I've always wanted to go to a love fest. This isn't exactly what I had in mind, but the truth is I wouldn't want to be anywhere else at this moment, which just shows you how important it is to get out of your mind and into your heart. My heart led me here today, as I know it's the same for all of you.

You see, I lost my heart to Timmy Russert the day I met him. And the entire time I knew him, he took care of it. He protected my heart when it needed protection. He nurtured it when it needed care. And he helped it grow. And he never, ever broke it. A rare man indeed. I remember so well the day I showed up to work at NBC News. I had been fired two months earlier by CBS News. That's another story. But I walked in these doors of 30 Rock, and I have to admit, I was wounded and quite scared. And Tim came up to me, put a big arm around me and said—took me to the side and he whispered—"Look, I was also educated by the nuns. I was educated by the Jesuits. I'm Irish Catholic, too. There aren't that many of us here in this building," he said. "But if we stick together, we'll be just fine."

I looked at him, and there was a little twinkle in his eye, but I knew he wasn't kidding. And I knew then and there that I had just gotten the last thing that I wanted in the world, but the thing I really needed: another brother.

You see, I have four brothers already, so I know a little bit from what I speak. Brothers have an uncanny ability to make you think that you're nothing without them. Somehow brothers make you believe that you need them to make every decision in your life, large and small. That you can't go anywhere without their protection or make any decision without their input. I'll bet Tim's sisters would agree that Tim was exactly this kind of brother.

I remember back when I scored an interview with Fidel Castro and I was going to Cuba. Tim came down from his vice president's office. He wasn't on the air at the time. And he came down to congratulate me. He sat down in the chair and started to talk to me.

And by the time he was finished, he had convinced me that I couldn't go to Cuba without him, this despite the fact that I had traveled all over the world interviewing people before I ever met Tim Russert. But he somehow convinced me that I couldn't make the trip without him. He went on to convince me that I couldn't even do the interview without him. That I didn't know how to interview, even though I had just come from anchoring a live morning show and interviewed scores of newsmakers on my own.

By the time he left my office, he had convinced me that it was he, not I, who had booked the interview, and that it was he who had actually sweated through all thirteen days of the Cuban Missile Crisis alongside my uncles in the White House.

I marveled. I thought to myself, "Isn't that so sweet of Timmy? He wants to help me. He wants to make me shine." I didn't get it. He just wanted to go to Cuba and meet Castro. He didn't care at all about me.

In fact, when we actually got to Cuba and Castro summoned us to his office in the middle of the night, Tim was the first one out of the door and the last one to leave the office. And when Castro actually said to me, "OK, now I'm ready to do the interview," Tim was sitting in the chair. And I said, "Tim, I'm doing the interview. Could you get up?"

He goes, "Oh, just checking the lighting for you. I wasn't planning on sitting here."

But he so loved being in the middle of the action. He so loved seeing history up close. And he loved to have stories to come back and share with everybody, to make you laugh, to make you feel as though you were there. Tim loved his life, and he loved life.

I'm sure every single person in this auditorium today has an extraordinary story about Tim. A story that would make us all laugh and a story that would touch us and probably make us cry. That's because Tim got into our lives. Deep into our lives. He knew about our troubles. He knew about our struggles. He knew about our triumphs. He knew about our families.

Not too long ago, he called me when he heard that my daughter was interested in applying to Boston College. And he said "Look, Maria, it's competitive at Boston College. You need to know people in Boston. You need to know people" —yes, yes. He said, "You need to know people in the Catholic Church. You need me if you want your daughter to get into BC."

I thanked him profusely and said, "Oh my God. You're so right. I grew up on the Cape. I don't know a person in Boston. And I've been educated in Catholic schools, and I don't know anybody in the church. Thank you, Tim. Please, make sure my daughter gets into Boston College." She didn't.

Anyway she's going to kill me for saying that. She got wait-listed. OK. Anyway, she's going to USC, one of the many fine colleges in the state of California. Anyway, but Tim liked to help. That's a true story. I'm sorry, Katherine.

But he loved helping people. He loved helping people who worked for him. He loved helping strangers. He loved anybody who he thought he could help. And with that same Russert radar, he just knew who among us needed his help.

When my uncle [Ted Kennedy] had a seizure a few weeks ago, the first phone call I got after my other brother Timmy was from Tim. He called me up and said, "How's Teddy doing?" And I talked to him. And then he said, "Now talk to me about you. Who's with you? How are you? What can I do for you? Are you all right?"

When my mother was going in and out of intensive care this past year, Tim kept tabs on her and on me. He talked with me about losing his own mother. He talked to me about what he felt, how hard it was for him. He talked to me about where he found support, about the role of his faith in that struggle. He shared his struggle with me so that mine would be a little bit easier.

And because he was so devoted to his dad, he always called to check on mine. Tim and [his wife] Maureen have a special place in my dad, Sarge's, life. And they would always call to find out how he was. And even when I would come into town and it was a Saturday night and invite them to come over, they always did. And my dad was always, and is always, so proud of Maureen, that she was one of the first women in this country to enlist in the Peace Corps, that she was so brave.

And every time she would come over, he'd marvel at her and the school that was named after her and the legacy that she created. And he'd always say, "I like that guy she married, as well." And every time Tim would come over, my mother would say when he left, "Now, that's the kind of jolly Irish Catholic boy I always thought you would marry. What happened?"

That's true. But that's another story, too.

Tim was family. And his family is our family. And it really touched me that after I left NBC News, Tim always made sure that I felt as though I were still a part of the NBC family. At the last presidential conventions, which were the first ones that I didn't work at, he called me on my cell phone and he said, "Look, I know you're here at the Republican convention, and I'm thinking you might be feeling a little out of sorts in this new role of yours. So come on up here to the booth and hang with Tom and I and we'll just kind of kibbitz. And bring your kids, and you'll be comfortable up here until you have to go down and hear Arnold's speech, where you'll sit with all the Republicans. But sit up here with us because you'll be comfortable here." And he was right.

He always made me feel comfortable, and I know every single person in this room can identify with that because he always wanted all of us to feel comfortable with what we were doing, with the stories that we were sharing with him. That's what he wanted us to feel.

And so here we are, feeling anything but comfortable, feeling lost, feeling sad, not understanding why we're here and Tim isn't. You know, every morning, I begin my day reading a prayer from St. Teresa, and it begins like this. It says, "May today there be peace within. May you trust God that you are exactly where you are meant to be."

Still, it is hard for us to comprehend why we are meant to be here and Tim is not. Having lived through more than a few losses that defy understanding, I've learned that asking why doesn't help. They only thing that does help is leaning on your friends and leaning on your family, opening your heart, crying, and keeping your loved one alive in your heart and alive in your stories. And it helps to have faith, like Tim.

All of us here were meant to witness Tim's life. We were meant to be touched by it. We were meant to be touched by his humor, by his love, by his faith, by his idealism, by his passion, and most of all, by his compassion. Tim Russert had a larger than normal heart. Maybe it's because we were all occupying so much space in it, with the biggest part reserved for his family, Maureen and Luke, his incredible sisters, his mom, and of course, Big Russ.

Maureen and Luke, I'd like to thank you for sharing Tim with everybody in this room, with everybody in this country. You were the light of his life. For me, as a woman, it was a beautiful thing to behold the love he had for you, for your family and the love that he had, the extraordinary capacity he had to love all of us and to make us feel loved.

Tim, I want to thank you up there in heaven for making room in your heart for me. I will be forever grateful.

A few years ago, when my cousin died, John, in an unexpected way, I was given a poem by a friend that helped me through some pretty dark days. It gave me some peace within whenever I thought about him in a faraway place, that I would be unable to see him or talk to him again. I read it many, many times and I thought I could share it with all of you today with the hope that it might also give you some peace within. It goes like this:

> *I stood watching as the little ship sailed out to sea. The setting sun tinted its white sails with a golden light. And as it disappeared from view, a voice at my side whispered, "He is gone." But the sea was a narrow one, and on the furthest shore, a little band of friends had gathered to watch in happy expectation. Suddenly, they caught sight of the tiny sail. And at the very moment when my companion had whispered, "He is gone," a glad shout went up in joyous welcome with the words, "Yes, here he comes!"*

God bless you. God bless you, Tim. Thank you.

IV. WE REMEMBER
Our Artists

EULOGY FOR ANDY WARHOL

by John Richardson
April 1, 1987
St. Patrick's Cathedral, New York, NY

Art historian John Richardson, along with artists Yoko Ono and Nicholas Love, were the speakers at a memorial Mass for Andy Warhol attended by more than two-thousand people. Richardson's focus on how Warhol's Catholicism influenced his life and work surprised many.

This was not the image Warhol created in the 1960s during his early days at the trendy and often scandalous Factory studio. The spirituality of the man Richardson knew was formed during childhood. Warhol's parents immigrated to Pittsburgh, Pennsylvania, from Austria-Hungary (now Slovakia), where his father became a coal miner. They raised their sons in a Byzantine Catholic parish. Warhol is buried in St. John the Baptist Byzantine Catholic Cemetery there, next to his mother and father.

After studying commercial art in Pittsburgh, Warhol's success as a New York magazine illustrator led to his launching the movement known as Pop art. His subject matter scandalized the established art world because it was commercial (soup cans, cola bottles, dollar bills) and celebrity-oriented (Marilyn Monroe, Judy Garland). Warhol's practice of making art out of his era's pop-culture icons (mushroom-shaped clouds, police dogs attacking civil rights workers, money, etc.) was dismissed as a joke and criticized as outrageous. Today, he is acknowledged as one of the most influential artists of the twentieth century. The Andy Warhol Museum opened as one of the four Carnegie Museums in Pittsburgh four years after his death.

Richardson's widely covered eulogy has also been criticized. A professor of religious studies at Virginia Commonwealth University dismissed "St. Andy" as a myth and lamented that this eulogy led to a serious study of Warhol's religious art. The studies examined Warhol's Christmas cards for Tiffany and Co., his images of the cross, and his series, "Eggs," reminiscent of Orthodox Easter images.

This eulogy and the reaction to it lead to the question of whether anyone can know the heart of someone in his or her final days or years— especially a celebrity whom we "know" only by the ways he or she is depicted in the media.

Perhaps it will suffice that another friend who knew Warhol primarily as a volunteer added this footnote to his memorial Mass card:

> Five hundred homeless and hungry New Yorkers will assemble on Easter Day at the Church of the Heavenly Rest, on Fifth Avenue at 90th Street. They will be served a delicious meal, and they will be treated as honored guests by some eighty volunteers. They will also be saddened by the absence of one who, with dedicated regularity, greeted them on Thanksgiving, Christmas, and Easter. Andy poured coffee, served food, and helped clean up. More than that, he was a true friend to those friendless. He loved these nameless New Yorkers and they loved him back. We will pause to remember Andy this Easter, confident that he will be feasting with us at a Heavenly Banquet, because he had heard another Homeless Person who said: "I was hungry and you gave me food... Truly, I say to you, as you did it to one of the least of these, my brothers and sisters, you did it to me."

> —The Reverend C. Hugh Hildesley,
> Church of the Heavenly Rest

Besides celebrating Andy Warhol as the quintessential artist of his time and place—the artist who held the most revealing mirror up to his generation—I'd like to recall a side of his character that he hid from all but his closest friends: his spiritual side. Those of you who knew him in circumstances that were the antithesis of spiritual may be surprised that such a side existed. But exist it did, and it's the key to the artist's psyche.

Never forget that Andy was born into a fervently Catholic family and brought up in the fervently Catholic *Ruska dolina*, the Ruthenian section of Pittsburgh. As a youth, he was withdrawn and reclusive, devout and celibate; and beneath the disingenuous public mask that is what he, at heart, remained. Thanks largely to the example of his adored mother, Julia, Andy never lost the habit of going to Mass more often than is obligatory. As fellow parishioners will remember, he made a point of dropping in on his local church, St. Vincent Ferrer, several days a week until shortly before he died.

Although Andy was perceived—with some justice—as a passive observer who never imposed his beliefs on other people, he could on occasion be an effective proselytizer. To my certain knowledge, he was responsible for at least one conversion. He also took considerable pride in financing a nephew's studies for the priesthood. And as you have doubtless read on your Mass cards, he regularly helped out at a shelter serving meals to the homeless and the hungry. Trust Andy to have kept these activities very, very dark.

The knowledge of this secret piety inevitably changes our perception of an artist who fooled the world into believing that his only obsessions were money, fame, and glamour, and that he was cool to the point of callousness. Never take Andy at face value. The callous observer was in fact a recording angel. And Andy's detachment—the distance he established between the world and himself—was above all a matter of innocence and of art. Isn't an artist usually obliged to step back from things? In his impregnable innocence and humility, Andy always struck me as a *yurodstvo*—one of those saintly simpletons who haunt Russian fiction and Slavic villages, such as Mikova in Ruthenia, whence the Warhols stemmed. Hence his peculiar, passive power over people; his ability to remain uncorrupted, no matter what activities he chose to film, tape, or scrutinize. The saintly simpleton side likewise explains Andy's ever-increasing obsession with folklore and mysticism. He became more and more like a medieval alchemist searching—not so much for the philosopher's stone as for the elixir of youth.

If in the sixties some of the hangers-on at the Factory were hell-bent on destroying themselves, Andy was not to blame. He did what he could to help, but nothing in the world was going to deter these lemmings from their fate. In any case Andy was not cut out to be his brother's keeper. That would hardly have been compatible with the existent detachment which was his special gift. However, Andy *did* feel compassion, and he *did*, in his Prince Myshkin way, save many of his entourage from burnout.

Though ever in his thoughts, Andy's religion didn't surface in his work until two or three Christmases ago, when he embarked on his series of Last Suppers, many of them inspired by a cheap plaster mock-up of Leonardo's masterpiece he bought on Times Square. Andy's use of a Pop concept to energize sacred subjects constitutes a major breakthrough in religious art. He even managed to give a slogan like "Jesus Saves" an uncanny new urgency. And how awesomely prophetic is Andy's painting—one of his very last—which announces: "Heaven and Hell Are Just One Breath Away!"

DANNY'S PROMISE:
IN MEMORY OF DANNY THOMAS

by Phil Donahue
February 8, 1991
Church of the Good Shepherd, Beverly Hills, CA

Among the eulogists at the funeral of Danny Thomas were two American Presidents (Reagan and Ford); comedy legends Milton Berle and Bob Hope; and Roger Cardinal Mahony, then Archbishop of Los Angeles. Another eulogist, television personality Phil Donahue, had a special relationship with Thomas: Donahue is married to his daughter Marlo, actress and author of the children's book Free to Be You and Me. *Donahue's tribute to his father-in-law uses all of the names by which Danny Thomas was known and loved before he became known to millions: Amos was an early Americanization of his original Lebanese name Muzyad.*

Danny Thomas was called a comedian in his early days doing stand-up in Detroit and Chicago clubs, but he always said he thought of himself as a storyteller. His act involved telling elaborate tales about quirky characters.

In 1940, the struggling storyteller prayed to be able to use his gift to make a living for his family. In gratitude, he promised he would build a shrine to St. Jude Thaddeus, patron of impossible causes. That shrine evolved to become a unique medical research hospital offering free treatment for children with cancer.

Danny told stories he'd never once dreamt of telling to make all that happen...about children with diseases for which there were no treatments in that era, mostly fatal cancers in which the best survival rate was 4 percent. Eventually, Danny came up with more stories to show his friends and fans how they could help.

While his talents blossomed into radio, film, and television work, as a star and as a producer, St. Jude Children's Research Hospital in Mem-

*phis, Tennessee, claimed as much of his energy as his career did. The hos-
pital became his life's work and remains his living legacy. After he raised
the money to begin construction, he organized Arab-American donors to
pledge to underwrite the operating cost of providing free medical care to
St. Jude patient-families. And he enlisted all of America—including its
children—to be a part of his answered prayer.*

*In 1985, Danny Thomas received the Congressional Gold Medal
from President Ronald Reagan in a White House ceremony. In 1991, he
died at the age of seventy-nine. He and his wife Rose Marie are buried in
a family crypt at the pavilion on the hospital grounds.*

*Five years after Danny's death, Dr. Peter Doherty, a St. Jude Hos-
pital immunologist, was awarded the Nobel Prize for Medicine. Through
the development of research and protocols, survival rates for the four most
common childhood cancers are now 94 percent (Acute Lymphoblastic Leu-
kemia, the most common childhood cancer); 85 percent (Meduloblasto-
ma—a brain tumor); and two at 90 percent (Hodgkin Lymphoma and
Wilms tumor (kidney)).*

*Today the work continues with the dedication of Danny's three
children, the American Lebanese Syrian Associated Charities organization which he founded to raise the hospital's operating funds, and the
many donors and volunteers who continue to be a part of Danny's dream
to build a shrine to St. Jude in Memphis and in the hearts of Americans.*

My father-in-law loved the religious jokes Bob Hope told
about him, that he had stained-glass windows in his car,
for example. And we believed them.

Somewhere over the years we came to think of him as more
holy than mortal. And this week he proved us wrong…and he broke
our hearts.

To those who gather in this magnificent demonstration of affection for this uncommon human being, may I extend to you the
gratitude of the Thomas family…and to be sure, the gratitude of

Danny Thomas as well...a street kid from Toledo, Ohio, who knew what it was like to be an outsider, would no doubt extend today his appreciation to those here gathered, as well as those who stand outside this crowded sanctuary.

To Glenn and to me, Danny and Rosie are the extraordinary extra gift that we got when we married into this family. To his nephews and nieces...and to Dionne and Jason, Tracy, Kristina, and Kate, he was the grandfather who lit up like a Christmas tree when they entered the room, as he did frequently and often during this last holiday season when we all gathered before him, together, for an entire family reunion in Connecticut, our most joyful and his last.

To Marlo and Terre and Tony he was just quite simply the best father there ever was...honor bright.

And to Rosie...his girl from day one...his girl now...and his girl forever. She loves ya, oh, how she loves ya, Muzyad. And how we need your help now to keep her well as she walks into the most painful moment of her life.

My father-in-law taught me lots of things...including the importance of knowing when to get off. And I shall not disappoint him now.

Amos, we agree with the sentiments of the simple man who approached you after a show that featured a galaxy of stars. He spoke for us when he said, "You was the best one."

We will not sing your theme today, Danny. It would bring a pain in our heart beyond our bearing. We will say, however, what you already know...Oh, Danny boy, we love you so.

THE ANGELS OF PATRICIA NEAL

by Terry Mattingly
August 18, 2010

Actress Patricia Neal was well-known for overcoming a series of severe strokes that left her in a coma when she was pregnant with her fifth child. Her husband Roald Dahl directed the long rehabilitation that taught her how to walk and talk again; she went on to receive television's Golden Globe, an Academy Award nomination, and Lifetime Achievement Awards in both film and stage.

In the early 1960s, the couple's young daughter died of measles, and an infant son suffered brain damage after his baby carriage was struck by a taxi. Neal later became an advocate for paralysis victims and was the public face of the Patricia Neal Rehabilitation Center in Knoxville, Tennessee, which serves patients with stroke, brain, and spinal cord injuries.

What is less well-known is that Neal lived her last thirty years in Edgartown, Massachusetts, a town with a resident population of 4,100. After her death there, the local newspaper depicted her as "a vigorous, generous force," an unpretentious hands-on neighbor devoted to friends and community. The paper's obituary recalled Neal's loyalty to their annual community fundraiser for its social services agency and her yard sales benefitting its substance abuse facility. She was depicted scooping ice cream at an annual benefit for the Catholic Church, and as a grand lady who loved to sit on her porch and talk to neighbors as they walked by. The paper noted that her three daughters were with her when she died, and that she is survived by ten grandchildren and a great-grandchild.

Neal is buried on the grounds of the cloister of Regina Laudis Abbey, Bethlehem, Connecticut, where she had found peace, consolation, and meaning to her life during its most turbulent years.

After her destructive affairs with married men, after the death of her first child, after an accident left her infant son brain-damaged, after the near-fatal strokes that struck months after her 1964 Oscar win, actress Patricia Neal faced yet another personal crisis that left her on the verge of collapse.

While her marriage to British writer Roald Dahl, the author of children's classics such as *James and the Giant Peach*, had long been troubled, Neal was shattered when she learned he was having an affair with one of her friends. They divorced in 1983.

In her 1988 memoir, *As I Am*, Neal admitted: "Frequently my life has been likened to a Greek tragedy, and the actress in me cannot deny that comparison."

That quotation captured the tone of the tributes published after Neal passed away on Aug. 8 at the age of 84. Broadway theaters dimmed their lights in honor of the Tony Award winner and critics sang the praises of one of Hollywood's ultimate survivors, an actress who literally learned to walk and talk again before returning to the screen to earn another Oscar nomination.

But Neal's story contained angels as well as demons. This is obvious in the overlooked passages in *As I Am* that described her conversion to Catholicism and her visits to the cloister of Regina Laudis (Queen of Praise) Abbey in Bethlehem, Conn., where the sisters helped her confess her sorrows and rage.

Finally, the abbess suggested that Neal move into the abbey for a month.

"Lady Abbess," said Neal, "I don't want to join up, you understand?"

The abbess sighed and said, "Believe me, we don't want you to, either. I don't think we could take it for more than a month."

As she arrived, Neal stubbed out the "last cigarette I would ever smoke."

A priest gave her a blessing and, she recalled, "I felt his cross blaze into my forehead.... I traded my street clothes for the black dress of the postulant and scrubbed off my makeup. I removed the rings from my fingers and covered my hair with a black scarf. I looked at the bare wooden walls of my cell.... I did not live the exact life of a postulant, but I did my best."

Neal went to church on time, followed the abbey's prayer regime, baked bread, remained silent during meals and, with the help of a spiritual director, began writing the journal that evolved into *As I Am*.

Behind closed doors, she unleashed her fury. At one point she screamed so many curses at her counselor that the sister finally cursed right back, urging Neal to be honest about her own faults and mistakes.

The actress finally voiced her secret pain. Monsignor Jim Lisante of Diocese of Rockville Centre (New York) later discussed with Neal the tragedies of her life and asked if there was any one event that she would change.

"She said, 'Forty years ago I became involved with the actor Gary Cooper, and by him I became pregnant. As he was a married man and I was young in Hollywood and not wanting to ruin my career, we chose to have the baby aborted,'" wrote Lisante, at the Creative Minority Report website. "She said, 'Father, alone in the night for over 40 years, I have cried for my child. And if there is one thing I wish I had the courage to do over in my life, I wish I had the courage to have that baby.'"

Several of the obituaries for Neal—including *The New York Times*—mentioned this episode in the context of her pain and regret. *The Washington Post* noted that late in life "she suffered periods of depression and suicidal thoughts before finding peace as a Catholic convert."

In the end, Neal decided that, "God was using my life far beyond any merit of my own making," allowing her to reach out to those who were suffering. "I learned that my damaged brain cannot reclaim what is dead. It has to create totally new pathways that allowed me to make choices I would never have made had I not suffered that stroke— choices that an infallible voice assures me will be blessed."

One final lesson from the abbess, wrote Neal, stood out: "There is a way to love that remains after everything else is taken from us."

HE'S COMIN' THROUGH: MILTON BATISTE

by Jason Berry
May 18, 2001

In considering the life and faith of jazz artist Milton Batiste, his eulogist places him within the history of the influence of New Orleans Catholics and American jazz. Trumpeter Batiste and many other prominent musicians came from the city's famed Seventh Ward, which houses the Josephite Corpus Christi-Epiphany Church and School where Batiste grew up.

Batiste's glorious jazz funeral described below occurred in the old New Orleans—before Hurricane Katrina in 2005. The homes of the five thousand parish members were devastated. Five years later, student groups still come to volunteer in the rebuilding effort. The church and rectory have been restored, but there was no way to salvage the school that once enrolled a thousand students.

Corpus Christi pastor Reverend John Harfmann, SSJ, said that "a little better than half" of the parishioners have come back. Those who reached the end of their lives in other states have often returned to be buried. Corpus Christi now has more than one hundred funerals a year.

With about seven hundred people attending weekend masses, the parish still has no gathering place. Father Harfmann hopes to build a Community Center with help from the government and friends of the parish. The Center will house a museum of the Seventh Ward.

Dirges are the songs of sorrow a brass band plays in ushering a coffin to the cemetery. The tolling of the dirges has a solemn dignity, shaping the image most people have of a jazz funeral. Trailed by limousines and a crowd of mourners, the musicians in dark pants, white shirts, dark ties and caps, their instruments glinting silver and gold in the sun, move in a slow procession. They follow the grand marshal in tuxedo or tails who sets the pace with sculpted steps, one foot out, another pulling behind in a slow drag, a hand holding the top hat across the sash on his chest.

Like the chorus in a Greek drama, the musicians articulate the consciousness of a community when someone is laid to rest.

So has it been in the century since jazz arose from working-class neighborhoods at the bottom of America, a melding of the sacred and profane, of Catholicism and jazz, as music moves between streets and sacred spaces. So it was in early April, when Catholic bandleader Milton Batiste was laid to rest after a jazz sendoff that, more than most, held a mirror to the epic of the music and the spiritual sensibility out of which it arose.

As the procession moves on, the trumpeter lays out the melody, playing a slow tempo, tunes like "Old Rugged Cross," a song carried out of slavery, or "Just a Closer Walk With Thee," now the most popular dirge, a hymn that found its way into the New Orleans street repertoire in the 1930s:

> *Just a closer walk with thee*
> *Grant it, Jesus, is my plea...*

With the trumpeter advancing the melodic line, the clarinet sings back an embroidered countermelody with the high pealing "widow's wail," a voice of lamentation and female woe. The bass drummer hits the hard, deep thuds of grief that anchor the backbeat; the trombone's pulsations strengthen the rhythm; the tuba and other instruments fill in a melding of cross-rhythms.

The wailing of the dirges quickens excitement in the second line, the spontaneous street dancers (many of whom never knew the deceased) who shuffle alongside the band. Their numbers grow in anticipation of that sharp shift when burial is done and the band breaks into an up-tempo song like "Didn't He Ramble?" that signals the "cutting loose" of the soul from earthly ties. When the band hits that up-tempo shift, hundreds of second liners explode into gyrations and a wave of high kicking prances, giving the dead a joyous sendoff. Bravura rhythms and irreverent dancing signal the soul's release, no longer a time to mourn, rather to celebrate—what Jelly Roll Morton called "the end of a perfect death."

Milton Batiste played a river of dirges and second line anthems during his sixty-six years. As lead trumpet in the Olympia Brass Band for thirty-nine years, the amiable Batiste, a dark, hefty, bearded man with an easy drawl and winning grin, was a beloved figure in the jazz community. From the mid-1970s into the 1990s, Olympia made thirty concert tours of Europe and a tour of Africa under State Department auspices. Olympia played for three presidents and Pope John Paul II on his 1987 visit to New Orleans.

Next door to Milton Batiste's home in the leafy Gentilly Woods neighborhood, he turned a shotgun house into a ramshackle studio. There he produced a line of CDs on Olympia and a stream of gospel singers and younger musicians just starting out.

His funeral on April 6, with a requiem Mass at Corpus Christi Church and a rollicking burial parade, brought an illustrious career into high relief, his career, like that of many New Orleans musicians, ending where it began—at a crossroads of jazz and the Catholic church.

New Orleans, now sixty-two percent African-American, has been a heavily Catholic city since its founding by the French in 1718. In recent years a quilt of black Protestant churches has drawn many worshipers. However, there is still a substantial black Catholic community, including many politicians. Corpus Christi was once the largest black parish in America. In the 1930s it had 18,000 members; today it's closer to 5,000. The church is in the Seventh Ward, on the downtown or downriver side of the French Quarter. The three black men who have been elected mayor since the civil rights era—Ernest "Dutch" Morial, Sidney Bartholomey, and Marc Morial

(Dutch's son)—grew up in the Seventh Ward, the hearth of Creole culture. The younger Morial is a graduate of Jesuit High School; Bartholomey was a seminarian in his youth.

The downtown Creole culture has its origins in the French-speaking free persons of color, many of them mulattoes or fair-skinned blacks, who came to New Orleans in the early 1800s following the war of liberation on the island of Haiti. In 1809, the city's population of 10,000 nearly doubled with the arrival of some 10,000 émigrés from Haiti who came via Cuba. A third were French, a third free persons of color, a third slaves belonging to both groups.

New Orleans was a crossroads of humanity, a melting pot before the term was coined.

The Spanish acquired the colony from the French in the late 1700s, only to return it in time for Napoleon to sell it as part of the 1803 Louisiana Purchase. Waves of Irish immigrants came in the 1820s and '30s, followed by a surge of Sicilians in the latter decades of the nineteenth century. As the Creole poet Marcus Christian wrote in 1968:

> *I am America epitomized*
> *A blending of everything*
> *Latin, Nordic and Negro*

Music was central to the urban character. In 1810 the city had three opera companies when New York had but one. As dance halls proliferated, so did the open-air Sunday gathering of slaves at a park called Place Du Congo, or, as English supplanted French as the local language, Congo Square. There, on a grassy commons behind the city proper, hundreds of slaves formed concentric circles—rings within rings—and danced to the rhythms of conga drums, stringed instruments and panpipes made of wood.

"Wherever in Africa the counterclockwise dance ceremony was performed," writes Sterling Stuckey in Slave Culture (1987), "the dancing and singing were directed to the ancestors and gods." Ring dances were burial ceremonies in the mother culture. As this ritual psyche took root in New Orleans it spawned a tradition of public dancing that honored the dead.

Brass bands were a European tradition that flourished in the raucous port. Military bands have played funeral marches in many cultures stretching back across time. By the 1880s, with blacks forming their own brass bands, waves of street dancers—spiritual descendants of the long-since dormant ring dancers of Congo Square—began following burial marches and parades for other occasions. Jazz arose in the early 1900s as the African genius for polyrhythm merged with European instrumentation and melody. Most of the darker blacks, who lived uptown, were descendants of slaves. The downtown Creoles came out of a tighter family structure and a tradition of self-reliance: Families of carpenters, brick masons, cigar makers and music teachers, among other artisans, created a sturdy economy of scale.

Most of the downtown Creoles were classically trained. The uptown blacks for the most part learned to play by ear, improvising on what they heard. Louis Armstrong, a grandson of slaves, learned to play by ear. Jelly Roll Morton, born into a comfortable Creole home, took music instruction.

"There was a caste system within the Negroes themselves," the late Danny Barker, a musician and author, explained. "The Catholics liked Creole music, which was refined, and the Protestants were closer to the blues shouting and the spirituals and screaming to the skies and the Lord. All the bands had a particular section of society where they entertained...and particular halls where they played."

A Creole bandmaster named James Brown Humphrey was a key figure in the development of jazz. In the 1890s he boarded the train each week, traveling to the outlying plantation areas where he gave music lessons to field workers and descendants of slaves. In time, some of his pupils moved to New Orleans, filling the ranks of brass bands in the early 1900s.

The music had a rougher side in the quasi-legal red light district known as Storyville, which operated from 1897 until 1917. Many musicians who played funerals or at church wakes found venues in the Storyville speakeasies with sawdust-spattered floors. Pianists played in the opulent bordellos in Victorian mansions. "One thing that always puzzled me," the trumpeter Lee Collins recalled in a memoir, "was that the prostitutes from the district would go to church and take flowers to put on the altar; they would never miss Mass. Maybe they had not altogether forgot the way they were brought up. Some of the girls that worked in the district came from fine old Creole families. Lots of them never went back home again... as they had brought great disgrace to their families."

Sorrowful hymns, sung in pews of Catholic as well as Protestant churches, worked their way into the repertoire of brass bands at the funerals. This gave the early jazz idiom a pronounced religious coloring. "When the Saints Go Marching In" was one of the most popular hymns, sung in slow tempo in the churches. In 1938 Louis Armstrong recorded the song at a parade beat, anchoring it forever as an anthem of the second liners.

Armstrong, though raised a Protestant, was baptized a Catholic. Paul Barbarin, a drummer from one of the most illustrious musical families (his sister was Danny Barker's mother) grew up on the edges of Storyville. So did the boisterous bandleader Louis Prima, whose family home lay just outside a Sicilian enclave in the rear of the French Quarter. George Lewis, the clarinetist whose tours of Japan in the 1960s exposed a vast new audience to traditional jazz, was a Catholic who imbued his reed with the beauty of the spirituals.

Aaron Neville, the Grammy-winning vocalist with huge biceps and a dagger tattooed on his cheek, is a gentle soul behind that menacing façade. He has publicly credited St. Jude, the patron of hopeless cases, for helping him overcome a heroin addiction. Jazz educator Ellis Marsalis is a lifelong Catholic whose sons Wynton, Branford, Delfeayo and Jason have national careers. The singer and film star Harry Connick, Jr. graduated from Jesuit High School. The list goes on.

Milton Batiste was a driving force in the rise of Olympia, the oldest of the city's marching bands. The group formed in the 1880s to perform for the Young Men Olympian, a black benevolent society that assured each member of a proper burial. The Olympia band underwent many changes, becoming an orchestra and a brass band again until World War II, when the group faded from the scene. In 1958 the saxophonist Harold "Duke" Dejan resurrected Olympia as a brass band.

Dejan, one of ten children from a Creole family, took lessons as a child from Lorenzo Tio, Jr., a legendary clarinetist with the Onward Brass Band. Dejan's first exposure to brass bands came as a teenager in the 1920s in a group affiliated with Holy Ghost Catholic Church, which is located in a central city ward. "We played up there where the organ sits, played the hymns for religious concerts," Dejan has recalled.

There is no written account of the church's role in the development of jazz. However, oral traditions suggest ambivalence if not downright opposition by church officials to the burial parades, which often turned flamboyant.

"At one time the Catholics didn't want no band for jazz funerals," Harold Dejan explained. "Then they thought of letting the band play, and changed it [for the] better."

The dramatic orations of pulpit preachers and surging choral singing of black Protestant churches were similar to the call-and-response pattern of early jazz ensembles. Although the early brass band funerals shared such dynamics, there was a spiritual idea as central to Catholicism as the African vision of many deities—the idea of the soul sent into the afterlife.

"I was an altar boy, and we had to read Latin," Batiste recalled in a 1997 interview. "It was a [different] type of music played in our churches than in the Baptist church or Lutheran church."

When Batiste was growing up in the 1940s, "It was unheard of to have a band in the Catholic church. This was blasphemy. As a matter of fact, when I was in grammar school [at] Corpus Christi—the teachers were sisters and the priest—they explicitly told us in more ways than one that we shouldn't attend these kinds of services."

Whether church officials issued some formal prohibition on brass band funerals in those years is unclear, but Batiste stressed that more than a few black Protestant preachers took a dim view of brass band funerals. "They didn't want that rowdy music that those guys were playing in the club in their church because it would tear down the significance of religious services. Which was wrong, because in the Bible it states, 'Let the trumpets blow, let the angels sing.' Well, how are the trumpets going to blow and the angels sing if we are not in church? 'Make a joyful noise unto the Lord'" [Psalm 98].

Resistance to the musical sendoffs began melting in the 1950s. Musicians had long referred to the rites as "a funeral with music." As film and TV cameramen began following the parades, a new term arose—jazz funerals.

"Duke" Dejan, a crusty chap with a gift for organization, recognized a burgeoning market for street jazz in the post-war years. Eureka, the dominant mid-century marching band, was cutting back on parades because the leader, trumpeter Percy Humphrey— a grandson of the influential early professor, James Brown Humphrey—had grown tired of marching. In 1961, a club called Preservation Hall opened in the French Quarter, providing a venue for the small community of traditional jazzmen.

As Eureka withdrew from the scene, a rare, beautiful expression of dirge-playing went with it. The overpowering eloquence and stately sadness is best heard on a famous 1951 recording *Eureka Brass Band: New Orleans Funeral and Parade* (American Music CD-70, 1992 reissue). The crafted military beat, the high, ethereal cries of the legendary clarinetists George Lewis and Willie Humphrey, Percy's brother, the tightly structured cadences, represent a pure form of the early brass music as rarely heard today.

Olympia's new leader stamped the group with his own name—

Dejan's Olympia—and in 1962 enlisted a young Milton Batiste as trumpeter. Milton became Duke's musical alter ego, getting the band into concert halls, nightclubs, festival grounds, parades and convention venues. In the 1980s, when Dejan suffered a stroke, Batiste assumed leadership of the group but in honor of his friend never made a move to change the name.

Dejan discarded certain of the old military marches, like "Washington Post" and "Under the Double Eagle," and added pop songs to the repertoire like "The New Second Line" and "Come on Baby, Let the Good Times Roll." Jazz purists who viewed the Eureka as a living link to the dawn of jazz were appalled. "We still play the old marches when they are occasionally requested," Batiste reflected with a tone of pragmatism in 1987. "Sousa marches were played in the 1930s for cornerstone layings, and naturally the clientele was different, mostly white people. Our repertoire had to change for the simple reason that the people we were playing for wanted to hear songs that were popular on the radio."

Olympia's following became as strong among whites as blacks. "To keep the music going and also to quote with our inner selves, we spruce up the old tunes," Batiste continued. "We like rhythm and blues so we put R&B and jazz together."

In addition to his many recording projects, Batiste loved to videotape parades and funerals in which he was not performing. He played the role of on-air host in a documentary by David Jones for WYES-TV, New Orleans, *Jazz Funerals*. The film included a segment in Wales, where Olympia played the funeral of an industrialist who had made provisions in his will for the New Orleans band to perform at his burial.

As Edgar Smith, the band's tuba player, puts it: "I'll almost classify the Olympia Brass Band as a minor religion."

Olympia's looser rhythms infused the New Orleans style with a sound tapping into gospel and rhythm and blues. In gathering these musical strands, Olympia fashioned a sound that was still traditional jazz, but with a little more sway and roll like the pop music sounds of the day.

For years, Olympia's distinctive style was well displayed at Preservation Hall.

As late as 1997, an eighty-seven-year-old "Duke" Dejan, slowed by a stroke, was still performing on Sunday nights as people crowded in like pilgrims at a shrine. Shoulder-tight on the creaky benches, they watched with a reverence for the authentic item—jazz as it had come down across a century in the city where it all began.

The musicians sat on chairs spanning the French windows, the guys so close to the front benches that you could touch their knees. Preservation Hall has no sound system; overhead lights illuminate the band; the house itself is dark. No beverages are sold, not even Coke. A sign says, "No Smoking." A five-dollar cover charge buys a ringside seat to history.

The stout and sturdy drummer, Nowell Glass, wearing sunglasses and a dark baseball cap, pounded the bass drum, launching "When the Saints Go Marching In" on an up-tempo drive. Milton Batiste raised his silver trumpet, pealed out the melody, and rocked back in his seat, tilting the horn skyward, as a bygone trumpeter once advised him, "So the sound will bounce off the walls and not get lost." As clarinet notes soared like birdsong in counter melody, the old bandleader, Dejan, rose to his feet, one hand resting on the walking cane, and stood like the rock of ages, his right fist raised and voice in clarion song: "Oh when the sun/Refuse to shine/Yes I want to be in that number/When the saints go marching in!"

In February of this year [2001], Dejan turned ninety-two. By then Milton Batiste was battling for his life, having gone into the hospital last summer with shortness of breath and circulation problems caused by diabetes. When he went home months later, his left leg had been amputated below the knee. Still, he kept his solid front, breathing hard, ever cheerful when visitors came around.

On March 29 he died.

The next day Olympia's drummer, Nowell "Pa-pa" Glass, died of heart complications at age seventy-two.

Although Dejan was mentally alert, he did not attend the funerals.

The oldest of eight children, Milton Batiste had gone to Corpus Christi grammar school, which is staffed by Josephite sisters and priests.

"We were a wealthy family, not in material but in love," his sister Mercedes said in a eulogy at the requiem Mass. "Every time we split something, we split it eight ways. The Batiste family [members] are a strong bunch of people. If one ate, all ate. Now Milton, he was beautiful—but he ate more than we did."

As laughter washed across the pews, she continued: "Milton ate with the trumpet, walked with the trumpet, slept with the trumpet."

Ruby, his wife of forty-seven years, sat stoically in the front pew, a slender woman who spoke the same easy drawl as Milton. When they married, each had a child by a previous marriage. Sheila was Milton's daughter. Richard Matthews was Ruby's son.

Matthews, a tall man with a long beard beginning to gray, is widely known as "King Richard"—Olympia's grand marshal, the figure in formal attire, his umbrella aloft, whose marching steps set the pace for a parade. Sitting in the pew with his own wife and children, staying close to Ruby through Milton's decline, Richard had assumed the role of Olympia's business manager with his mother.

Grandchildren, nieces, nephews and siblings filled a dozen pews.

Outside the church on the sidewalk and grassy neutral ground of St. Bernard Avenue, three thousand people waited for the coffin to come into the sun-splashed morning. On many a day like this, Milton had played "King Richard" and marched and Ruby had watched.

The pallbearers in flowing white robes with golden trim were members of the Young Men of Labor, a black organization dedicated to preserving the tradition of brass band burials. Trumpeter Gregg Stafford, a member of the organization and leader of the Young Tuxedo Brass Band, played a majestic version of "Flee as a Bird," TK one of the oldest dirges, as the religious service concluded. Then he took his place with the pallbearers as they carried the casket out of the church. A gauntlet of horns and reed instruments on either side of the steps formed an arch, playing "Old Rugged Cross."

The pallbearers lifted the coffin into a white nineteenth-century horse-drawn hearse with glass panels. Just ahead, on the flatbed of a second buggy, his trumpet rested on a hill of flowers, a silver vessel shrouded by red, yellow and green. Now the drivers coaxed the horses, and the parade began.

People were holding photographs of Milton as the crowd strutted down St. Bernard Avenue, following the band of thirty musicians drawn from a range of local brass bands. Schoolchildren from Corpus Christi stood on the sidewalk, some no doubt seeing their first jazz funeral.

Kid Merv Campbell, a trumpeter who had made his first recordings under Milton Batiste, wept as he walked, playing his horn, moving the melody.

Brightly colored umbrellas began opening as the band broke into "Just a Little While to Stay Here." Umbrellas were an icon of royalty transposed from Africa to the street parades of New Orleans.

The band and waves of people coursed along beneath warm, sunny skies, stopping traffic at intersections and magnetizing people from the steps and stoops and bars as the flow of people turned onto North Claiborne Avenue.

Then the band broke into one of Milton's compositions, "No, It Ain't My Fault," with a rolling tuba line simulating the call "Nooooo" and the horns blasting back the response. The crowd was surging now, people whooping and clapping as they reached the funeral home where the wake had been held. From here the cortege would head to a distant cemetery.

Second liners were jumping for a last look as the pallbearers hoisted the casket out of the buggy and into a limousine for the final ride.

"Yes, sir!" cried a man. "Send him on!"

"It's all right!" cried another. "Don't hold him! He's comin' through! Let him go!"

"I'll meet you later on!" cried a third. "Well done, well done."

Three thousand people were dancing under the overpass of the interstate that traverses North Claiborne as the limousines with the family members and closest friends drove away.

"Milton did everything he could to make sure traditional jazz was preserved," his sister Mercedes said in the eulogy. "Milton's music will live on and play on. Olympia will live with us forever."

WIT AND WISDOM ON THE REFRIGERATOR DOOR: ERMA BOMBECK

by D.L. Stewart and Anne Gasior
April 23, 1996

If an entire city can mourn, it seems that Dayton, Ohio, did just that upon the death of one of its most beloved citizens, Erma Bombeck. For days, Dayton papers carried remembrances of the favorite humorist of her generation. The tribute below captures the affinity between Erma and her hometown especially well.

Bombeck's ties to Roman Catholic University in Dayton were especially strong. After an unsuccessful freshman year at Ohio University, Athens, where she was rejected for the campus newspaper, she enrolled at RCU. Erma once told how her English professor there, Brother Tom Price, changed her life: "He was a man who saw each student individually. And he knew I wanted to write.... And I told him I didn't have time because I worked a part-time job to come [t]here. And he said, 'Go home and do something for [the University magazine].'" She told of sliding her article under his door, and that later when he saw her outside the cafeteria: "He said three words to me, that's all, just three words...this would sustain me the rest of my life, I think. He looked at me and said: 'You can write.'"

She converted to Catholicism at age twenty-two, and was a lifetime trustee of the university where her talent had been discovered and encouraged. Her archives are permanently stored at RCU.

The Bombeck credo was, "If you can't make it better, you can laugh at it," and she loved to laugh, even—especially—at herself. After writing the book When You Look Like Your Passport Photo It's Time to Come Home, *she looked at her own passport photo, laughed, and submitted it to be on the book's cover. The front cover.*

Throughout a stellar career, Erma understood the difference between fame and success: "Madonna is one; Helen Keller is another." The

*end of her life was marked by a characteristic courage, particularly during
a five-year wait for a donated kidney that never arrived.*

*She once expressed a hope that by the time of her death she would be
ready to answer God's questions, "What have you got left of your life? Any
dreams that were unfulfilled? Any unused talent that we gave you when
you were born that you still have left? Any unsaid compliments or bits of
love that you haven't spread around?" by saying "I've nothing to return. I
spent everything you gave me."*

Dayton's Erma Bombeck, whose greatest tributes hang on
refrigerator doors throughout the world, died Monday following a long battle with polycystic kidney disease that cul-
minated in a kidney transplant. She was 69....

In Dayton, a legion of friends and fans mourned.

"She was so up, so enthusiastic that everything would work
out," said Shirley Fleischman, who visited with Mrs. Bombeck in
Arizona just before her a transplant. "She was a wonderful friend
and a great listener."

Perhaps it was those qualities that made her column so beloved
by millions of fans in more than a dozen countries from Ireland to
Australia. For 32 years, she wrote about family life and everyday issues.

"I like to imagine that after a person has read our waters are
polluted, the world is in flames, streets are crime-ridden, drugs are
rampant, she'll read how the dryer returns only one sock from every
two I put in and I tell my kids, 'The other one went live with Jesus'
and maybe smile," Mrs. Bombeck said in a 1990 *Dayton Daily News*
interview.

Mrs. Bombeck was born in Dayton on Feb. 21, 1927, to Erma
and Cassius Fiste. Her father died when she was 9, and two years later her mother married Albert Harris, who became a second father to
Erma. Mrs. Bombeck graduated from Emerson Junior High School

and Patterson Vocational High School. After enrolling briefly at Ohio University, where a guidance counselor advised her to "forget about writing," she attended the University of Dayton and graduated in 1949 with a bachelor's degree in English.

While at UD, she searched for spiritual guidance, converted to Catholicism, wrote columns for the college magazine and met her future husband, William Bombeck, whom she married after graduation. Bill, a high school teacher, went on to become the principal at Roth High School. They had three children. ...The Bombeck family lived in Centerville and then in Bellbrook before moving to Paradise Valley, Ariz., in 1971.

In her adopted desert home, Bombeck was very generous, contributing time and money to a number of charitable organizations.

But though she moved away, Mrs. Bombeck always kept a piece of her heart in Dayton. She served on the board of trustees at the University of Dayton from 1984-1987, and spoke at many campus events, including a writers' workshop.

Writing was something Mrs. Bombeck could certainly talk about. She began her journalism career in 1944 with the Dayton *Journal* as a copy girl. She worked as a reporter at the *Journal Herald* after graduating from college, but it wasn't until 1964, when she was hired by the *Kettering-Oakwood Times*, that she began to write about family life. The column was called "Zone 59," a reference to the zip code of her home on Cushwa Drive in Centerville. She was paid $3 a week for it.

In 1965, *Journal Herald* editor Glenn Thompson offered her $50 to write two columns a week, and she began writing "At Wit's End," wry observations on motherhood and household events. Reflecting on disappearing socks, septic tanks and "waxy yellow build-up" propelled Mrs. Bombeck from a local column into national syndication. Three weeks after it was first published in Dayton, the column was picked up by the Newsday Newspaper Syndicate and was reprinted in 38 newspapers. Within five years it appeared in 500 papers. At her peak, it appeared in 900 newspapers and had an estimated 30 million readers.

She wrote, co-wrote and contributed to at least 15 books even after she began giving herself home dialysis four times a day. She was a regular on "Good Morning America" for 11 years. She is a member of the Ohio Women's Hall of Fame, holds dozens of honorary degrees, including an honorary doctor of humane letters from the University of Dayton, and has been named to *Good Housekeeping* magazine's list of the world's most admired women. In 1984, she was the subject of a *Time* magazine cover story.

But her greatest honor was a faithful readership that clipped her columns and taped them to their refrigerator doors so they could reread her wit and wisdom.

"I would rather hang from a 100 refrigerator doors than in the Louvre," she said in a 1990 interview.

Her innate and irrepressible sense of humor made it all happen. But, as she liked to point out: "Humor is like a Chinese dinner. People can't remember it two minutes after they've laughed."

Perhaps that was not the case with Mrs. Bombeck, whose humor seemed to endure.

"She was twice as funny in conversation as in her columns and books,' said Brother Raymond L. Fitz, president of UD and a longtime friend of Mrs. Bombeck's. "Her humor always made us, in some sense, realize the frailty of our human life. At the same time, she could raise criticisms of institutions (in society). She had a good sense of social justice and the role of women in society."

It was that wisdom and sensitivity in her writing that separated her from the Erma "wannabes" who appeared in countless local newspapers. One of her columns that drew the most public response, in fact, was a Mother's Day column that paid tribute to the mothers of handicapped children.

"The mail came by the box full," she said of that column. "None of the humorous columns ever approached that."

Still, it was the humor in her columns and books that brought Mrs. Bombeck fame and gave her the most satisfaction. "Anybody can make you cry," she told a biographer in 1992. "But laughter, that's much more difficult."

AN UNWIELDY RADIANCE OF SPIRIT: FLANNERY O'CONNOR

by Katherine Anne Porter
1964

Katherine Anne Porter was a Pulitzer-Prize-winning writer who phoned this tribute from her sick bed, sharing her unrehearsed thoughts with the editor of a memorial book honoring Flannery O'Connor. Though necessarily brief and conversational, it conveys Porter's admiration for O'Connor's genius, her spirit, and her Catholic faith—which Porter shared.

O'Connor's father died when she was fifteen of a disease that would also one day claim her life. She was diagnosed with lupus at age twenty-six, and her first novel was published the next year. She struggled as a novelist, short-story writer, and essayist while living in a small, Georgia town with her mother and a huge collection of exotic and ordinary birds. She communicated by letter with countless friends and fellow writers until her death at age thirty-nine.

O'Connor's fiction portrayed lost and often grotesque individuals touched by divine grace. Her stories, set in the Bible belt where she lived, dealt with questions of morality and grace. Her comic sensibility and realistic view of humanity was distinctive, prohibiting the preachiness and sentimentality often found in other writing of her era that dealt with religious themes.

She was the first fiction writer born in the twentieth century to have her collected works published by the Library of America. She also reviewed over one hundred books for Georgia diocesan newspapers and gave talks on how faith can inform one's writing.

I saw our lovely and gifted Flannery O'Connor only three times over a period, I think, of three years or more, but each meeting was spontaneously an occasion and I want to write about her just as she impressed me.

I want to tell what she looked like and how she carried herself and how she sounded standing balanced lightly on her aluminum crutches, whistling to her peacocks, who came floating and rustling to her, calling in their rusty voices.

I don't want to speak of her work because we all know what it was and we don't need to say what we think about it but to read and understand what she was trying to tell us.

Now and again there hovers on the margin of the future a presence that one feels as imminent—if I may use stylish vocabulary. She came up among us like a presence, a carrier of a gift not to be disputed but welcomed. She lived among us like a presence and went away early, leaving her harvest perhaps not yet all together gathered, though, like so many geniuses who have small time in this world, I think she had her warning and accepted it and did her work even if we all would like to have had her stay on forever and do more.

It is all very well for those who are left to console themselves. She said what she had to say; I'm pretty certain that her work was finished. We shouldn't mourn for her but ourselves and our loves.

After all, I saw her just twice—memory has counted it three— for the second time was a day-long affair at a Conference and a party given by Flannery's mother in the evening. And I want to tell you something I think is amusing because Flannery lived in such an old-fashioned southern village very celebrated in southern history on account of what took place during the War. But in the lovely, old, aerie, tall country house and the life of a young girl living with her mother in a country town so that there was almost no way for her knowing the difficulties of human beings and her general knowledge of this was really very impressive because she was so very young and you wondered where—how—she had learned all that. But this is a question that everybody always asks himself about genius. I want to just tell something to illustrate the southern custom.

Ladies in Society there—that particular society, I mean—were nearly always known, no matter if they were married once or twice, they were known to their dying day by their maiden names. They were called "Miss Mary" or whoever it was. And so, Flannery's mother, too; her maiden name was Regina Cline and so she was still known as "Miss Regina Cline" and one evening at a party when I was there after the Conference, someone mentioned Flannery's name and another—a neighbor, mind you, who had probably been around there all her life—said, "Who is Flannery O'Connor? I keep hearing about her." The other one said, "Oh, you know! Why that's Regina Cline's daughter: that little girl who writes." And that was the atmosphere in which her genius developed and her life was lived and her work was done. I myself think it was a very healthy, good atmosphere because nobody got in her way, nobody tried to interfere with her or direct her and she lived easily and simply and in her own atmosphere and her own way of thinking. I believe this is the best possible way for a genius to live. I think that they're too often tortured by this world and when people discover that someone has a gift, they all come with their claws out, trying to snatch something of it, trying to share some thing they have no right even to touch. And she was safe from that: she had a mother who really took care of her. And I just think that's something we ought to mention, ought to speak of.

She managed to mix, somehow, two very different kinds of chickens and produced a bird hitherto unseen in this world. I asked her if she were going to send it to the County Fair. "I might, but first I must find a name for it. You name it!" she said. I thought of it many times but no fitting name for that creature ever occurred to me. And no fitting word now occurs to me to describe her stories, her particular style, her view of life, but I know its greatness and I see it—and see that it was one of the great gifts of our times.

I want to speak a little of her religious life though it was very sacred and quiet. She was as reserved about it as any saint. When I first met her, she and her mother were about to go for a seventeen day trip to Lourdes. I said, "How I wish I could go with you!" She said, "I wish you could. But I'll write you a letter." She never wrote that letter. She just sent a postcard and she wrote: "The sight of Faith and affliction joined in prayer—very impressive." That was all.

In some newspaper notice of her death, mention of her portrait with her favorite peacock was made. It spoke of her plain features. She had unusual features but they were anything but plain. I saw that portrait in her home and she had not flattered herself. The portrait does have her features, in a way, but here's something else. She had a young softness and gentleness of face and expression. The look—something in the depth of the eyes and the fixed mouth, the whole pose fiercely intent—gives an uncompromising glimpse of her character. Something you might not see on first or even second glance in that tenderly fresh-colored, young, smiling face; something she saw in herself, knew about herself, that she was trying to tell us in a way less personal, yet more vivid than words.

The portrait, I'm trying to say, looked like the girl who wrote those blood-curdling stories about human evil—NOT the living Flannery whistling to her peacocks, showing off her delightfully freakish breed of chickens.

I want to thank you for giving me the opportunity to tell you about the Flannery O'Connor I know. I loved and valued dearly her work and her strange unworldly radiance of spirit in a human being so intelligent and so undeceived by the appearance of things. I would feel too badly if I did not honor myself by saying a word in her honor: it is a great loss.

THE INVISIBLE ARTIST:
SCULPTOR FREDERICK HART

by Tom Wolfe
2000

Sculptor Frederick Hart has been called "The American Michelangelo and Rodin of our time." Pope John Paul II viewed Hart's The Cross of the Millennium, *a retelling of the ancient mystery as a translucent acrylic sculpture seemingly made of pure light, and pronounced it, "A profound theological statement for our day." Yet Hart seemed to be a genius born too late, producing rich, realistic art in an era where critics disdained that style, an era that disagreed with film director Ingmar Bergman's lament that, "Art lost its basic creative drive the moment it was separated from worship."*

For Hart, it was art that led him to worship, and later into the Catholic Church, where he found not only worship and art but grace, beauty, truth, and even theology, more than the sum of their parts. His first masterpiece, Ex Nihilo *("out of nothing"), depicts the biblical Creation, and forms the west façade at the main entrance of the Washington National Cathedral. He came to the Cathedral as a mail clerk, watched Italian master artists at work there, and began to carve in his spare time. The neophyte also enrolled in courses at the Cathedral to understand the stories the sculptures told.*

Hart has been called a "master storyteller." The stories his unfashionable yet classically beautiful figures tell are meant to direct the viewer's imagination toward an appreciation of human life and the core values of civilization, while striving for an additional transcendent "story," a "thrust of spirit intentionally wrought through high craft to embody a meaning considered far more important than the meaning of art itself." This at a time when critics saw art itself as the goal of adulation.

Acknowledging how out of step he was with the art critics of his day, Hart unapologetically designed his work as a "refutation of the ni-hilism, abstraction, and deliberate destruction of the ideals of Grace and Beauty that characterize much of the art of the twentieth century."

While working on commissioned sculptures for the Vietnam Veter-ans Memorial, NASA, the U. S. Capitol and U. S. Senate Office Build-ings, and for private individuals, such as the Prince of Wales, Hart made time to create and donate pieces to Operation Smile International, which provides service to children who need reconstructive surgery; America's Veterans of Foreign Wars; the Design Industries Foundation for AIDS; and (with Jay Hall Carpenter) the Veterans Memorial in Warrenton, Virginia, among others. Hart viewed it all as an attempt to restore to America's public memorials an art worthy of a great nation.

In December of 1997, Hart sued Warner Brothers after portions of his Ex Nihilo *were used in the film* Devil's Advocate *as a bas relief on the character Satan's penthouse wall. The suit claimed that misusing this religious work violated Hart's moral rights to the integrity of his work; prejudiced the artist's honor and reputation; denigrated the experience of all viewers of seeing the original at the National Cathedral; and—as the most prominent image in the promotion of the movie—falsely im-plied that the artist himself endorsed the film. Hart suffered a stroke two months before the suit was won, and Warner Brothers announced that it would cease its misuse and remove Hart's images from the film.*

Frederick Hart said that his dream for the twenty-first century was for art to: "renew its moral authority by redirecting itself to life rather than art...[to] again touch our lives, our fears, our cares. It must touch our dreams and give hope to the darkness." He did not live to see the new century, but his art remains for the ages.

Author Tom Wolfe's eulogy to Hart echoes another aspect of Ingmar Bergman's lament, one about those who create. In his nihilistic world of the mid-twentieth century, the individual "has become the highest form and the greatest bane of artistic creation," Bergman wrote, contrasting those creators to an earlier era's artists of "invulnerable assurance and natural humility" because their work was bonded with worship. The awe-filled artist sees—as did Frederick Hart—the ability to create as a gift.

⌒⌒

Frederick Hart died at the age of fifty-five on August 13, 1999, two days after a team of doctors at Johns Hopkins discovered he had lung cancer, abruptly concluding one of the most bizarre stories in the history of twentieth-century art. While still in his twenties, Hart consciously, pointedly aimed for the ultimate in the Western tradition of sculpture, achieved it in a single stroke, then became invisible, and remained as invisible as Ralph Ellison's invisible man, who was invisible "simply because people refused to see me."

Not even Giotto, the twelve-year-old shepherd boy who was out in the meadow with the flock one day circa 1280 using a piece of flint to draw a picture of sheep on the face of a boulder, when the vacationing Florentine artist Cimabuè happened to stroll by and discover the baby genius—not even Giotto could match Frederick Hart's storybook rise from obscurity.

Hart was born in Atlanta to a failed actress and a couldn't-be-bothered newspaper reporter. He was only three when his mother died, whereupon he was packed off to an aunt in a part of rural South Carolina where people ate peanuts boiled in salty water. He developed into an incorrigible Conway, South Carolina, juvenile delinquent, failed the ninth grade on his first try and got thrown out of school on his second. Yet at the age of sixteen, by then a high-school dropout, he managed to universal or at least Conway-wide amazement, to gain admission to the University of South Carolina by scoring a composite thirty-five out of a maximum thirty-six on an ACT college entrance test, the equivalent of a 1560 on the College Boards.

He lasted six months. He became the lone white student to join 250 black students in a civil rights protest, was arrested, then expelled from the university. Informed that the Ku Klux Klan was looking for him, he fled to Washington.

In Washington he managed to get a job as a clerk at the Washington National Cathedral, a stupendous stone structure built in the Middle English Gothic style. The Cathedral employed a crew of Italian masons full-time, and Hart became intrigued with their skill at stone carving. Several times he asked the master carver, an Italian named Roger Morigi, to take him on as an apprentice, but got nowhere. There was no one on the job but experienced Italians. By and by, Hart got to know the crew and took to borrowing tools and having a go at discarded pieces of stone. Morigi was so happily surprised by his aptitude, he made him an apprentice after all, and soon began urging him to become a sculptor. Hart turned out to have Giotto's seemingly God-given genius—Giotto was a sculptor as well as a painter—for pulling perfectly formed human figures out of stone and clay at will and rapidly.

In 1971, Hart learned that the Cathedral was holding an international competition to find a sculptor to adorn the building's west facade with a vast and elaborate spread of deep bas-reliefs and statuary on the theme of the Creation. Morigi urged Hart to enter. He entered and won. A working-class boy nobody had ever heard of, an apprentice stone carver, had won what would turn out to be the biggest and most prestigious commission for religious sculpture in America in the twentieth century.

The project brought him unimaginable dividends. The erstwhile juvenile delinquent from Conway, South Carolina, was a creature of hot passions, a handsome, slender boy with long, wavy light brown hair, an artist by night with a rebellious hairdo and a rebellious attitude who was a big hit with the girls. In the late afternoons he had taken to hanging about Dupont Circle in Washington, which had become something of a bohemian quarter. Afternoon after afternoon he saw the same ravishing young woman walking home from work down Connecticut Avenue. His hot Hart flame lit, he introduced himself and asked her if she would pose for his rendition of the Creation, an array of idealized young men and women rising nude from out of the chaotic swirl of Creation's dawn. She posed. They married. Great artists and the models they fell in love with already accounted for the most romantic part of art history. But probably no model in all that lengthy, not to say lubricious, lore was ever so stunningly beautiful as Lindy Lain Hart. Her face and figure were to recur in his work throughout his career.

The hot-blooded boy's passion, as Hart developed his vision of the Creation, could not be consummated by woman alone. He fell in love with God. For Hart, the process began with his at first pragmatic research into the biblical story of the Creation in the Book of Genesis. He had been baptized in the Presbyterian Church, and he was working for the Episcopal Church at the Washington National Cathedral. But by the 1970s, neither of these proper, old-line, in-town Protestant faiths offered the strong wine a boy who was in love with God was looking for. He became a Roman Catholic and began to regard his talent as a charisma, a gift from God. He dedicated his work to the idealization of possibilities God offered man.

From his conception of *Ex Nihilo*, as he called the centerpiece of his huge Creation design (literally, "out of nothing"; figuratively, out of the chaos that preceded Creation), to the first small-scale clay model, through to the final carving of the stone—all this took eleven years.

In 1982, *Ex Nihilo* was unveiled in a dedication ceremony. The next day, Hart scanned the newspapers for reviews…*The Washington Post*…*The New York Times*…nothing…nothing the next day, either… nor the next week…nor the week after that. The one mention of any sort was an obiter dictum in the *Post's* Style (read: Women's) section indicating that the west facade of the Cathedral now had some new but earnestly traditional (read: old-fashioned) decoration. So Hart started monitoring the art magazines. Months went by…nothing. It reached the point that he began yearning for a single paragraph by an art critic who would say how much he loathed *Ex Nihilo*…anything, anything at all…to prove there was someone out there in the art world who in some way, however slightly or rudely, cared.

The truth was, no one did, not in the least. *Ex Nihilo* never got ex nihilo simply because art worldlings refused to see it.

Hart had become so absorbed in the "triumph" that he had next to no comprehension of the American art world as it existed in the 1980s. In fact, the art world was strictly the New York art world, and it was scarcely a world, if world was meant to connote a great many people. In the one sociological study of the subject, *The Painted Word*, the author estimated that the entire art "world" consisted of some three thousand curators, dealers, collectors, scholars, critics and artists in New York. Art critics, even in the most remote outbacks of the heartland, were perfectly content to be obedient couriers of the word as received from New York. And the word was that School of Renaissance sculpture like Hart's was nonart. Art worldlings just couldn't see it.

The art magazines opened Hart's eyes until they were bleary with bafflement. Classical statues were "pictures in the air." They used a devious means—skill—to fool the eye into believing that bronze of stone had turned into human flesh. Therefore, they were artificial, false, meretricious. By 1982, no ambitious artist was going to display skill, even if he had it. The great sculptors of the time did things like have unionized elves put arrangements of rocks or bricks flat on the ground, objects they, the artists, hadn't laid a finger on (Carl Andre); or prop up slabs of Cor-Ten steel straight from the foundry, edgewise (Richard Serra); or they took G. E. fluorescent light tubes straight out of the box from the hardware store and arranged them this way and that (Dan Flavin); or they welded I-beams and scraps of metal together (Anthony Caro). This expressed the material's true nature, its "gravity" (no stone pictures floating in the air), its "objectness."

This was greatness in sculpture. As Tom Stoppard put it in his play *Artist Descending a Staircase*, "Imagination without skill gives us contemporary art."

Hart lurched from bafflement to shock, then to outrage. He would force the art world to see what great sculpture looked like.

By 1982, he was already involved in another competition for a huge piece of public sculpture in Washington. A group of Vietnam veterans had just obtained congressional approval for a memorial that would pay long-delayed tribute to those who had fought in Vietnam with honor and courage in a lost and highly unpopular cause. They had chosen a jury of architects and art worldlings to make a blind selection in an open competition; that is, anyone could enter, and no one could put his name on his entry. Every proposal had to include something—a wall, a plinth, a column—on which a hired engraver could inscribe the names of all 57,000-plus members of the American military who had died in Vietnam. Nine of the top ten choices were abstract designs that could be executed without resorting to that devious and accursed bit of trickery: skill. Only the number-three choice was representational. Up on one end of a semi-circular wall bearing the 57,000 names was an infantryman on his knees beside a fallen comrade, looking about for help. At the other end, a third infantryman had begun to run along the top of the wall toward them. The sculptor was Frederick Hart.

The winning entry was by a young Yale undergraduate archi-tectural student named Maya Lin. Her proposal was a V-shaped wall, period, a wall of polished black granite inscribed only with the names; no mention of honor, courage or gratitude; not even a flag. Absolutely skillproof, it was.

Many veterans were furious. They regarded her wall as a gi-gantic pitiless tombstone that said, "Your so-called service was an absolutely pointless disaster." They made so much noise that a com-promise was struck. An American flag and statue would be added to the site. Hart was chosen to do the statue. He came up with a group of three soldiers, realistic down to the aglets of their boot strings, who appear to have just emerged from the jungle into a clearing where they are startled to see Lin's V-shaped black wall bearing the names of their dead comrades.

Naturally enough, Lin was miffed at the intrusion, and so a make-peace get-together was arranged in Plainview, New York, where the foundry had just completed casting the soldiers. Doing her best to play the part, Lin asked Hart—as Hart recounted it—if the young men used as models for the three soldiers had complained of any pain when the plaster casts were removed from their faces and arms. Hart couldn't imagine what she was talking about. Then it dawned on him. She assumed that he had followed the lead of the ingenious art worldling George Segal, who had contrived a way of sculpturing the human figure without any skill whatsoever: by covering the model's body in wet plaster and removing it when it began to harden. No artist of her generation (she was twenty-one) could even conceive of a sculptor starting out solely with a picture in his head, a stylus, a brick of moist clay and some armature wire. No artist of her generation dared even speculate about...skill.

President Ronald Reagan presided at a dedication ceremony unveiling Hart's *Three Soldiers* on Veterans Day 1984. The next day Hart looked for the art reviews...in *The Washington Post...The New York Times*...and, as time went by, in the magazines. And once more, nothing...not even the inside-out tribute known as savaging. *Three Soldiers* received only so-called civic reviews, the sort of news or feature item or picture captions that say, in effect, "This thing is big; it's outdoors, and you may see it on the way to work, and so we should probably tell you what it is." Civic reviews of outdoor representational sculpture often don't even mention the name of the sculptor. Why mention the artist since it's nonart by definition?

Hart was by no means alone. In 1980, a sculptor named Eric Parks completed a statue of Elvis Presley for downtown Memphis. It was unveiled before a crowd of thousands of sobbing women: it became, and remains, a tremendous tourist attraction; civic reviews only. And who remembers the name of Eric Parks? In 1985, a sculpture named Raymond J. Kaskey completed the second-biggest copper sculpture in America—the *Statue of Liberty* is the biggest—an immense Classical figure of a goddess in a toga with her right hand outstretched toward the multitudes. *Portlandia* she was called. Tens of thousands of citizens of Portland, Oregon, turned out on a Sunday to see her arrive by barge on the Willamette River and get towed downtown. Parents lifted their children so they could touch her fingertips as she was hoisted up to her place atop the porte cochere of the new Portland Public Services Building: civic reviews only. In 1992, Audrey Flack completed *Civitas*, four Classical goddesses, one for each corner of a highway intersection just outside a moribund mill town, Rock Hill, South Carolina. It has been a major tourist attraction ever since; cars come from all directions to see the goddesses lit up at night; a nearby fallow cotton field claiming to be an "industrial park" suddenly a sellout; Rock Hill comes alive; civic reviews only.

Over the last fifteen years of his life, Hart did something that, in art-world terms, was even more infra dig than *Ex Nihilo* and *Three Soldiers*: he became America's most popular living sculptor. He developed a technique for casting sculpture in acrylic resin. The result resembled Lalique glass. Many of his smaller pieces were nudes, using Lindy as a model, so lyrical and sensual that Hart's Classicism began to take on the contours of Art Nouveau. The gross sales of his acrylic castings have gone well over $100 million. None was ever reviewed.

Art worldlings regarded popularity as skill's live-in slut. Popularity meant shallowness. Rejection by the public meant depth. And truly hostile rejection very likely meant greatness. Richard Serra's *Tilted Arc*, a leaning wall of rusting steel smack in the middle of Federal Plaza in New York, was so loathed by the building's employees that 1,300 of them, including many federal judges, signed a petition calling for its removal. They were angry and determined, and eventually the wall was cut apart and hauled away. Serra thereby achieved an eminence of immaculate purity: his work involved absolutely no skill and was despised by everyone outside the art world who saw it. Today many art worldlings regard him as America's greatest sculptor.

In 1987, Hart moved seventy-five miles northwest of Washington to a 135-acre estate in the Virginia horse country and built a Greek Revival mansion featuring double-decked porches with twelve columns each; bought horses for himself, Lindy, and their two sons, Lain and Alexander; stocked the place with tweeds, twills, tack and bench-made boots; grew a beard like the King of Diamonds'; and rode to the hounds—all the while turning out new work at a prolific rate.

In his last years he began to summon to his estate a cadre of like-minded souls, a handful of artists, poets and philosophers, a dedicated little *derrière garde* (to borrow a term from the composer Stefania de Kenessey) to gird for the battle to take art back from the Modernists. They called themselves the Centerists.

It wasn't going to be easy to get a new generation of artists to plunge into the fray yodeling, "Onward! To the center!" Nevertheless, Hart persevered. Since his death certain...signs...have begun, as a sixties song once put it, blowing in the wind...the suddenly serious consideration, by the art world itself, of Norman Rockwell as a classical artist dealing in American mythology...the "edgy buzz," to use two nineties words, over the sellout show at the Hirschl & Adler Gallery of six young representational painters known as "the Paint Group," five of them graduates of America's only Classical, *derrière-garde* art school, the New York Academy of Art...the tendency of a generation of serious young collectors, flush with new Wall Street money, to discard the tastes of their elders and to collect "pleasant" and often figurative art instead of the abstract, distorted or "wounded " art of the Modern tradition...the soaring interest of their elders in the world of the once-ridiculed French "academic" artists Bouguereau, Meissonier, and Gérôme and the French "fashion painter" Tissot. The art historian Gregory Hedberg, Hirschl & Adler's director of European art, says that with metronomic regularity the dawn of each new century has seen a collapse of one reigning taste and the establishment of another. In the early 1600s, the Mannerist giants (for example, El Greco) came down off fashionable walls, and the Baroque became all the rage; in the early 1700s, the Baroque giants (Rembrandt) came down, and the Rococo went up; in the early 1800s, the Rococo giants (Watteau) came down, and the Neoclassicists went up; and in the early twentieth century, the Modern movement turned the Neoclassical academic giants Bouguereau, Meissonier, and Gérôme into joke figures in less than twenty-five years.

And at the dawn of the twenty-first century in the summer of 1985, the author of *The Painted Word* gave a lecture at the Parrish Museum in Southampton, New York, entitled "Picasso: The Bouguereu of the Year 2020." Should such turn out to be the case, Frederick Hart will not have been the first major artist to have died ten minutes before history absolved him and proved him right.

V. WE REMEMBER
Those Who Served Us

SERVANT OF INCURABLE CANCER PATIENTS: ROSE HAWTHORNE LATHROP

by Julian Hawthorne
September, 1928

Julian Hawthorne and his sister Rose were two of Nathaniel and Sophia Hawthorne's three children. Discomfort with his Puritan great-grandfather's participation in the Salem Witch Trials and his own exploration of sin and redemption infused Nathaniel's writing—from his popular The House of the Seven Gables *and* The Scarlet Letter *to numerous short stories.*

The Hawthornes lived in Concord, Massachusetts, where among their friends were writers Ralph Waldo Emerson, Henry David Thoreau, Henry Wadsworth Longfellow, Herman Melville, Dr. Oliver Wendell Holmes, and U. S. President Franklin Pierce. After Nathaniel met Abraham Lincoln, he made the President the focus of an essay, "A Peaceable Man," which ran in the Atlantic Monthly *in 1862.*

Rose was a Unitarian when she met and married George Lathrop, an Episcopalian. They eventually joined the New York City literary and artistic milieu, where George—a former Atlantic Monthly *editor—was then a novelist, poet, and essayist. The couple relocated to the more affordable New London, Connecticut, in 1887, and four years later revealed their conversion to Catholicism. The news was met with shock among their former New York society friends, who viewed Catholicism as a faith of the servant class of immigrants. (Indeed, the only Catholics Rose had known well while growing up were her family's servants.) The tone of the widespread newspaper coverage of their conversion ranged from condescension to hostility, often accompanied by distorted theories concerning their motives.*

Years before they had become Catholics, Rose prevailed upon George to have their only child baptized in a Catholic church. That boy died of diphtheria at age five, a devastating blow that also seemed to be a spiritual turning point for Rose. Although the couple began cowriting articles, one involving the mission of a religious order, their new interests did not bring them together in any other way. Rose, who had long been drawn to the useful good works of dedicated sisters, moved into a New York tenement and began caring for women who were dying of cancer. People of her era—even doctors—believed that cancer was contagious, so the afflicted, especially the impoverished, could find neither nursing nor housing.

At age forty-nine, Rose, now widowed, founded the order of the Dominican Sisters of Hawthorne, later incorporated into The Servants of Relief for Incurable Cancer. She took the name Mother Alphonsa. By December, 1909, when she and longtime coworker Sister Rose took their final vows, they had cared for more than one thousand patients in their two sanctuaries. The two women pioneered the field of compassionate advocacy and palliative care for the dying, today known as hospice. After fifteen years of their order's service, with none of the Hawthorne Sisters contracting the disease, they also proved to the medical community that cancer was not contagious.

Before her death, Mother Alphonsa opened homes in New York City and Hawthorne, New York; her successor Mother Rose opened homes in Philadelphia, Pennsylvania; Fall River, Massachusetts; Atlanta, Georgia; and St. Paul, Minnesota. Today, the Dominican Sisters of Hawthorne maintain four facilities: in Hawthorne, New York; Atlanta; Philadelphia; and in Kenya. Continuing the example of their founder by preaching only through their work, they accept patients regardless of creed or color and do not accept fees, supporting their work solely through donations.

As the last surviving Hawthorne sibling, Julian wrote affectionately of his sister Rose, especially when recalling their happy, younger days. Both had known difficulties—including the death of a child and chronic debt—before finding the work that best suited them. Julian had floundered as an engineer, and late in life he was separated from the mother of their nine children. He seemed to find his niche as a writer, but although he had many books and articles published, he never approached his father's literary or financial success.

At age sixty-six, Julian spent a year in the Atlanta Penitentiary for defrauding investors of 3.5 million dollars in a Ponzi scheme involving phony mining stocks. Rose showed her support throughout his trial and incarceration, even going to Washington, D.C., to petition President Woodrow Wilson for his parole.

Although she didn't succeed in that effort, Rose's unwavering love throughout this time affected her brother profoundly, as is evident from his eulogy some fourteen years later. Julian didn't share the faith that led his sister to give up the pleasures of beauty, art, and world travel so that she might serve suffering humanity. He aligns himself with his supposed readers when he says that Rose's choice was "to us...incomprehensible."

That he loved and admired Mother Alphonsa is, however, incontrovertible.

My sister Rose, last-born of Nathaniel Hawthorne's three children, lived seventy-five years; nearly two thirds of that span passed in the seclusion of her own family; the remainder, emerging to unsought distinction in the love and honor of many. The latter part of such a career arouses interest in its beginnings; and since I am now the only surviving person qualified to portray her earlier phase, I feel myself under a certain obligation to attempt this sketch of my sister's infancy and girlhood.

No one familiar with her as a girl could have foreseen what her maturity was to be; the change was abrupt and strange. Conditions for the departure were no doubt present, but hidden—even perhaps from herself. Yet her choice may have revealed her true nature more accurately than did her youth: the chemistry of growth is occult.

She was born in May 1851, in Lenox, on the Berkshire hills: a child of Spring, and Spring never perished from her nature. She was hearty, vigorous, and impetuous, blue-eyed and rosy, with the auburn hair of that temperament. "A bright and healthy child," wrote her father, two months after her birth, "and neither more nor less handsome than babies generally are. I think I feel more interested in her than I did in the other children at the same age, from the consideration that she is to be the daughter of my age—the comfort (at least so it is to be hoped) of my declining years." He was forty-seven, and was to die when Rose was in her thirteenth year.

She took her stand at once as a personage of dignity and importance; she was aggressive, quick-tempered, joyous, and confident. A breeze of purpose went with her; she was passionately affectionate, but independent; imperious, but generous. Her disappointments and indignation were frequent, but she could never be long dejected; she felt the richness of the world, and her thirst for high adventure would not be balked. She saw love in the faces of those about her, and supposed that earth and air were made of nothing else, and that it was her birthright.

She came at a happy hour of the family fortunes, after *The Scarlet Letter* had made its mark and the drab life in Salem could be exchanged for the freedom of the hills. Rose's petals expanded in the breezy sunshine; sky, mountain, lake, and forest were her familiars; good angels had been her god-mothers. Her father, in a happy vein, forthwith wrote *The Wonder-Book* and *Tanglewood Tales*; and all went well. After two years the family removed to Concord, and thence to England, where, and on the Continent, seven more years were to pass. Rose at fourteen, though never outside the family circle, had seen more of the world than had most of her age—England, France, Italy, Portugal, and Madeira; had even, at Lisbon, had the entrée of the little Portuguese Court there, and had stamped her foot when an attaché had failed to comprehend her orders, and shouted, with flashing eyes, "Understandey?" The princess rôle suited her very well.

But she was only five years old then. Later she felt the mightiness of London and the exhilaration of Paris; and in Rome and Florence she gamboled in the Coliseum and the Palace of the Cæsars, picked up treasure-trove in the Forum, found green lizards for her brother, who was her constant companion at the time and was making a natural-history collection. They climbed over the ruins of twenty centuries, and walked over the Campagna on the broad pavements

on which Roman armies had tramped homeward from their victories. On rainy days they would visit the sculptures and pictures of the
Vatican, or stroll about the vast jeweled spaces of the great Church,
observing the mystic performances of the priests before the altars
and listening to the enchanted music that wove invisible patterns
in the upper air. Especially interesting were the confessionals, little
booths set up here and there, into which would enter tortured sinners, emerging after a time with brightened face and lightened steps.
And the priest, wiping his shaved brow, would glance after them
with a placid smile: one more reverse for the enemy of mankind! My
sister and I never discussed religion; we were in a state of holy awe
on the subject; and, though we had gathered the impression that the
Roman Catholics were somehow in error, we didn't know why, and
were affected by the warm splendor of their performances.

Rose, I think, was less touched by form than by color, and the
long array of antique sculpture in the Vatican did not hold her as it
did her companion, though she "liked" the great Apollo, his patrician
air of beautiful disdain. The child was an innate patrician; seemed to
have a private understanding with royalty; had a sympathetic enjoyment of high ceremonies, and was extremely fastidious in her tastes.
Ugliness, dirt, disharmony, revolted her, and she averted herself from
them with a haughty disgust. In view of her after career, this trait of
hers must be emphasized.

II

Her father was an imaginative writer, her mother an artist, and
Rose inherited creative ardor, but lacked the ability to give her aspirations satisfactory projection. She painted, she wrote, she played the
piano and sang; but the restraint of rules was irksome to her in all
things. Her conceptions, as Browning might say, broke through language and escaped; in all her girlish products there were an impassioned surge and exaltation, the purpose flagrant, but the rendering
obscure. The gift of expression in art, much as she could appreciate it
in others, was beyond her own control. Something else was needed
to satisfy her soul and release her energies. She was to be a woman

grown before the solution to her riddle appeared.

She did not find it in society; she was very critical of others, and would endow this or that person with virtues which they lacked or with faults of which they were innocent; vehemently repented, afterward, her errors of judgment, but prone as ever to repeat them. She had no girl confidantes; and, in spite of her beauty and charm, she disturbed rather than won her male acquaintance. She might drape them in imaginative glories, or condemn them unheard and misunderstood; the ground failed beneath their feet and they were fain to retire, mystified; there would be no enlightenment on her part. One might almost say that she never really met people at all, for all her impersonal cordiality and resource. If she ever had a love affair, it was in some region of the imagination beyond the scope of daily life. She could have been a queen of love; but she bandaged her eyes with rainbows and could not see realities. She was prone to pregnant silences when others were chatting, but her eyes would speak. She took more from her father than from her mother.

The freedom and scope of natural scenery and things delighted her; here were a beauty and breadth not subject to criticism; they afforded space for her ideals. During our stay at English Leamington, one spring, she and her brother would walk up an acclivity, a mile or two outside the town, where grass and foliage were profuse and free as when Chaucer sang, and there were hedges of hawthorn bordering the rust paths. We gathered armfuls of the thick-growing red and white blooms, and Rose would carry them home through the sober streets, her rosy face smiling through the clusters.

Imagination so possessed her that in her childhood she mistook its creations for facts, and would come out of her retirements and marvelous tales of what she had seen and adventured; her wise father and mother were too wise to insist upon discrepancies between truth and fable. During our sojourn at the haunted castle of Montauto, outside Florence, Rose and her companion loved to wander through the great empty rooms, with the dim lights and soft shadows, listening for secret sounds and seeing gliding figures. In the *podere*—the estate appertaining to the house—we would wander hand in hand among the vines and fig trees, fauns and nymphs treading soundlessly at our side. If we recognized our own make-believe, it only added to the charm. The credulities of childhood may bear good fruit in later years.

On a visit to her free hospital sixty years after this, I recalled to her these child experiences. She sat on the wooden verandah of her house of love and charity, the clear American sunshine falling upon her: a devout Catholic, a band of white folded across her forehead, black robes falling about her in long folds, a rosary on her breast. Her cheeks were still rosy and her eyes blue, her lips tender and resolute. "I was chasing will-o'-the-wisps in those days," she said, with a smile and a sigh. If it were a sin, her father-confessor would gently have absolved her. Her mother supplied his rôle in the early years; when Rose had done wrong, she was not rebuked, but her mother would draw her into seclusion, leading her, in silence, into contemplation of the Good and True, until the barriers would give way and tears came forth. The Lord of Heaven Himself might look through the mother's face in those moments.

In Concord, in her teens, she did not attend Sanborn's famous boys' and girls' school; and the decline and death of our father ended her childhood, and left her perplexed and taciturn. She had never before faced irreparable loss and grief, and deep emotion, in her, had not learned how to give or to receive sympathy; and religious consolations seemed, perhaps, too conventional for her need. We cannot lift the veils that cover these human withdrawals. Her abounding health and energy, incongruous with her spiritual mood, puzzled her; soul and body were at odds. The music, dancing, and light-hearted chatter of the Concord young people discomposed her sense of social values; she would be present at their merrymakings, but without hearty merriment; the feelings that really dominated her were incommunicable.

By a fortunate chance, Dio Lewis's seminary for young ladies was opened in Lexington (neighboring Concord) at about this time, and Rose and her sister Una went there. It was, really, a school of physical exercise, according to Lewis's system, affording young

women their first opportunity in this country to cultivate their bodies and live by rules of health. Only young 'ladies' were admitted; all
went well; a delightful and wholesome organization was created. The
girls wore a distinctive dress suitable for outdoor hikes and sports;
they prospered greatly and were happy; it was a remarkable anticipation of a freer age. Una and Rose were greatly benefitted, and Lewis
made a small fortune; but after two years the big old frame building
which housed them (it had been a hotel) burned to the ground; it
was never rebuilt, and for fifty years the physical education of American young women was allowed to lapse. Mrs. Hawthorne, with her
three children, removed to Dresden, in Saxony, and a new era began,
by the end of which Rose had entered her twentieth year.

In the German city things wore a more practical aspect; the
American and English society in these foreign places felt more freedom than at home; there were good music, good pictures, pleasant
outdoor life, open-air concerts in the Grosser Garten and Sächsische
Schweiz, hard by. Rose began to understand the society idea; but before three years the Franco-Prussian War took me to New York and
the mother and daughters to London, where they were to meet the
Brownings and other old friends—an agreeable interlude, until the
mother's final illness began, the gravity of which I did not realize until a cablegram told me she was dead. A young fellow whom we had
known in Dresden happened to be about leaving for London, and
would escort the two girls back to America; but, after what seemed a
very brief interval, a short letter from him informed me that he and
Rose had become man and wife.

III

George Lathrop was even younger than his wife; neither of
them was yet twenty years old. But the episode does not belong to
the theme I am here treating; it was an error, not to be repaired. Its
significance here is in the fact that it obliterated whatever dreams of
a happy marriage state Rose might have had (based upon the flawless
felicity of her father's and mother's union), awakening her, instead,

to the rôle of endurance, difficult for her temperament of buoyant independence. Pride helped her, and her native habit of reticence in vital matters. Not until some twenty years later did she become a widow; a son had died in infancy.

Strong natures are perfected by strong measures. Rose was relentlessly tested. Beautiful, gifted, impetuous, imperious, and fastidious, the way to perversity was broad before her. Her friends were over prone to indulge and defer to her, and generous impulse could not protect her from selfishness. She might have made a brilliant figure before the world, but the heights above the world are reached by suffering.

Midway on their path, these young people were converted to Catholicism, surprising their friends even more than by their marriage—a daughter of the Puritans to embrace the faith pre-eminent for church authority, which had driven the Pilgrims to New England! Rose herself believed that the leaven had long been working in her, and that her childish experience in Rome had given hints of what was to come. We often interpret our present by our past. Her zeal was great; she had found a way to use her highest energies. But some few years were yet to pass before she found the means for the total self-surrender and devotion which were indispensable.

Her first step was to seek a nurse's certificate in a hospital. There she worked for a year, overcoming all the obstacles and tests which are designed to prove to the utmost the sincerity and constancy of the applicant. With the winning of her diploma, her future was in her hands. She knew the stories of the saints and martyrs of the Church, and nothing less than the extreme would satisfy her thirst for self-sacrifice. Whatever was most abhorrent to the instincts of the flesh, that must she embrace; whatever was most hopeless and forlorn in human fate, that must she love and assuage. All that had given joy in her life must be banished for the sake of a purer joy. In no figurative sense, but literally, must she accept the stern injunction, "Sell what thou hast, and give to the poor...and follow me!"

She did not beguile herself with ecstatic emotions; she realized what she did; she had abundant common sense. But she was resolved that her regeneration should be unfaltering and permanent. Nor would she seek the solace of mortal sympathy, but would pass through her fires, like the martyrs of the Church before her, with humility and cheerfulness. How be other than cheerful, since the indulgences of earth become a stench in the nostrils, but the fragrance of Heaven is immortal? She held no pose of sanctity, but was a plain working woman, diligent and faithful in the duties she had undertaken. Work, in increasing measure, was always to do, and she did it to the very end.

No other disease is more painful or repulsive than cancer, more hideous to see or torturing to endure. When the sufferer's poverty prevents him from commanding medical care and leaves him to perish unattended, human misery can hardly go further. Rose's plan was simple: she would attend those only who were paupers and had been given up as hopeless cases by the doctors. They came to her, not to be healed, but to die. But till death came they received every attention and tenderness that love and skill could give, and breathed an atmosphere of human love, to many of them an experience without precedent. Rose had a little money of her own, and she spent it in renting a floor of a building in the slums of east New York and supplying it with cots; she could not pay for help, and at first she worked alone. By and by another young woman visited her, and became her voluntary assistant and her friend. Other persons, learning of the strange enterprise, made occasional contributions. Presently she was able to enlarge the accommodations and to care for more patients.

As time went on, other unselfish helpers came, but not all found courage to remain. The enterprise, too, teetering continually on the brink of collapse for lack of means to carry it on, seemed to survive by miracle only; but always, even at the last moment, money would be sent it from unknown sources to supply the desperate need; the workers prayed, and their prayers were answered—they could assign no other reason, and they held faith in the efficacy of prayer. But by slow degrees the almost incredible fact of the hospital became known to one and another, and personally confirmed, the supplies became larger and more frequent. A larger building was rented, and at last it became practicable to acquire a refuge for the moribund paupers, in an airy and wholesome New York suburb; more recently it has been redesigned and constructed on a broader plan. Long before this the Mother Church had taken cognizance of the Home, and a date was appointed for the formal consecration. Rose looked forward with joy to this consummation of her hopes; but when, one night, she had composed herself to happy sleep, she did not awaken the next morning when the Sisters came to call her. Mother Alphonsa was gone; but she had lived long enough to see her work well done, and promising to endure, perhaps, as long as the need which it relieved.

IV

Circumstances took me far from her neighborhood in the latter years of her life; I could visit her but at long intervals. It happened usually in spring, cool sunshine falling on the porch we sat in; and our talk was not about the Home, nor about their joining the Church; and but once or twice did she lead me through the wards, perhaps wishing to spare me even a sight of what monopolized her whole existence. But we chatted of old times, and of the children who had arisen in our later age, whom she ardently loved, and who loved her. Once she gave me some little books of the Lives of the Saints; and once, when I was departing for India, to investigate the plague and famine there, she put about my neck a tiny metal effigy which had, she said, been blessed by the Holy Father, and would shield me from harm.

Upon the whole, I found her, in this later phase, naïve and childlike, like the little girl who had been my playmate, but with a difference. The passions of her nature, doubtless as urgent as ever, centered no longer round her personal fate and interests, for in her own view she no longer existed. She lived, labored, and prayed only for those incarnations of mortal misery which she had drawn about her. Formerly she looked forward to the splendid carnival of human life, to a career in art, in society, to a bountiful and happy marriage.

Those aspirations had been uprooted like weeds in a garden, and she had planted in their place flowers of deathless root: the lights of Carnival were quenched in the dawn of a purer festival. As she sat before me in her black robes, she was not sad to look at; cheerfulness emanated from her like a fragrance, as I remember it in her mother; and, like her, she was low-voiced, tranquil, and fearless. As with her father, too, her face would now and again be traversed by lights and shades of eloquent thought and feeling. But within all was the vivid, innocent sister who had been my companion long ago.

Does it seem a pity that a nature so finely organized to give pleasure to the world and to receive it should willfully confine itself to such as it were the poorest and most barren of human creatures? Is it not better to establish and illustrate the beauty of the life of the world than, for such an alternative, to turn one's back upon it?

Persons competent to answer such questions must needs do so in terms which to us are incomprehensible. They have learned, at a price, things which we do not know. They have felt a joy and seen a beauty in whose existence we are impotent to believe; and for the least of these, having once tasted them, they would not exchange the kingdoms and the glory of all the earth. Such divine beauty and joy are all about us, always; but we cannot be aware of them, for, though the veil be transparent, our eyes are blind.

The seers, on the other hand, are shy and humble, and stammer and retire when interrogated. They are not proud of their knowledge, but feel themselves to be the very paupers of Creation. "What am I in the pure and lovely light of the Holiness of God?" It is vain to argue with such persons; but, if you examine them narrowly, you may find upon their hands and feet the marks of the nails.

IMPERILED MEN: MOURNING CAG

by Andre Dubus

Everything we know about the deceased is in this eulogy, which lacks even his name. He was called by the acronym CAG, referring to his role as a Navy pilot (commander of a Carrier Air Group). The commander's suicide caused every man aboard the ship to reconsider the added perils faced by some of their mates. It is possible that Dubus' compassion for CAG deepened over the years. This tribute was written over thirty years later, after Dubus had acquired life-altering afflictions.

Dubus was born in Louisiana to a Cajun-Irish Roman Catholic family. After graduating from college in 1958, he spent six years in the Marine Corps, where he met CAG aboard a submarine tender. Dubus was thirty-one before he established himself as a writer with his first novel, The Lieutenant.

At age fifty, he stopped his car to help two injured motorists. As he was assisting the disabled brother and sister to the edge of the highway, an oncoming car swerved into them. Dubus pushed the sister out of the way to safety, but the brother was killed. Dubus was seriously injured and spent the rest of his life in a wheelchair, suffering amputation, hospitalizations, infections, and clinical depression.

His Catholic faith deepened during this time and was revealed in his work. This eulogy to his commander appears in his book, Meditations from a Movable Chair, *published in 1999, the year of Dubus' death.*

He was a Navy pilot in World War II and in Korea and, when I knew him in 1961 for a few months before he killed himself, he was the commander of the Air Group aboard an aircraft carrier, and we called him by the acronym CAG. He shot himself with his thirty-eight-caliber revolver because two investigators from the Office of Naval Intelligence came aboard ship while we were anchored off Iwakuni in Japan, and gave the ship's captain a written report of their investigation of some of CAG's erotic life. CAG held the rank of commander then; he was a much-decorated combat pilot, and his duty as CAG was one of great responsibility. The ship's executive officer, also a commander, summoned CAG to his office, where the two investigators were, and told him that his choices were to face a general court marital or resign from the Navy. Less than half an hour later, CAG was dead in his stateroom. His body was flown to the United States; we were told that he did not have a family, and I do not know where he was buried. There was a memorial service aboard ship, but I do not remember it; I only remember a general sadness like mist in the passageways.

I did not really know him. I was a first lieutenant with the Marine Detachment; we guarded the planes' nuclear weapons stored belowdecks, ran the brig, and manned one of the antiaircraft gun mounts. We were fifty or so enlisted men and two officers among a ship's crew of thirty-five hundred officers and men. The Air Group was not included in the ship's company. They came aboard with their planes for our seven-month deployment in the western Pacific. I do not remember the number of pilots and bombardier-navigators, mechanics and flight controllers, and men who worked on the flight deck, but there were plenty of all, and day and night you could hear planes catapulting off the front of the deck and landing on its rear.

The flight deck was a thousand feet long, the ship weighed seventy thousand tons, and I rarely felt its motion. I came aboard in May for a year of duty and in August we left our port in San Francisco Bay and headed for Japan. One night on the voyage across, I sat in the wardroom drinking coffee with a lieutenant commander. The long tables were covered with white linen; the wardroom was open all night because men were always working. The lieutenant commander told me that Russian submarines tracked us, they recorded the sound of our propellers and could not be fooled by the sound of a decoy ship's propellers, they came even into San Francisco Bay to do this; and our submarines did the same with Russian carriers. He said that every time we tried in training exercises to evade our own submarines, we could not do it, and our destroyers could not track and stop them. He said, "So if the whistle blows, we'll get a nuclear fish up our ass, in the first thirty minutes. Our job is to get the birds in the air before that. They're going to Moscow."

"Where will they land afterward?"

"They won't. They know that."

The voyage to Japan was five or six weeks long because we did not go directly to Japan; the pilots flew air operations. Combat units are always training for war; but these men who flew in planes, and the men in orange suits and ear protectors who worked on the flight deck during landings and takeoffs, were engaging in something not at all as playful as Marine field exercises generally were. They were imperiled. One pilot told me that, from his fighter bomber in the sky, the flight deck looked like an aspirin tablet. On the passage to Japan, I became friendly with some pilots, drinking coffee in the wardroom, and I knew what CAG looked like because he was CAG. He had dark skin and alert eyes, and he walked proudly. Then in Japan, I sometimes drank with young pilots. I was a robust twenty-five-year-old, one of two Marine officers aboard ship, and I did not want to be outdone at anything by anyone. But I could not stay with the pilots; I had to leave them in the bar, drinking and talking and laughing, and make my way back to the ship and sleep and wake with a hangover. Next day, the pilots flew; if we did not go to sea, they flew from a base on land. Once I asked one of them how he did it.

"The pure oxygen. Soon as you put on the mask, your head clears."

It was not simply the oxygen, and I did not understand any of these wild, brave, and very efficient men until years later when I read Tom Wolfe's *The Right Stuff*.

Months after CAG was dead, I saw another pilot die. I worked belowdecks with the Marine Detachment, but that warm gray afternoon the entire ship was in a simulated condition of war, and my part was to stand four hours of watch in a small turret high above the ship. I could move the turret in a circular way by pressing a button, and I looked through binoculars for planes or ships in the hundred-and-eighty-degree arc of our port side. On the flight deck, planes were taking off. Two parallel catapults launched planes straight off the front of the ship, and quickly they rose and climbed. A third and fourth catapult were on the port side where the flight deck angled sharply out to the left, short of the bow. From my turret, I looked down at the ship's bridge and the flight deck. A helicopter flew low near the ship, and planes were taking off. On the deck were men in orange suits and ear protectors; on both sides of the ship, just beneath the fight deck, were nets for these men to jump into, to save themselves from being killed by a landing plane that veered or skidded or crashed. One night, I inspected a Marine guarding a plane on the flight deck; we had a sentry there because the plane carried a nuclear bomb. I stepped from a hatch into the absolute darkness of a night at sea, and into a strong wind that lifted my body with each step. I was afraid it would lift me off the deck and hurl me into the sea, where I would tread water in that great expanse and depth while the ship went on its way; tomorrow they would learn that I was missing. I found the plane and the Marine; he stood with one arm around the cable that held the wing to the deck.

In the turret, I was facing aft when it happened: men in orange were at the rear of the flight deck; then they sprinted forward and I moved my turret toward the bow and saw a plane in the gray sea, and an orange-suited pilot lying face down in the water, his parachute floating beyond his head, moving toward the rear of the ship. The plane had dropped off that third catapult and now water covered its wing, then its cockpit, and it sank. The pilot was behind the ship; his limbs did not move, his face was in the sea, and his parachute was filling with water and starting to sink. The helicopter hovered low and a sailor on a rope descended from it; he wore orange, and I watched him coming down and the pilot floating and the parachute sinking beneath the waves. There was still some length of parachute line remaining when the sailor reached the pilot; he grabbed him;

then the parachute lines tightened their pull and drew the pilot down. There was only the sea now beneath the sailor on the rope. Then he ascended.

I shared a stateroom with a Navy lieutenant, an officer of medical administration, a very tall and strong man from Oklahoma. He had been an enlisted man, had once been a corpsman aboard a submarine operating off the coast of Russia, and one night their periscope was spotted, destroyers came after them, and they dived and sat at the bottom and listened by sonar to the destroyers' sonar trying to find them. He told me about the sailor who tried to save the pilot. In the dispensary, they gave him brandy, and the sailor wept and said he was trained to do that job, and this was his first time, and he had failed. Of course he had not failed. No man could lift another man attached to a parachute filled with water. Some people said the helicopter had not stayed close enough to the ship while planes were taking off. Some said the pilot was probably already dead; his plane dropped from the ship, and he ejected himself high into the air, but not high enough for his parachute to ease his fall. This was all talk about the mathematics of violent death; the pilot was killed because he flew airplanes from a ship at sea.

He was a lieutenant commander and I knew his face and name. As he was being catapulted, his landing gear on the left side broke off and his plane skidded into the sea. He was married; his widow had been married before, also to a pilot who was killed in a crash. I wondered if it was her bad luck to meet only men who flew; years later, I believed that whatever in their spirits made these men fly also drew her to them.

I first spoke to CAG at the officers' club at the Navy base in Yokosuka. The officers of the Air Group hosted a party for the officers of the ship's company. We wore civilian suits and ties and gathered at the club to drink. There were no women. The party was a matter of protocol, probably a tradition among pilots and the officers of carriers; for us young officers, it meant getting happily drunk. I was doing this with pilots at the bar when one of them said: "Let's throw CAG into the pond."

He grinned at me as I looked to my left at the small shallow pond with pretty fish in it; then I looked past the pond at CAG, sitting on a soft leather hair, a drink in his hand, talking quietly with two or three other commanders sitting in soft leather chairs. All the pilots with me were grinning and saying yes, and the image of us lifting CAG from his chair and dropping him into the water gave me joy, and I put my drink on the bar and said: "Let's *go*."

I ran across the room to CAG, grabbed the lapels of his coat, jerked him up from his chair, and saw his drink spill onto his suit; then I fell backward to the floor, still holding his lapels, and pulled him down on top of me. There was no one else with me. He was not angry yet, but I was a frightened fool. I released his lapels and turned my head and looked back at the laughing pilots.

Out of my vision, the party was loud, hundreds of drinking officers who had not seen this, and CAG sounded only puzzled when he said: "What's going on?"

He stood and brushed at the drink on his suit, watching me get up from the floor. I stood not quite at attention but not at ease either. I said: "Sir, I'm Marine Lieutenant Dubus. Your pilots fooled me." I nodded toward them at the bar. CAG smiled. "They said: 'Let's throw CAG into the pond.' But, sir, the joke was on me."

He was still smiling.

"I'm very sorry sir."

"That's all right, Lieutenant."

"Can I get the Commander another drink, sir?"

"Sure," he said, and told me what he was drinking, and I got it from the bar, where the pilots were red-faced and happy, and took it to CAG, who was sitting in the chair again, along with the other commanders. He smiled and thanked me, and the commanders smiled; then I returned to the young pilots and we all laughed.

Until a few months later, on the day he killed himself, the only words I spoke to CAG were greetings. One night, I saw him sitting with a woman in the officers' club, and I wished him good evening. A few times, I saw him in the ship's passageways; I recognized him seconds before the features of his face were clear: he had a graceful, athletic stride that dipped his shoulders. I saluted and said good morning, sir, or good afternoon, sir. He smiled as he returned my salute and greeting, his eyes and voice mirthful, and I knew that he was seeing me again pulling him out of his chair and down to the floor, then standing to explain myself and apologize. I liked being a memory that gave him sudden and passing amusement.

On a warm sunlit day, we were anchored off Iwakuni, and I planned to go with other crew members on a bus to Hiroshima. I put on civilian clothes and went down the ladder to the boat that would take us ashore. I was not happily going to Hiroshima; I was going because I am an American, and I felt that I should look at it, and be in it. I found a seat on the rocking boat, then saw CAG in civilian clothes coming down the ladder. There were few seats remaining, and he chose the one next to me. He asked me where I was going, then said he was going to Hiroshima too. I was relieved and grateful; while CAG was flying planes in World War II, I was a boy buying saving stamps and taking scrap metal to school. On the bus, he would talk to me about war, and in Hiroshima I would walk with him, and look with him, and his seasoned steps and eyes would steady mine. Then from the ship above us the officer of the deck called down: "CAG?"

CAG turned and looked up at him, a lieutenant junior grade in white cap and short-sleeved shirt and trousers.

"Sir, the executive officer would like to see you."

I do not remember what CAG said to me. I only remember my disappointment when he told the boat's officer to go ashore without him. All I saw in CAG's face was the look of a man called from rest back to his job. He climbed the ladder, and soon the boat pulled away.

Perhaps when I reached Hiroshima, CAG was dead; I do not remember the ruins at ground zero, or what I saw in the museum. I walked and looked, and stood for a long time at a low arch with an open space at the ground, and in that space was a stone box that held the names of all who had died on the day of the bombing, and all who had died since because of the bomb. That night, I ate dinner ashore, then rode the boat to the ship, went to my empty room, climbed to my upper bunk, and slept for only a while, till the quiet voice of my roommate woke me: "The body will be flown to Okinawa."

I looked at him standing at his desk and speaking into the telephone.

"Yes. A thirty-eight in the temple. Yes."

I turned on my reading lamp and watched him put the phone down. He was sad, and he looked at me. I said: "Did someone commit suicide?"

"CAG."

"CAG?"

I sat up.

"The ONI investigated him."

Then I knew what I had not known I knew, and I said: "Was he a homosexual?"

"Yes."

He told me two investigators from the Office of Naval Intelligence had come aboard that morning and had given the captain their report. The investigators were with the executive officer when he summoned CAG to his office and showed him the report and told him that he could either resign or face a general court-martial. Then CAG went to his room. Fifteen minutes later, the executive officer phoned him; when he did not answer, the executive officer and the investigators ran to his room. He was on his bunk, shot in the right temple, his revolver in his hand. His eyelids fluttered; he was unconscious but still alive, and he died from bleeding.

"They ran?" I said. "They ran to his room?"

Ten years later, one of my shipmates came to visit me in Massachusetts; we had been civilians for a long time. In my kitchen, we were drinking beer, and he said: "I couldn't tell you this aboard ship, because I worked in the legal office. They called CAG back from that boat you were on, because he knew the ONI was aboard. His plane was on the ground in Iwakuni. They were afraid he was going to fly it and crash into the sea and they'd lose the plane."

All thirty-five hundred men of the ship's crew did not mourn. Not every one of the hundreds of men in the Air Group mourned. But the shock was general and hundreds of men did mourn, and each morning we woke to it and it was in our talk in the wardroom and in the passageways. In the closed air of the ship, it touched you, and it lived above us on the flight deck, and in the sky. One night at sea, a young pilot came to my room; his face was sunburned and sad. We sat in desk chairs, and he said, "The morale is very bad now. The whole Group. It's just shot."

"Did y'all know about him?"

"We all knew. We didn't care. We would have followed him into hell."

Yes: they would have followed him diving in tunnels to the flaming center of the earth. When he was their leader, they were ready every day and every night to fly with him from a doomed ship, and follow him to Moscow, to perish in their brilliant passion.

THE GREAT HEART OF THOMAS P. "TIP" O'NEILL

by Thomas P. O'Neill III
January, 1994

Tip O'Neill, the son of a bricklayer, was educated in parochial schools in North Cambridge, Massachusetts. He graduated from Boston College in 1936 and became a member of the Massachusetts State Legislature at the age of twenty-one. Combining what his biographer John A. Farrell called "street smarts with a Jesuit education," O'Neill served in the U. S. House of Representatives for thirty-four years and as Speaker of the House from 1977-1987. He was known throughout his career for repeating his father's slogan, "All politics is local."

At his funeral, Catlin O'Neill read Matthew 5:1-13, saying that her grandfather considered it "the greatest political speech ever written":

When Jesus saw the crowds, he went up the mountain; and after he sat down, his disciples came to him. Then he began to speak, and taught them, saying:

"Blessed are the poor in spirit, for theirs is the kingdom of heaven. Blessed are those who mourn, for they will be comforted. Blessed are the meek, for they will inherit the earth. Blessed are those who hunger and thirst for righteousness, for they will be filled. Blessed are the merciful, for they will receive mercy. Blessed are the pure in heart, for they will see God. Blessed are the peacemakers, for they will be called children of God. Blessed are those who are persecuted for righteousness' sake, for theirs is the kingdom of heaven. Blessed are you when people revile you and persecute you and utter all kinds of evil against you falsely on my account. Rejoice and be glad, for your reward is great in heaven, for in the same way they persecuted the prophets who were before you."

In describing my dad, I once heard Leo Diehl say, "You know, you haven't lived till you have met Tip O'Neill." I think all of us really believed that he would live forever and that this really wasn't ever supposed to happen. Don't you wish just once more he could appear suddenly, here in this church, his great heart filling a living room, a House chamber, a ballpark, or us. Just the other night, that great heart of his filled a very small room at the Brigham and Women's Hospital.

We were sitting together eating coffee ice cream with Heath Bar crunch topping. Every once in a while he would spit out one of the larger chunks. We were talking about Boston College football. God, did B. C. make him happy this year.

"That Foley kid," he said, talking about our great quarterback. "Foley's really a North Cambridge kid, you know." I looked at him a little askance and he said, with such pride and with pleasure, "Tommy, you know who his grandmother is, Foley's grandmother? Verna, from Verna's Doughnut Shop." Well, Verna's Doughnut Shop was just across the street from this church, a landmark in this neighborhood for many, many years. "Tommy," he said, and these were among his last words, "Do you remember how good those honey-dipped doughnuts were? God, those honey-dipped doughnuts." Well, I treasure those words now because they bring back the eagerness and the pleasure and the joy he took in everything that he loved: honey-dipped doughnuts, cigars, coffee ice cream, Boston College, B. C. football, the Red Sox, a good card game, this neighborhood, his whole life.

You loved Tip O'Neill. We all did. It is my great privilege, on behalf of his family, to remind you today how much he loved you. As an Irish-American male, maybe he didn't always make that feeling clear, how much pleasure and joy he took in being your friend, your colleague, your Congressman, your father, your husband, your Pop-Pop. And he loved America, the welcome it gave his immigrant forebears, and the promise it makes to his grandchildren.

Mr. Vice President [Al Gore], your presence here representing this country is very precious to us. I want you to know that he loved your dad, and he loved you.

Of course, Tip O'Neill loved the Democratic party. Your presence here, Senator [Ted] Kennedy, Speaker [Tom] Foley, and so many others of his fellow Democrats, honors our dad, and again we are so very grateful. But to tell you the truth, for Tip O'Neill, who embodied for at least a time, maybe even saved the values of our party, your presence is quite fitting.

As for you Republicans, well, as a Catholic my father always believed, hate the sin, but love the sinner. Especially President Reagan, his beloved nemesis. It was Reagan, as Dad told, and loved to call him, who taught our father a new motto, "Trust, but verify." And while President Reagan applied it to the Soviets, Tip O'Neill applied it to the Republicans. What our dad enjoyed most about President Reagan, of course, was their common Irish roots. Ballypareen, Dad would say, citing the Irish village that President Reagan's people came from, which means, he would always add, "Valley of the Small Potatoes." Our father was serious about his love of Ireland, which is why he would be very grateful to you, John Hume, not only for being here today but for your efforts on behalf of peace, how it filled his heart and made him so very, very proud.

Our father was an unusual Irish American. He was an Irishman without a dark side. Entirely positive in his outlook, he always wished people well, everybody. He had no envy, he had no spite. "Remember," he would say, "today's enemies are tomorrow's friends." This week he has often been described as the last of a breed, but the truth, especially in this town, is that he was the beginning of something, not the end: a politics which defends working people but does not depend on class resentment; a politics that loves justice and hates no one.

Our father loved being from Cambridge, North Cambridge, Barry's Corner, St. John's Parish, and all of it. We have all heard the stories, so many stories, all week long, from people like John the cobbler and Frank the barber.

But also our father loved being from the town that boasts of Harvard College, even though, through his father's life and most of his own, Harvard was in another world. And after the rest of the world had noticed this Mick from North Cambridge, finally, Harvard got it. When he received the honorary degree in 1987, I remember how moved he was. But not so much by the degree itself; what really moved him was the standing ovation that those Harvard students gave him that afternoon following his remarks.

One of the miracles of his public life was how the young people loved him, as deeply as the elderly did. When he saw all those young students opening their hearts to him, he went back to the podium, this man whose father had laid those bricks, this man who himself had mowed that grass, and he said to those young people, "It is because of you I am here in Harvard Yard as a member of your community."

"Yesterday's enemies," he might have said, "are today's friends."

Friends, God, how he loved his friends. All politics is local, right. But what our father also believed, all politics is personal, going back to that movie script of a campaign against Mike LoPresti in 1952, when our father's personal connections brought together the likes of Henry Owens, Blandina Ruffo, Chick Artesani, Lennie Lamkin, Red O'Connell, to forge the kind of cross-ethnic coalition that would be our father's trademark; the last of a breed. I think I can talk for everybody when I say that I hope not.

Our father's approach to national and international politics was personal as well. His emphasis on the government's role in providing quality education to ordinary people came in large part from his own sister Mary, our Aunt Mary, who was a pubic school teacher and among the first of the female principals in public schools in Massachusetts.

He responded to the great crises of his era in personal terms, too, helping to end an American war in Vietnam, largely because it was killing our young, the sons of the working class; helping to prevent one in Nicaragua and in El Salvador as Joe Moakley—and Joe, you got it exactly right. My father's Aunt Annie was a Maryknoll nun named Sister Eunice. His life-changing high school teacher was also a nun named Sister Agatha. So when the nuns were murdered in El Salvador, my father didn't have to wonder what side he was going to be on. And when Jesuits were murdered by death squads, my father felt it, as a man whose whole life was a gift from the Jesuits.

Personal, local, my brothers and my sisters and I learned our politics at the kitchen table on Russell Street. We all treasure the memory of that table, how everybody from Barry's Corner showed up there. Later in his fancy offices in Washington, they were like that, too, everybody always being made to feel welcome.

I think our father's genius was that he felt toward everybody who came to his table, or who came into his office, the way he felt towards us, his family, his kids, his first constituents. Loving America and the Democrats, Boston, B. C., Cambridge, the elderly, the kids, it was all a version, his version of how he loved his family.

And oh, how he loved us. How he loved you, Kippy, and Michael, and you, Susan, God did he love you, and you, Rosemary, and you, Chip, and you, Jackie, and you, Joanne, and all of you grandchildren, you were Pop-Pop's very own honey-dipped doughnuts.

But the man's core, the pulse of his huge heart, the cushna Machree, as the Irish would say, was Mommy, his high school sweetheart, his lifelong love, the great source of his braveness. All the world knows how he loved you; most importantly, you do, too.

My father always said that if he hadn't married Millie, he probably would have gone into the church and become a priest. If that is the case, Your Eminence, I am afraid that Tip O'Neill would have been Boston's Cardinal Archbishop all of these years.

The church, our father loved the church. He loved this church and he loved God, who has now called him home.

But the main thing I want to leave with you is how much Tip O'Neill loved all of you. If he could, if this casket were a magic suitcase out of which he could appear just one last time, he would offer you this last gift, this poem of Curley's that you all have heard him recite a thousand times, with that great voice of his, that heart, both of which would fill a space like this.

Around the corner I have a friend,
in this great city that has no end.
Yet days go by and weeks rush on,
and before I know it, a year is gone.
And I never see my old friend's face,
for life is a swift and terrible race.
He knows I like him just as well
as in the days when I rang his bell
and he rang mine.
We were younger then,
and now we are busy, tired men.
Tired with playing a foolish game,
tired with trying to make a name.
Tomorrow, I say, I will call on Jim
just to show that I am thinking of him.
But tomorrow comes and tomorrow goes,
and the distance between us
grows and grows.
Around the corner yet miles away:
"Here is a telegram, sir; Jim died today."
And that's what we get and deserve
in the end,
around the corner, a vanished friend.

Thank you, everybody.

THE ANGEL OF AA:
SISTER MARY IGNATIA

by "Bill W."
August, 1966

While many Americans today know that the eulogist "Bill W." and "Dr. Bob" founded Alcoholics Anonymous, few people know there was a third—female—AA pioneer. Although she was the only one of the three who was not an alcoholic, she has remained more anonymous to AA history than have "Bill W." and "Dr. Bob."

The three came together at a turning point in their lives in the era when America had responded to a crisis of rampant alcoholism by enacting Prohibition. In 1928, Sister Mary Ignatia's doctor said that she needed to end the accumulated stress of her twenty-year career as a musician. She was sent to Akron, Ohio, to start over in hospital work. There she met Dr. Bob and Bill, who were also trying to start over: with sobriety.

By the time she became the hospital's head of admissions, Ignatia developed a new interest and had been quietly trying nutrition-based treatment for those alcoholics who came into the emergency room at night. Hospitals did not admit them because alcoholism was viewed solely as a moral failure; jail was the only authorized place to put a drunk.

Prohibition had long given way to the Great Depression by 1939, the year that this eulogy describes Ignatia and Dr. Bob's collusion to admit an alcoholic patient. St. Thomas eventually became the first hospital in America to provide detoxification in a full-treatment atmosphere.

Bill's tribute below does not deal with the greatest difficulties Ignatia faced, because they came from within her Church. Neither he nor Dr. Bob were Catholics, so they were likely not aware of these pressures. But a true appreciation of her work requires an understanding of her struggle to reconcile the dictates of her heart with those of her religious superiors.

After Dr. Bob died in 1950, Ignatia's duties multiplied. Much of her time was spent replying to inquiries for information and guidance from other hospitals, although Catholic hospitals were often uncomfortable with her link to AA's "Higher Power" spirituality. This discomfort, along with financial pressures (partly caused by Ignatia's charity admissions), led to her ouster. After twenty-four years at St. Thomas, Sister Ignatia was transferred to a big city hospital under orders from the Archbishop and her Mother Superior not to speak publicly outside of her workplace. At age sixty-three, she found herself starting over once again, this time at St. Vincent's Charity Hospital in Cleveland. She arrived without a job title; there were also no facilities for treating alcoholics.

The following year, Archbishop Richard J. Cushing of Boston asked the Cleveland Archbishop if Sister Ignatia could speak to an audience of priests at a National Clergy Conference on Alcoholism. The answer was no. In 1953, the idea of any woman addressing the Catholic clergy on a spiritual matter may have personally appalled her Archbishop; he could have perceived it as a threat to his clerical authority. That conference also hinted at the drinking problems of Catholic clergy, which the Church wanted to deal with internally, by admonishing prayer and self-control. The worst cases were sent away for a lengthy retreat in New Mexico or New Jersey, out of view.

Unaware of these machinations, a group of women chose Sister Ignatia as its "Catholic Woman of the Year 1954." The National Council of Catholic Women had no idea how their award would roil the Cleveland archdiocese. For Ignatia's superiors could hardly forbid her to address a group of women (who had already announced their selection to the national press).

In her acceptance speech, Ignatia listed ways that society—from spouses to the church—could help alcoholics, humanely rather than punitively. She also talked of the special challenges alcoholic women face (even Dr. Bob struggled with the idea of women in AA). Widespread coverage of this event continued to complicate Ignatia's relationship with her superiors. She was also treating alcoholic nuns, an even greater potential scandal.

Ignatia's most powerful critics—her religious superiors—had authority over her. But the love of the broader community was even more powerful. Her recovering alcoholics could not be silenced. Cleveland, in fact, then had more AA members than any other city in America, many of whom she had personally treated in Akron.

Now they not only insisted upon a hospital ward in Cleveland for those they were mentoring, they built one themselves. The city's AA members—engineers, carpenters, electricians, painters, attorneys, businessmen—came forth to remodel and furnish St. Vincent's annex. Doctor-members and AA priests joined their efforts. One recovering priest said that Sister Ignatia had once told him that alcoholic doctors and priests were "the hardest nuts to crack. Whenever I get my hands on one, he stays here [in the AA ward] twice as long." She also had a great fondness for them. The courageous AA priests had to counter the hierarchy's point of view: "Should a priest tarnish the Church's reputation by joining AA?" They accepted a Jesuit's answer: that the Church doesn't need saving nearly as much as the alcoholic does, and that, "God's cause is often hurt by people who are trying to save God."

They all celebrated the opening of Rosary Hall Solarium on December 8, 1952. Years later, in 1960, Ignatia addressed an audience of 1,700 at AA's twenty-fifth anniversary celebration. President John F. Kennedy's White House sent a letter acknowledging her contribution to American life. To this day, Rosary Hall remains a premier addiction treatment center.

On the morning of her funeral, a popular Cleveland radio broadcaster, knowing that travelers coming to pay their respects had filled downtown hotel rooms, gave a tribute to Sister Ignatia that ended with: "It's long been a saying among Alcoholics Anonymous that if the Catholic Church doesn't canonize her, the Protestants will make her a saint."

By then, however, her religious superiors had finally developed a full appreciation for Sister Ignatia. An archdiocesan vicar asked her Mother Superior to begin interviewing all who had known Sister Ignatia, and to preserve all of her papers, implying that he anticipated her future canonization.

Shortly before Dr. Bob died, a reporter asked, "Who is this woman, Sister Ignatia?" Dr. Bob took time to formulate his reply, perhaps thinking (correctly) that it might be the last thing he said about her publicly:

"In my book, Sister Ignatia is the type of person who's born once every hundred years in this world."

Sister Mary Ignatia, one of the finest friends that we of AA shall ever know, went to her reward Friday morning, April 1, 1966. Next day, the Sisters of Charity of St. Augustine opened their Mother House to visitors. More than one thousand of them signed the guest book in the first two hours. These were the first of many who during the two days following came to pay their respects to Sister.

On Monday, at high noon, the Cathedral at Cleveland could barely seat its congregation. Friends in the city and from afar attended the service. The Sisters of Charity themselves were seen to be seated in a body, radiant in their faith. Together with families and friends, we of AA had come there in expression of our gratitude for the life and works of our well-loved Sister. It was not really a time for mourning, it was instead a time to thank God for His great goodness to us all. In its affirmation of the faith, the Mass was of singular beauty; the more so to many, since it was spoken in English....

For those thousands of men, women and children whose lives had been directly touched and illumined by Sister, it would perhaps not be needful to write this account of her. Of Sister, and of the Grace she brought to all these, they already know better than anyone else. But to the many others who have never felt her presence and her love, it is hoped this narrative may be something for their special investigation.

Born in 1889 of devout and liberty-loving parents, Sister entered into this world at Shanvilly, County Mayo, of the Emerald Isle. The famed poet Yeats, born nearby, once remarked that the strange beauty of County Mayo had been specially designed to raise up poets, artists, heroes and saints. We can little doubt that even when Ignatia was aged six, and her parents had emigrated from Ireland to Cleveland, she was already beginning to manifest many a sterling virtue.

Soon the child began to reveal unusual musical talents, both of piano and voice. A few years later she was seen giving lessons at the home of her parents. During 1914, she became possessed of a great desire to become a religious. In this year she joined the Community that many of us AAs know so well....

But even then, as ever since, Sister was frail, exceeding frail. By 1933 the rigors of her music teaching had become too great. She had a really serious physical breakdown. Her doctor put to her this choice: "You will have to take it easy. You can either be a dead music teacher or a live Sister. Which is it going to be?"

...Ignatia accepted a much quieter and less distinguished assignment [as] registrar at St. Thomas Hospital in Akron, Ohio.... [I]t was wondered if she could manage even this much. That she would live to the age of seventy-seven was not believable; that she was destined to minister to 15,000 alcoholics and their families in the years to come was known only to God.

Sister serenely carried on at the admissions desk [for years, during which time] Group One at Akron, and Group Two in New York had been in slow and fitful growth since 1935....

AA'S SUDDEN GROWTH

In 1939 the scene changed abruptly. In the spring of that year the AA book was first printed, and *Liberty* magazine came up with an article about our society in the early fall. This was quickly followed by a whole series of remarkable pieces which were carried by The Cleveland *Plain-Dealer*.... The mere two dozen AAs then in town were swamped by frantic pleas for help. Despite this rather chaotic situation, the Cleveland membership burgeoned into several hundreds in a few months.

Nevertheless the implications of this AA population explosion were in some ways disturbing, especially the lack of proper hospital facilities. Though the Cleveland hospitals had rallied gallantly to this one emergency, their interest naturally waned when bills often went unpaid, and when ex-drunks trooped through the corridors to do what they called "Twelfth Step" work on sometimes noisy victims just arrived. Even the City Hospital at Akron, where Dr. Bob had attended numerous cases was showing signs of weariness... [so he] decided to visit St. Thomas and explain the great need for a hospital connection that could prove permanently effective. Since St. Thomas was a church institution, he thought the people there might envision a fine opportunity for service where the others had not. And how right he was!

SISTER IGNATIA LEARNS OF AA

But Bob knew no one in authority at the hospital. So he simply betook himself to "Admissions" and told the diminutive nun in charge the story of AA, including that of his own recovery. As this tale unfolded, the little sister glowed. Her compassion was deeply touched and perhaps her amazing intuition had already begun to say, "This is it." Of course Sister would try to help, but what could one small nun do? After all, there were certain attitudes and regulations. Alcoholism had not been reckoned as an illness; it was just a dire form of gluttony!

Dr. Bob then told Sister about an alcoholic who then was in a most serious condition. A bed would simply have to be found for him. Said Mary Ignatia, "I'm sure your friend must be very sick. You know, Doctor, this sounds to me like a terrible case of indigestion." Trying to keep a straight face, Dr. Bob replied, "How right you are—his indigestion is most terrible."...Sister immediately said, "Why don't you bring him in right away?"

The two benign conspirators were soon faced with yet another dilemma. The victim proved to be distressingly intoxicated. It would soon be clear to all and sundry that his "indigestion" was quite incidental. Obviously a ward wouldn't do.... Sister declared, "I'll have a bed moved into our flower room. In there, he can't disturb anyone." This was hurriedly done, and the "indigestion" sufferer was already on his way to sobriety and health.

Of course...the "indigestion" pretense simply couldn't last.

Somebody in authority would have to be told, and that somebody was the hospital's Superior....She went along, and a little later she boldly unfolded the new project before the St. Thomas trustees. To their everlasting credit they went along too—so much so that it was not a great while before Dr. Bob himself was invited to become a staff physician at St. Thomas, a bright example indeed of the ecumenical spirit.

Presently a whole ward was devoted to the rehabilitation of alcoholics, and Sister Ignatia was of course placed in immediate charge. Dr. Bob sponsored the new cases into the hospital and medically treated each, never sending a bill to pay. The hospital fees were very moderate and Sister often insisted on taking in patients on a "pay later" basis....

Together Ignatia and Dr. Bob [opened the ward to] visiting AAs from surrounding groups who, morning to night, told their stories of drinking and of recovery. There were never any barriers of race or creed; neither was AA nor Church teaching pressed upon any.

WITH INFINITE TENDERNESS

Since nearly all her strenuous hours were spent there, Sister became a central figure on the ward. She would alternately listen and talk, with infinite tenderness and understanding. The alcoholic's family and friends received the very same treatment. It was this most compassionate caring that was a chief ingredient of her unique Grace: it magnetically drew everyone to her, even the most rough and obstinate. Yet she would not always stand still for arrant nonsense. When the occasion required, she could really put her foot down. Then to ease the hurt, she would turn on her delightful humor. Once, when a recalcitrant drunk boasted he'd never again be seen at the hospital, Sister shot back, "Well, let's hope *not*. But just in case you *do* show up, please remember that we already have your size of pajamas. They will be ready and waiting for you!"

As the fame of St. Thomas grew, alcoholics flocked in from distant places. After their hospitalization they often remained for a time in Akron to get more first-hand AA from Dr. Bob and from

Akron's Group Number One. On their return home, Sister would carry on an ever mounting correspondence with them.

We AAs are often heard to say that our Fellowship is founded upon resources that we have drawn from medicine, from religion and from our own experience of drinking and of recovery. Never before nor since those Akron early days have we witnessed a more perfect synthesis of all those healing forces. Dr. Bob exemplified both medicine and AA; Ignatia and the Sisters of St. Augustine also practiced applied medicine, and their practice was supremely well animated by the wonderful spirit of their Community. A more perfect blending of Grace and talent cannot be imagined.

It should never be necessary to dwell, one by one, upon the virtues of these magnificent friends of AA's early time—Sister Ignatia and co-founder Dr. Bob. We need only recollect that "by their fruits we shall always know them."

PASSING OF DR. BOB

Standing before the Cleveland International Convention of 1950, Dr. Bob looked upon us of AA for the last time.... Ten years has slipped by since the day when he and Sister had bedded down that first sufferer in the St. Thomas flower room. In this marvelous decade Sister and Dr. Bob had medically treated, and had spiritually infused *five thousand alcoholics*. The greater part of these had found their freedom under God.

In thankful recollection of this great work, we of AA presented to the Sisters of Charity of St. Augustine and to the Staff of the St. Thomas Hospital a bronze plaque, ever since to be seen in the ward where Sister and Dr. Bob had wrought their wonders. The plaque reads as follows:

IN GRATITUDE
The friends of Dr. Bob and Anne S.
affectionately dedicate this memorial to the
Sisters and staff of St. Thomas Hospital at Akron,
birthplace of Alcoholics Anonymous.
St. Thomas Hospital became the first religious institution ever to open

its doors to our society. May the loving devotion of those
who labored here in our pioneering time be a bright and wondrous
example of God's Grace everlastingly set before us all.

Visitors at St. Thomas today often wonder why this inscription says not a word about Sister Ignatia. Well, the fact was, she wouldn't allow her name to be used. She had flatly refused; it was one of those times when she had put her foot down! This was of course a glowing example of her innate and absolutely genuine humility. Sister truly believed that she deserved no particular notice; that such Grace as she might have could only be credited to God and to the community of her sisters.

This was indeed the ultimate spirit of anonymity. We who had then seen this quality in her were deeply affected, especially Dr. Bob and myself. Hers came to be the influence that persuaded us both never to accept public honors of any sort. Sister's example taught that a mere observance of the *form* of AA anonymity should never become the slightest excuse for ignoring its *spiritual substance*.

Following Dr. Bob's death, there was great concern lest Sister might not be allowed to continue her work.... However, nothing happened for a time. Assisted by surrounding AA groups, Sister continued to carry on at St. Thomas. Then suddenly in 1952, she was transferred to St. Vincent Charity Hospital at Cleveland, where… she was [eventually] placed in charge of its alcoholic ward. At Akron a successor was named…the work there would continue.

The ward at "Charity" occupied part of a dilapidated wing, and it was in great need of repair.... Substantial contributions flowed in. In their spare hours, AA carpenters, plumbers and electricians set about redoing the old wing—no charge for their services. The beautiful result of these labors of love is now known as Rosary Hall.

Again the miracles of recovery from alcoholism commenced to multiply. During the following fourteen years, an astonishing 10,000 alcoholics passed through the portals of Rosary Hall there to fall under the spell of Mary Ignatia, and of AA. More than two-thirds of all these recovered from their dire malady, and again became citizens of the world. From dawn to dark Sister offered her unique Grace to that endless procession of stricken sufferers. Moreover, she still found time to minister widely to their families and this very fruitful part of her work became a prime inspiration to the Al-Anon Family Groups of the whole region....

Toward the close of her long stewardship there were brushes with death. Sometimes I came to Cleveland and was allowed to sit by her bedside. Then I saw her at her best. Her perfect faith, and her complete acceptance of whatever God might will was somehow implicit in all she said, be our conversation gay, or serious. Fear and uncertainty seemed entire strangers to her. On my leave-taking, there was always that smiling radiance; always her prayerful hope that God might still allow her a bit more time at Rosary Hall. Then a few days later I would learn that she was back at her desk. This superb drama would be re-enacted time after time. She was quite unconscious that there was anything at all unusual about it.

Realizing there would come the day which would be her last, it seemed right that we of AA should privately present Sister with some tangible token that could, even a little, communicate to her the depth of our love. Remembering her insistence, in respect of the Akron plaque, that she would not really like any public attention, I simply sent word that I'd like to come to Cleveland for a visit, and casually added that should her health permit, we might take supper together in the company of a few of her stalwart AA friends and co-workers. Besides, it was her fiftieth year of service in her community.

On the appointed evening, we foregathered in one of the small dining rooms at Charity Hospital. Plainly delighted, Sister arrived. She was barely able to walk. Being old-timers all, the dinner hour was spent in telling tales of other days. For her part, Sister regaled us with stories of St. Thomas and with cherished recollections of Anne and co-founder Dr. Bob. It was unforgettable.

Before Sister became too tired we addressed ourselves to our main project. From New York, I had brought an illuminated scroll... written on behalf of our AA Fellowship worldwide. I stood up, read the scroll aloud, and then held the parchment for her to see. She was taken by complete surprise and could scarcely speak for a time. In a low voice she finally said, "Oh, but this is too much—this is too good for me."

Our richest reward of the evening was of course Ignatia's delight; a joy unbounded the moment we assured her that our gift need not be publicized; that if she wished to stow it away in her trunk we would quite understand.

It then seemed that this most memorable and moving evening was over. But there was to be another inspiring experience. Making light of her great fatigue, Sister insisted that we all go up to Rosary Hall, there to make a late round of the AA ward. This we did, wondering if any of us would ever again see her at work in the divine vocation to which she had given her all. For each of us this was the end of an epoch; I could think only of her poignant and oft-repeated saying, "Eternity is now."

The scroll given to Sister may now be seen at Rosary Hall. This is the inscription:

IN GRATITUDE
FOR SISTER MARY IGNATIA
ON THE OCCASION OF HER GOLDEN JUBILEE

Dear Sister,

We of Alcoholics Anonymous look upon you as the finest friend and the greatest spirit we may ever know.

We remember your tender ministrations to us in the days when AA was very young. Your partnership with Dr. Bob in that early time has created for us a spiritual heritage of incomparable worth.

In all the years since, we have watched you at the beside of thousands. So watching, we have perceived ourselves to be the beneficiaries of that wondrous light which God has always sent through you to illumine our darkness. You have tirelessly tended our wounds; you have nourished us with your unique

*understanding and your matchless love. No greater gifts of
Grace than these shall we ever have.*

*Speaking for AA members throughout the world, I say:
"May God abundantly reward you according to your blessed
works—now and forever."*

In devotion,
Bill W.
March 25, 1964

THANK GOD FOR THE LIFE OF ELLY CHOVEL!

by Reverend George A. Garcia
September 4, 2007
St. Hugh Catholic Church, Coconut Grove, FL

The celebrant at this funeral Mass, along with the pallbearers and mourners, were part of a significant American story that few outside Florida remember today. Father Garcia refers to his fellow "Pedro Pans" throughout his eulogy. These were children who comprised the largest exodus of child refugees in the history of the Western Hemisphere. Starting in December, 1960, more than 14,000 children were sent—mostly on planes, a few on boats—to Miami from Cuba without their parents.

Elly Chovel arrived at age fourteen with her younger sister. Thirty years later, in 1991, she became a driving force in founding Operation Pedro Pan Group, Inc., an organization dedicated to reuniting its members as adults in order to help other children in need, particularly those without parents.

Sharing and archiving memories is also important to the group's mission. Elly shared her own memory of the day her mother bid her and her sister a tearful goodbye at the Havana airport. Their mother told them to look out the window for her special farewell as the plane took off. She thought it would make her stand out in the crowd of other parents. But the girls never had the heart to tell their mother that they were on the wrong side of the plane, so they never saw her red umbrella.

The exodus was a response to Fidel Castro's new regime in Cuba, which had begun closing Catholic churches and schools and expelling priests and nuns from the country. Reports of teenagers coming back from Castro's mandatory camps, where they had been required to join the Communist "Youth Pioneers," and told to alert authorities if their parents deviated from Party mandates, increased parental fears.

Meanwhile in Miami, Monsignor Bryan Walsh, director of Catho-

lic Charities, was establishing a process of receiving and placing the children with the cooperation of the U. S. State Department. To help handle the growing influx of émigrés, he asked Florida's Protestant and Jewish families to take in children as well. Ultimately, he appealed to 110 Catholic charity agencies in thirty-five other states for help. The Irish priest became a beloved mentor to Elly and a surrogate father to thousands. The Pedro Pan organization has pledged "to honor the sacrifice of our parents and this noble nation that welcomed us, and the person who made it all possible, Monsignor Bryan O. Walsh."

Everyone involved believed the children and parents would be reunited in a relatively short time. But the Cuban Missile Crisis of October, 1962, dashed those hopes.

The children grew up in America instead, some staying with relatives who had previously settled in the U. S., but most (an estimated 8,000) were placed in foster homes, orphanages, and Catholic boarding schools to begin their lives in exile. Often siblings were not able to be placed together, but Elly and her sister were assigned to the same foster home outside of Buffalo, New York. Five years later, they were reunited with their parents in Miami.

Thirty-five years later, Elly returned to Cuba carrying a red umbrella "as a sign of hello rather than goodbye," she said. She was one of a thousand Cuban-Americans allowed to return for Pope John Paul II's visit to the land which had once made attending Mass a criminal act. There, the Pope spoke about family and human rights, and as he paid tribute to those who had fled the country of their birth and those, now dead, who could never return, Elly opened her red umbrella. "I do believe in miracles," she told a reporter when recalling that moment. "After the Cuban people have tasted a little bit of freedom, they can never be pushed back again."

Pedro Pans who became prominent Americans include Mel Martinez, former U. S. Senator; Carlos Eire, the Yale University professor of history and religious studies who won a National Book Award for his memoir, Waiting for Snow in Havana; and Miami Bishop Felipe Estevez, who concelebrated Elly Chovel's requiem Mass.

Dear Archbishop Favalora, Bishop Estevez, my brothers and sisters in Christ:

Every time the Christian community gathers together to celebrate the Eucharist, we gather together for thanksgiving. We thank God our Father, for the gift of salvation in Jesus Christ and the blessings the Lord gives us daily.

Today we come together to give thanks to God for our sister Elly (Vilano) Chovel, who has finished her pilgrimage and testimony on this earth. We commend her to the Lord whose love she knew well. We pray for her whole family, her children and grandchildren, that they may receive the gift of consolation only God can give us.

We thank God for all the blessings she received: the blessings of life, family and friends, faith, hope, and love, and especially her calling to minister to the Pedro Pan adults, through the Operation Pedro Pan Group which she founded and took her all over the country with great love and dedication.

At Msgr. Brian Walsh's funeral Mass, some of us Pedro Pan priests accompanied Msgr.'s casket from the altar to the entrance of the church. It was a very powerful experience for me, for then I realized what a tremendous influence one person can have on the lives of thousands! And Msgr. Walsh inspired Elly to do the same, to minister to the Pedro Pans, and she accepted that call with great dedication. Recalling her work, the words of Jesus come to mind: "Jerusalem, Jerusalem, how many times I yearned to gather your children together as a hen gathers her brood under her wings."

Elly was a loving mother hen to all Pedro Pans and others, and the Pedro Pan Group showed this in creating Camp Matecumbe Park and the Msgr. Bryan Walsh Children's Village, made possible with generous help from many Pedro Pans.

Reviewing Melinda Lopez' play *Sonia Flew*, about the Pedro Pan experience, Elly wrote:

"As one of the 14,000 Pedro Pans, I feel blessed to have the opportunity to grow up in a democracy where diversity is respected and encouraged and freedom of speech is an undeniable right." I will forever be thankful to Msgr. Walsh, my mentor, for his support and understanding of our need to share, to uncover our history, forming a bond that has helped us heal and move forward.

And it was this "ministry of healing" Elly sought with all her strength. She knew in her own life the sufferings experienced by all Pedro Pans: separation from parents, adjustment to a new, welcoming, but different culture, nation and language, and the struggle of growing up away from family created wounds that needed to be healed.

We thank the Lord for all the love Elly was willing to give to so many. We thank the Lord for a generous life, whose generosity extended to the end as she donated her body organs to bring healing and life to others.

We thank the Lord for the challenges and blessings Elly received during her journey to the Kingdom.

We thank the Lord for her work on world peace and reconciliation.

We pray she will receive the words of her Lord: "Well done, good and faithful servant, because you were faithful in small things, come and receive the blessings of the Kingdom." The New Jerusalem, "where there shall be no more death or mourning, crying out or pain, for the former world has passed away."

And Elly, like Martha, will reply: "I believe you are the Messiah, the Son of God: he who is to come into the world."

May eternal light shine on her forever and may the consolation of the Lord descend on all her relatives and friends. Amen.

IN THE IRISH TRADITION:
DANIEL PATRICK MOYNIHAN

by Lawrence J. McCaffrey
September, 2003

Among those who paid tribute to Daniel "Pat" Moynihan at his memorial service were then–New York Governor George E. Pataki; former New York Mayor Edward Koch; then–Attorney General Eliot Spitzer; former senators Alfonse D'Amato, Bill Bradley and Bob Kerrey; and Moynihan's daughter, Maura. Hillary Clinton, who succeeded Moynihan in the Senate, had previously read her tribute into the Congressional Record.

Moynihan's place on the liberal-to-conservative spectrum is still debated—he served both Democratic and Republican presidents. Media and colleagues both admired and criticized him over the years, but biographer Godfrey Hodgson's claim that Moynihan "had the respect of all and the love of many" on both sides of the aisle was evident in the eulogies that were given for him.

Moynihan used to say that he was "baptized a Catholic and born a Democrat," and Lawrence J. McCaffrey's eulogy explores the Irish-Catholic faith that guided a career marked by compassion for the poor and outrage over political corruption.

At age ten, Daniel was the eldest of three children when his father abandoned the family during the Great Depression. His mother struggled between welfare and work but managed to keep the children in Catholic grammar school. Patrick and his brother Mike shined shoes in Times Square to help out.

Gentleman is the word most frequently used to describe Moynihan. Yet this gentle man was known for a significant breach of etiquette—during a Papal audience with Pope Paul VI in 1965. Contrary to protocol, Moynihan addressed the Pope, saying, "Holy Father, we hope you will not forget our friends the Jews." This startled the cardinals and bishops and everyone who was present. Pope Paul VI had declined to retract the Church's ancient insistence on the collective guilt of the Jews for the crucifixion of Christ, so Moynihan's unabashed plea was premeditated. He knew he would have only a moment—while kneeling before the Pope—to make his appeal.

Moynihan's memorial service was sponsored by the Jewish Community Relations Council of New York in appreciation of his friendship. It was to be over thirty years before Moynihan's petition was satisfactorily addressed: A subsequent Pope, John Paul II, made a series of apologies to victims of the Inquisition, of the Holocaust, and to all Jews who had suffered because of what Catholics and the Church had done or failed to do throughout the years.

During and after his four terms in the United States Senate, Moynihan shaped the public debate on a broad spectrum of issues through his writing and oratory. The Almanac of American Politics *described him as "the nation's best thinker among politicians since Lincoln, and its best politician among thinkers since Jefferson." Columnist George F. Will once claimed that Moynihan "wrote more books than most senators have read."*

Writer and editor James Q. Wilson said that Moynihan's epitaph would be that he brought to every task "luminous intellect, personal conviction, deep historic knowledge, the eye of an artist, the pen of an angel, and above all, an incorruptible devotion to the common good."

I learned of Daniel Patrick Moynihan's death in the midst of reading Christopher M. Finan's biography of Alfred E. Smith. Highly favorable remembrances from politicians and distinguished journalists indicated how Moynihan represented the advance of Catholic Irish-America since Smith's defeat in the 1928 presidential election. Conservatives as well as liberals lavished praise on the late senator. In a syndicated March 30 column in the *Chicago Sun-Times*, George Will, a long time admirer, rated him as the "most penetrating political intellect to come from New York since Alexander Hamilton, who, like Moynihan, saw over the horizon of this time, anticipating the evolving possibilities and problems of a consolidated, urbanized nation. A liberal who did not flinch from the label, he reminded conservatives that the Constitution's framers 'had more thoughts about power than merely its limitations.'"

In the April 1 *National Review*, William F. Buckley, Jr., perhaps the most revered, certainly the most articulate conservative, lamented some of Moynihan's political thoughts and actions but praised his "shrewd and original insights," and pictured him as "always a shining light, giving pure pleasure as a lyrical social philosopher and wit." Representing a more recent and rigid conservative generation, William Kristol, editor of the *Weekly Standard*, on April 7 lauded Moynihan's humanity and generosity. He noted that although he once worked for him in the United Nations and during his Senate campaigns, they had drifted apart politically. Still, Kristol "remained proud to claim some relationship of debt and obligation to him. He was a kind benefactor and a gentle instructor, who put friendship ahead of partisanship, generosity ahead of ideology. I think about him a lot, always with admiration, gratitude, and indeed love."

Al Smith remained popular in New York City, but by the time of his death in October, 1944, he had lost a great deal of national respect and affection. Newspaper comments on his life and career did not match Moynihan's glowing eulogies. Although they ended their lives with different reputations, these New York, Irish-Catholic Democrats had a similar beginning. Both lost male parents at any early age. Alfred was ten when his father died. Daniel Patrick was ten when his father deserted his wife and children. Consequently, their families suffered periods of poverty. After years of physical labor, including a stint in the Fulton Street Fish Market, politics provided Smith with an avenue to success. A product of Tammany Hall, he became a powerful voice in New York's State Assembly, its four-term governor, and the first Catholic to run for the American presidency. His social policies in the Assembly and governor's office served as precedents for Franklin D. Roosevelt's New Deal.

At the 1920 and 1924 convention, Roosevelt nominated Smith as the Democratic candidate for the highest office in the land. The party selected others, but his outstanding record as New York governor won him the prize in 1928. Considering the nation's apparent prosperity, there was little chance that Smith could have defeated Herbert Hoover, his Republican opponent. However, a national wave of anti-Catholicism figured in Smith's embarrassing margin of defeat—he even failed to carry his own state. A considerable number of Protestants from all classes and vocations questioned whether Roman Catholicism, with its authoritarian, superstitious nature, could be successfully integrated into American institutions and values. The bigotry evident in his 1928 loss and the Democratic decision to pass him over in 1932, in favor of Roosevelt, his successor as New York governor, embittered Smith. For a brief period he supported FDR but then, contradicting the precedents he established in Albany, Smith criticized the New Deal as oppressive big government. He endorsed Alfred Landon and Wendell Wilke in the 1936 and 1940 presidential elections. As a group, the Irish and other Catholics remained loyal Democrats, but 1928's no-Popery crusade intensified their defensiveness and insecurity, increasing self-doubts that they would ever achieve American equality.

Unlike Smith, who left school to work at fourteen and learned politics by diligent study, observation, careful listening, and the selection of talented advisors, many of them women such as Belle Moskowitz and Frances Perkins, education propelled Moynihan's career. His brilliant, quick mind was evident when he finished first in his graduating class at Benjamin Franklin High School in East Harlem.

He labored for a time as a longshoreman and attended the City College of New York. In 1944 Moynihan enlisted in the Navy, which sent him to Tufts University for Officer's Training and a degree in naval science. After his 1947 honorable discharge, he took advantage of the G. I. Bill to earn a B. A. from Tufts in 1948 and an M. A. in its Fletcher School of Law and Diplomacy the following year. Moynihan spent 1950-51 as a Fulbright Scholar at the London School of Economics. He earned his Ph.D. from Tufts in 1961 and a law degree in 1968. When Moynihan entered politics, other Americans viewed the Irish more favorably than they did in Al Smith's time. Beginning in the 1930s, domestic and foreign events and issues and popular entertainment lessened anti-Catholicism. People of various faiths and ethnicity suffered together during the Depression. World War II joined them in common patriotism. Catholics contributed more than a fair share to the armed forces, easing doubts of their patriotism. Movies with popular stars such as Spencer Tracy, Pat O'Brien, Bing Crosby, and Preston Foster, playing charming priests as effective social workers or heroic army and navy chaplains, challenged the incompatibility of Americanism and Catholicism.

About twenty-five percent of FDR's government appointees were Catholics, mostly Irish. Beginning with his first term, Americans became familiar with Irish Catholics in prominent positions. Three have been speakers of the House of Representatives, two Senate majority leaders, a number of Cabinet members and Supreme Court justices. And, in 1960, John F. Kennedy became president of the United States. His election, occupancy of the White House, and national and international popularity erased most of the doubts of Irish and other Catholic Americans concerning their first-class citizenship. A 1979 *U. S. News and World Report* poll of 1,439 prominent Americans ranked Senator Edward M. Kennedy, Speaker of the House, Thomas P. (Tip) O'Neill, and George Meany, President of the AFL-CIO, as the second, third, and fourth most powerful people in the country. Probably the Irish-American with the greatest and most liberal impact was William J. Brennan, Jr., son of immigrant parents. From his appointment in 1956 to his retirement in

1990, he was the most influential member of the Supreme Court.

Moynihan began his political career in 1953, assisting in the New York City mayoral campaign of Robert F. Wagner. From 1955 to 1958, he was on the staff of New York Governor Averell W. Harriman, first as a speechwriter then as chief aide. In 1955, he married a co-worker in the Harriman campaign, Elizabeth Brennan.

During 1959 and 1960, Moynihan served as a member of the New York State tenure Commission. From 1959 to 1961, Moynihan left academic life to become an undersecretary of labor in John F. Kennedy's administration, remaining on under Johnson. In 1963, he coauthored with Nathan Glazier *Beyond the Melting Pot: Jews, Italians, and Irish of New York City*, a rebuttal to the thesis that assimilation would undermine the significance of religion and ethnicity in American political life. It was the first of eighteen books that bore his name. In 1965, Moynihan wrote a paper, "The Negro Family: The Case for National Action," taking the position that absentee fathers and illegitimate births were main causes of African-American poverty and social disorder, and doubting that welfare checks could solve the crisis. Reacting to his analysis of one aspect of a difficult problem, a number of liberals accused Moynihan of racism. In time, experts in and out of politics credited him with prophetic insight.

The same year that he wrote "The Negro Family," Moynihan left the Department of Labor to run for president of the New York City Council. A primary loss sent him off to Wesleyan University. In 1966, he left Middletown, Connecticut, to accept the directorship of the Harvard-Massachusetts Institute of Technology Joint Center for Urban Studies.

Although he opposed the war in Vietnam and supported Eugene McCarthy's and Robert F. Kennedy's 1968 challenges to President Lyndon Johnson's leadership, the next year Moynihan took leave from the Joint Center for Urban Studies to serve as an advisor to President Richard Nixon on domestic affairs. His rather glib proposal that the racial issue needed a period of "benign neglect" offended liberals, black and white. But he was far from insensitive to African-America's woeful situation. In his "benign neglect" comment Moynihan was suggesting that thoughtful analysis rather than angry and harsh rhetoric would be more effective in confronting poverty and prejudice. He demonstrated his own concern with and involvement in the problems of black America when he advised the president to push a guaranteed family income as a less expensive and demoralizing, more dignified and productive alternative to the existing welfare system. Nixon passed Moynihan's idea on to Congress, where it died from inaction. In 1970, Moynihan returned to Cambridge but in 1973 accepted a presidential appointment as ambassador to India. In 1975, President Gerald Ford named him United States ambassador to the United Nations where he offended some liberals by hawkish stances against the Soviet Union and Communism but won the affection of American Jews by his vigorous defense of Israel. In 1976, New York voters elected Moynihan to the first of his four terms as senator. Politically astute Elizabeth Brennan Moynihan managed her husband's campaigns.

After the Northern Ireland civil-rights campaign evolved into civil war, Moynihan, along with Senator Edward M. Kennedy, New York's Governor Hugh Carey, and House Speaker Tip O'Neill (the Big Four), urged Irish-Americans to identify with constitutional approaches to peace and justice in the Six Counties and not to donate money to those espousing violence. To him the Irish Republican Army represented thuggery....

In 1980, he foresaw the collapse of the Soviet Empire and urged the government to spend more on domestic problems than military equipment. He criticized the Reagan administration's mucking around in Latin America and its comic opera Grenada "rescue" and President George H. Bush's 1989 invasion of Panama and 1991 war on Iraq. The younger Bush's preemptive attack on Iraq violated Moynihan's respect for international law.

In 2000, Moynihan decided not to seek a fifth senate term. Although spending a great deal of time with his wife at a family home in Pindars County, upstate New York, and writing in a nearby one-room schoolhouse, he didn't retire from the public scene. Moynihan reentered the academic world as a professor at Syracuse

University's Maxwell School (2001) and as a senior scholar at the Woodrow Wilson International Center for Scholars (2001-2003). He also agreed to serve on President George W. Bush's Social Security Commission. Moynihan died on March 26 from complications resulting from surgery on a busted appendix. He is survived by his wife and sons, Timothy and John, daughter Maura, and two grandchildren.

Compared to Edward M. Kennedy, probably one of the most effective and productive senators in American history, Moynihan did not leave a rich legislative legacy, but as Adam Clymer points out in his detailed March 27 *New York Times* obituary, he was an effective member of the Senate, especially in serving the needs of New York constituents. He was a powerful member, at times chair, of the Finance, Environment and Public Works, and Intelligence Committees. In the late 1970s, Moynihan and fellow New Yorker Senator Jacob K. Javits authored legislation that saved New York City from bankruptcy. In 1991 and '92, he shifted much of highway financing in the direction of urban mass transit, and procured a retroactive five billion dollars to reimburse New York for its State Thruway, constructed before the Eisenhower administration launched the Interstate Highway System. Believing that the national capital deserved beauty, Moynihan played a major role in restoring dingy areas of the city. He deserves credit for many of the architectural improvements on Pennsylvania Avenue, the thoroughfare between the Capitol building and the White House. But Moynihan's major impact on American government policies and conduct was in the realm of ideas. According to Clymer, he "was less an original researcher than a bold, often brilliant synthesizer whose work compelled furious debate and further research." The senator's agile and perceptive mind ranged over a wide range of subjects, domestic and foreign, but he had a special interest in the social problems of urban America.

When it came to votes in the Senate, Moynihan was a dependable Democrat but not a party hack. He and Bill Clinton weren't always on the same track. Early in the administration, Moynihan told the president that the welfare issue should have priority over health care. He also protested the 1996 Welfare Bill, insisting that it would have disastrous effects on millions of children. Moynihan irritated many on the left by describing so-called partial birth abortion as infanticide. As a member of the Intelligence Committee, he was disturbed by the excessive secrecy of some government agencies. Moynihan spent much of his time pondering social security, how to maintain the program's financial stability and improve its benefits. In regard to the former, he suggested extending retirement age beyond sixty-five, and, concerning the latter, he departed from party orthodoxy by suggesting that workers should have the right to invest part of their Social Security contributions in stocks and bonds. Perhaps the recent fluctuations in the stock market might have led him to a different conclusion.

In "The Irish" chapter of *Beyond the Melting Pot*, Moynihan criticized Irish politicians of the past for not properly applying the political power they so skillfully acquired: "They ran the city, but the parochialism and bureaucracy that enabled them to succeed in politics prevented them from doing much with government.... They never thought of politics as an instrument of social change."

With his well dressed, fashionable appearance, social sophistication, education, comprehensive knowledge; cosmopolitan view of the world, personal and public integrity, and colorful, erudite language, Moynihan seemed strikingly different from New York's George Washington Plunkett, Chicago's Johnny Powers, Boston's Michael Lomasney, Frank Skeffington and his crowd of followers in Edwin O'Connor's *The Last Hurrah*, and yes, Al Smith. But appearances and vocabulary were deceiving. In his view of what politics could and couldn't do he was closer to Plunkett, Powers, Lomasney, Skeffington, and Smith than he was to the hard-line ideological liberals he served with in the Senate. Moynihan's Irish walking hats were more representative of his value core than the Savile Row suits he sometimes wore.

According to Mickey Kaus (*Slate*, March 27), he enjoyed a songfest with Irish working-class men in a seedy Sommervile saloon, and at his Arlington National Cemetery Interment, where

Maura Moynihan read a verse from Dylan Thomas, she mentioned her father enjoyed drinking with the Welsh poet in Greenwich Village's White Horse Tavern (Clymer, *New York Times*, April 1).

[That] Irish chapter...was more the product of academic reflection than his experience as a practicing politician. From the latter, he must have discovered that greedy-for-votes, graft-tolerant Irish politicians, who provided jobs, bail money, coal, food baskets, and medical and funeral expenses for a variety of ethnic constituents, did a great deal more to achieve social change than Anglo-Protestant "progressives" whose idea of reform had more to do with prohibiting alcohol, gambling, and prostitution than improving the life of the poor. Martin F. Nolan pointed out how Moynihan enjoyed reading Plunkett's description of reform movement as "mornin' glories—looked lovely in the mornin' and withered up in a short time, while the regular machines went on flourishin' forever like fine old oaks." (*Boston Globe*, March 28).

While Moynihan rejoiced in the liberal label, his thought process was different than many who carry that designation. His definitions of and recipes for social justice came from his ethnicity and religion rather than ideological absolutes. He relied on facts more than theories, seeing things as they are rather than how they should be. As Irish and Catholic, Moynihan believed that government had obligations to the sick, poor, old, and physically handicapped. But unlike ideological liberals in academia and politics, he realized that imperfect people could never achieve a perfect society. Moynihan's ethnic and religious realism was expressed in his comments following the assassination of JFK: "I don't think there is any point in being Irish if you don't know the world is going to break your heart eventually." Although he didn't believe that politicians and intellectuals could produce a society without economic or social blemish, perhaps they could make it somewhat better—at least they should try. Moynihan had faith in government as an instrument of positive change, but also feared its potential as an instrument of oppression and violator of personal freedom and secrecy, and he distrusted Washington's bureaucracy. While Moynihan approached politics in a flexible, pragmatic way, he had high standards concerning personal conduct. He had more confidence in government intervention in the social than in the moral order, and worried about the disintegration of traditional institutions, especially the family, and misbehavior in the white as well as the black community. In "Defining Deviancy Down," an essay in the 1993 winter issue of *American Scholar*, he deplored liberal tolerance and public apathy that led to social disorder.

Intelligent, articulate, witty, and charming, Moynihan decorated the American political landscape. He was what a senator should be and seldom is, a representative of the people who could see the complexity of issues, suggest a variety of approaches to domestic and foreign policy challenges, work with people from both parties for the common good, and, while serving his constituents, place the country's needs at the top of his priority list. Although Moynihan was much better educated, more honorable, and far more sophisticated than the first and second generation of Irish-American politicians who functioned in graft-ridden urban machines, he inherited their ethnic and religious collectivism, which viewed government as a friend not an enemy of the American dream of freedom and opportunity. Post-1932 people such as Senators Moynihan, Gene McCarthy, Philip Hart, George Mitchell, Mike Mansfield, and Justice William Brennan may have represented a shift in style of Irish-American politics but not a change in its essential values and purpose. However, looking at the present American main stream, which includes Catholic ethnics, whose focus is on the individual rather than the common good, Moynihan may have been one of the last communal Irish liberals in Congress, but as Martin Nolan wrote in his Boston *Globe* tribute: "Because of his generous heart and diligent mind and because of his confidence in faith, family, and country, the reputation of Daniel Patrick Moynihan, like a fine old oak, will flourish forever."

VI. WE REMEMBER
Those Who Showed Us the Way

DIDN'T HE SHOW US THE WAY?
JOSEPH CARDINAL BERNARDIN

by Msgr. Kenneth Velo
November 18, 1996
Holy Name Cathedral, Chicago, IL

When he arrived in Chicago in 1982, then-Archbishop Joseph Bernardin asked anyone who had ever been hurt by the Church to contact him. He spent the rest of his days responding to the calls and letters he received. He also reached out to members of the Jewish community who had been harmed by the Church. His humble attempts at reconciliation endeared him to a city, and eventually, to a nation.

Two lines in this eulogy filled the cathedral with laughter, although appreciating them on paper requires some imagination. Picture Holy Name Cathedral's altar draped with gold and white linens; red-mitred cardinals from all over the world; formally garbed singers and musicians; front pews filled with recognizable dignitaries and global leaders.

It is time for the homily. A man climbs to the lectern. Dressed in a priest's plain, black suit with white collar, he is unknown to the vast majority of mourners and the television audience. He begins by welcoming everyone, those in the church and those listening over radio and TV, greeting all as "family and friends."

Pause.

"Perhaps you're wondering who I am," he says, causing a roar of laughter. He then identifies himself as "Father Velo, the regular driver," as he is known to the Cardinal's then-ninety-two-year-old mother who lives in a nursing home.

It feels so good to laugh at this moment. It is reassuring to be in the hands of this eulogizer, and the audience quickly understands why he has endeared himself to the Cardinal.

The next explosion of laughter comes when Msgr. Velo describes waking up the Cardinal when they arrived at a destination. He mimics the Cardinal combing his hair, saying, "Our objective is to get out of here as quickly as possible."

Well, one might have had to be there for that one, to see Msgr. Velo's spot-on impersonation of the just-awakened, husky-voiced Cardinal. The mourners' laughter was not merely from surprise over Father Velo's skilled imitation, but because they were delighted—for a fleeting second—that the Cardinal had been brought to life in such a very human moment.

The "false accusation" mentioned in the eulogy refers to a young man's claim to have been sexually abused by the Cardinal, an accusation which the accuser eventually retracted.

Cardinal Bernardin's service was marked by reaching out to AIDS victims and fellow cancer patients, and by guiding Church thinking on a "seamless garment ethic" regarding the value of life, which included abolishing capital punishment and modern warfare, along with abortion and euthanasia. Shortly before the Cardinal died of pancreatic cancer at age sixty-eight, President Bill Clinton awarded him the Presidential Medal of Freedom. The canonization process for his sainthood cause is now underway.

Whether you're in the first pew or the thirtieth pew of this great cathedral, whether you're participating through the public address system or seated in the auditorium, whether you're listening on the radio as you travel the Dan Ryan Expressway or sitting in a kitchen in Rogers Park, whether you're watching television coverage of this funeral service in a nursing home in Waukegan, a living room in Calumet City, or a classroom on Chicago's West Side—today, this day, you are all dignitaries, for God has touched you through the life of Cardinal Bernardin, and I greet you as family and friends.

Perhaps you're wondering who I am. Let me introduce myself the way that Mrs. Bernardin, the Cardinal's ninety-two-year-old mother, knows me. I am Father Velo, the regular driver.

And one of the greatest compliments His Eminence paid me through the years was just to fall asleep in the car. He would travel the city's streets, sometimes make phone calls, but he would usually fall asleep toward the end of our journey.

I would say, "Cardinal, we're here. We've arrived." The comb would come out of the pocket and the event, the ceremony, the dinner, whatever, would begin, but not before he said to me, "Our objective is to get out of here as quickly as possible."

Somewhere over Greenland in mid-September, the Eminence showed me his funeral plans. I began to cry. I saw the things he had listed. I saw my name. I saw the name of Cardinal [Roger] Mahony, whom he asked to celebrate this Mass of Christian burial.... As I cried, he said, "Don't worry. I have cried too."

...Cardinal Bernardin was many things to people, but he was a teacher. He taught lessons of life, and I'd like to talk about Cardinal Bernardin in the context of one of his favorite prayers, a prayer he kept in the pocket of his suit and used at all sorts of different times. It was the prayer of St. Francis of Assisi: "Lord, make me an instrument of your peace."

He brought people together. He worked hard at doing that. He had the gift of resilience. It was on a trip with some of his bishop friends when he took a moped. He went out. There was an accident. They found him in brambles and thorns with the wheels turning up and around, and he said, "I finally got the knack of it."

...He was a man of humility. He told a story of being on vacation. He was far away from Chicago, dressed in casual clothes, walking the aisles of a grocery store to prepare for the evening meal. A man saw him. "Oh, I can't believe you're here. Do you have one minute to see my wife? She's in the parking lot, one minute."

The Cardinal said, "He recognized me." He walked down the aisle, walked through the grocery store turnstile. He walked into the parking lot. The man said, "My car is over there. There is my wife." He walked up to the car. The man said, "Helen, look who's here! Dr. Kresnick!"

People know him now. They know him now, and they loved

him.... To you, my brothers and sisters who are part of this great archdiocese, didn't he teach us? Didn't he show us the way?

He took hard stands...nuclear disarmament, health care for the poor, racial injustice. He stood on the Capitol steps against partial-birth abortions. And in his last days, during his own suffering, he spoke out loud and clear to the Supreme Court about assisted suicide. Didn't he teach us? Didn't he show us the way?

...Every day in the quiet of his chapel when we were privileged to celebrate the Eucharist, there was always one prayer.... He prayed for an increase of vocations to the priesthood and the religious life. There are many young boys and girls, men and women, whom I'm sure are listening as we speak this very moment. You see how fulfilling and satisfying his life was and how yours could be as you offer you life and service to others.

...He put himself into everything.... He seldom said no. He would write thank-you letters for thank-you letters. He would give himself to priests and people....

Even when most people would have gone on disability after the news of cancer, our friend started a new ministry and reached out to cancer patients with notes and phone calls and visits and care. Priest once more, for he knew "it is in giving that we receive."

...And who will ever be able to forget that false accusation? And let us never forget his forgiveness, the Cardinal's forgiveness from the very first moment and that wonderful reconciliation, which he spoke of time and time again. For he knew that "it is in pardoning that we are pardoned."

I was with him in the examination room when he was told that he had an aggressive form of cancer. The doctor said it most likely would be his life-ending event. In those situations, he calmly dealt with this, for he was embracing a friend. Yes, he was embracing death as a friend, for he knew that it was "in dying that we have been born to eternal life."

I know there are many people watching, viewing, standing with us at this hour. But I ask you to allow me just a few words with the Cardinal. You see, it's been a long, long and beautiful ride.

Cardinal, Eminence, you're home. You're home.

THE WORK OF DEMOCRACY: CÉSAR CHÁVEZ

by Mario T. Garcia
2007

The importance of César Chávez transcends his work as a labor organizer, although he achieved unheralded victories in that role in support of farm workers. Chávez is seen as a great spiritual and civil rights leader, called by some the "Chicano Moses." As the most recognized Latino figure in U. S. history, the United States Postal Service honored Chávez with a commemorative stamp in 2003.

Eulogist Mario T. Garcia is a professor of history and Chicano studies at the University of California, Santa Barbara. He is the author of several books on Mexican-American leaders, and compiled and edited The Gospel of César Chávez: My Faith in Action. *His introduction to the book was a more extensive version of the eulogy below.*

César Chávez is one of the great figures in the history of the United States in the twentieth century and, I maintain, one of its great spiritual figures. César—as most who knew him simply called him—accomplished what no other U. S. labor leader had been able to do: successfully organize farm workers. Others had tried and had given up, saying that it was almost impossible to unionize these workers because, among other things, they were always migrating and their lack of permanency did not lend itself to organization. Others gave up due to the strong opposition by growers backed by their supporters in government and law enforcement who decried and destroyed any effort to have their workers unionized. Unionization, the growers believed, would deprive them not only of a cheap labor source, but, perhaps even more significant, of a perceived manageable labor force.

César Chávez overcame these obstacles, beginning in 1965... in California, the country's richest agricultural state with the largest number of farm workers. These mostly Mexican and Filipino workers joined what became the United Farm Workers (UFW). For almost thirty years until his death in 1993, César labored and struggled to support and enhance the working and living conditions of these... "forgotten Americans" [who] fed the country through their labor, yet reaped little of the fruits of their labor....

At an even-larger level César...stood for a recognition that the work of American democracy was, and still is, not over. In César's time, Mexican Americans and other Latinos were still marginalized and neglected Americans.... Not just as farm workers, but as urban workers in industries and services, Mexican Americans were segregated in low-skill jobs, historically referred to as "Mexican jobs"... that paid menial and, in too many cases, unlivable wages that had been historically labeled "Mexican wages." Further segregated in urban barrios with inadequate housing and public facilities, Mexican Americans had to send their children to segregated and inferior so-called "Mexican schools"...[W]hile Mexican Americans...worked hard and asked for no handouts, they were not integrated into the folds of American democracy....

This, however, would not be the same for many of the children [of Mexican immigrants who were] born and raised in the United States, and who as U. S. citizens were more cognizant of their rights and clearer on their expectations for opportunities to integrate into American society. This generation of Mexican Americans by the 1930s and beyond forged the first significant although dispersed civil rights movement in Chicano history....

An important aspect of this generational struggle was that thousands of Mexican Americans fought bravely in World War II.... The "good war" not only socialized them to the goals of the conflict centered on the defense of democracy, but motivated many of them after the war to no longer tolerate anything less than democracy at home....

It is out of this historical context that the story of César Chávez emerges.

⸺⸻

César Chávez was born on March 31, 1927, in the San Luis Valley near Yuma, Arizona, the child of hard-working Mexican American small farmers. His parents had both been born in northern Mexico but had lived in the United States for many years. His mother and grandmother, who lived with them, particularly socialized him and his four siblings. It was these devout Catholic women who influenced César to be nonviolent, to care about the welfare of others, and to give to those in need, [which] laid the foundation for César's profound spirituality.

But the family struggled, especially during the Great Depression. Not able to pay his property taxes, César's father saw his farm taken over by the state, and he had to later sell it for very little. César's parents had no choice but to leave Arizona in 1939 with their family and migrate, along with many other Americans, to seek a better fortune in California.... Following the crops, the Chávez family lived in one labor camp after another, often with little food and little shelter...[César] recalls attending thirty-seven different elementary schools. He dropped out after the eighth grade....

César enlisted in the Navy in 1944 when he turned seventeen.... He saw service in the Pacific but with little actual combat. Upon being released, he returned to...Delano...[and] married his girlfriend Helen Fabela.

Soon thereafter César and Helen, along with their developing family that would include eight children, moved to urban San Jose, where they lived in an east side barrio called "Sal Si Puedes" or "Get Out If You Can." César would later turn that around to invent his famous mantra "Sí Se Puede" ("Yes it can be done").

[In San Jose] César met Father Donald McDonnell at his local church. Fr. Donald...took on the responsibility of completing the education that César had never had.... He gave César copies of key social justice doctrines of the Catholic Church such as *Rerum Novarum* (*On the Condition of Labor*). Issued in 1891...this papal pronouncement focused on the importance of providing dignity and respect to the new industrial labor force created by industrial capitalism in western Europe and the United States, a theme [that] would become a major emphasis of César's future work....

In addition, Fr. Donald had César read the biography of Gandhi.... César was highly impressed by Gandhi's use of nonviolence as not only a moral principle, but as a key strategy that successfully achieved the independence of India from the British Empire.... Nonviolence would, in turn, become a central tenet of the farm workers' struggle.

As a Franciscan, Fr. Donald further impressed on César the life of St. Francis, especially Francis' embracing of sacrificing for others. Influenced by St. Francis, César would likewise sacrifice his own life for the liberation of his people. The education of César Chávez by Fr. Donald...reinforced many of the same principles that his mother and grandmother had taught him: nonviolence, helping those in need, sacrificing for others, respect for others and for one's self.

It was Fr. Donald who was also responsible for César meeting another key influence on his life: Fred Ross. Ross was a community organizer for the Chicago-based Industrial Areas Foundation, which since the war had been active in organizing in labor and minority communities.... [After] César...accompanied the organizer to several house meetings in the barrio, César had found his mission in life....

Together César, [Helen], and a small band of committed organizers launched in 1962 the National Farm Workers Association in the San Joaquin Valley.... Slowly but deliberately, [they] began to meet with workers and their families in their homes to discuss the importance of a union and what it could do for them....

After almost three years of organizing, César and the union were confronted with a new challenge. A smaller union of predominately Filipino workers affiliated with the AFL-CIO decided to go on strike against the major table grape growers in the Central Valley. They approached César and asked for his union to join the strike.... His members...[voted] overwhelmingly to join the Filipinos. This would become the longest strike in U. S. agricultural history, lasting five long years. Yet one cannot understand this significant struggle by interpreting it only as a labor one. This was also a spiritual struggle enveloped by Mexican-American Catholic beliefs, symbols, and traditions. It was not only a bread-and-butter campaign, but also one for the souls of the workers.

As the strike progressed...César came up with the idea of a march from Delano to Sacramento in the spring of 1966.... [He] saw it as a *peregrinación*...a penitential pilgrimage to atone for one's sins and strengthen one's faith.... Not only a personal pilgrimage but a collective one. He knew that the strike would be long and hard. The *peregrinación* would prepare the farm workers for this.

With the banner of Our Lady of Guadalupe at the head of the pilgrimage accompanied by the U. S. and Mexican flags, César, the farm workers, and their supporters...marched for twenty-five days to Sacramento.... [César] planned the pilgrimage to conclude during Holy Week and to arrive in Sacramento on Easter Sunday. César and the workers had suffered, but the resurrection was at hand.

The pilgrimage, as César had hoped, brought much media attention to the strike. Yet he knew that marches alone would not bring the growers to the bargaining table. Only pressure, especially economic pressure, would do this. César proposed a boycott of table grapes.... With the names of labor and religious people who might help them, the boycott representatives, paid only five dollars a week, successfully plotted the boycott. Over the next two years, various city councils and other local governing bodies throughout the country and abroad voted to endorse the boycott. In addition, hundreds of...students, many of them Chicanos, picketed supermarkets in their communities to convince consumer not to buy nonunion grapes. The impact was significant. The sale of table grapes decreased dramatically.

Despite the success of the boycott, the union still underwent many hard times, and workers began to doubt that they could win.

Some even began to consider...violence.... César decided that he had to do something to reemphasize the importance of nonviolence that he had earlier committed the movement to support.... [H]e decided to go on a twenty-five-day fast in 1968 to suffer for the principle of nonviolence. He moved into a small shelter on the union's property of the Forty Acres and fasted and prayed. Masses and interfaith services were held for him. Soon hundreds...came to visit him and to join in partial fasting with him. César's fast squashed what dissent had appeared.

A weak and exhausted but spiritually strengthened Chávez ended his fast on March 10, 1968.... César invited Senator Robert Kennedy to join him as he broke his fast by taking Holy Communion. Kennedy had been the first important national politician to endorse the strike. As they both received Communion, the symbolism could not have been more striking. Here was a poor farm labor organizer of Mexican-American Catholic background alongside a wealthy Irish-American Catholic politician, the heir to the Kennedy legacy. César knew that to defeat the growers the farm workers needed allies from other sections. His joint Communion with Bobby Kennedy symbolized the achievement of this alliance. Senator Kennedy's assassination a few months later after his stunning victory in the California Democratic presidential primary deeply shocked César. He and the union had worked hard for Kennedy's victory and hoped to see him in the White House.... César and the farm workers had lost a close and personal friend.

But César and the union carried on. By the summer of 1970... the growers finally decided to negotiate [and] signed contracts.... Victory had been achieved.... It marked the first time that farm workers in the United States had successfully unionized. One year earlier César had graced the cover of *Time* magazine, the first Mexican American ever to do so.... He was now a nationally-recognized labor and civil rights leader.... [A]fter the initial contracts expired.... César would again go on numerous and extensive fasts that undoubtedly hurt his health. Yet *la lucha*—the struggle—continued....

To understand the success of the movement one needs to understand César's organizing themes and strategies....

César, first and foremost, stressed the dignity of farm workers and their right to unionize....

César employed the image of the *Virgen de Guadalupe*, not only the patroness of Mexico and of the Americas, but historically in Mexico the symbol of liberation movements.... Finally, he reached out and encouraged clergy, Catholic, Protestant, and Jewish, to join the movement. These expressions of religious sentiment and spirituality reflected not only César's own deep faith, but his political awareness that linking religion to the struggle was one effective way of blunting the charge that he and his movement were Communist inspired. This worked, for how could the *Virgen de Guadalupe* be a Communist?

...[I]n his organizing [César] stressed that his union movement was not just a labor struggle, but also a movement for social justice.... For human rights, civil rights, and, above all, for the dignity of the workers...based on the principle of nonviolence....

I want to share with you some of my own personal reflections on César Chávez. I did not know him personally very well. Of course, as he did for those of my generation—the Chicano generation of the 1960s—he served as an inspiration. His leadership and struggle motivated the new generation of Mexican Americans, proudly and defiantly calling themselves the barrio term "Chicano." Many received their baptism in political activism by making their own personal *peregrinación* to Delano to meet César and to see how they could help *la causa*. Many then returned to their communities to support the grape boycott as well as to launch the urban-based Chicano movement....

The Chicano Generation challenged the system on the meaning of democracy, a Chicano meaning based on an equitable sharing of the nation's wealth and privileges and respect and equality of opportunity for all ethnic groups. This challenge would be manifest in educational struggles, political representation, an anti-Vietnam War movement, struggles against police brutality and legal discrimination, protection for undocumented immigrants, equal rights for Chicana women, and a Chicano cultural and literary renaissance including the establishment of Chicano studies programs in universities.

I became Chicano in this period.... I would see and meet César during this time, as he would often speak on college campuses. Later, after I received my doctorate in history, and accepted an appointment at the University of California, Santa Barbara, I would again see César over the years as he visited UCSB to speak to large audiences about the continued strikes and boycotts, and increasingly about the harmful effects of pesticides in the fields that harmed the workers and harmed consumers....

Later, in the early 1990s when I briefly taught at Yale University, César [came] to speak on campus.... I welcomed him to a packed audience of students, faculty, and staff.... The scene was filled with contradictions. Here was César, a small, Indian-looking, modest leader of farm workers with his usual checkered shirt, the kind you buy at Penney's or Sears, in this elite and smug environment. The image remains vivid in my memory.

One has to remember that despite César's legendary status over the many years of his struggle he was not the usual image of a charismatic and vociferous leader. He was anything but that. He was a very modest and humble farm worker with little formal education who spoke softly and with little emotion. It was hard to look at him superficially and believe that he was one of the most important labor and civil rights leaders in the country's history. Yet he was. His personal power and influence were internal. It had to do, I believe, with his spirituality. He radiated a certain spiritual quality. You sensed that this was a man of principles based on his deep faith.

The next time I encountered César, regrettably, was at his funeral. He died on April 23, 1993. His funeral was a week later in Delano. Thousands attended. Many were farm workers or the children and grandchildren of farm workers. Many were veterans of the UFW struggles and of the Chicano movement. High school and college students were bussed in by their schools. Political and religious figures attended, such as representatives of the Kennedy family, Jesse Jackson, former California governor Jerry Brown, and many others. Cardinal Roger Mahony of Los Angeles said the Mass. I went with a colleague and two graduate students. It was an eventful day. It was not somber. People were celebrating the life and contributions of César. The UFW flag with its bold eagle was quite visible, as were other signs and banners. It was as if the early days of the union were being reenacted. It was a hot and dusty day in the Central Valley that made the long funeral march that resembled the *peregrinación* of 1966 rather difficult. But as in any pilgrimage one expects to suffer, and so we did, remembering what César himself had suffered and what he had given to us. When it all concluded toward late afternoon, we were exhausted, thirsty, and hungry, but we knew—I knew—that we had to be there. This was history and collective memory, and I had to be a part of it. Through César's life we examined our own.

THE POSTER BOY FOR HOPE: RON SANTO

by Monsignor Dan Mayall
Holy Name Cathedral, Chicago, IL
December 10, 2010

In Chicago, the name Ron Santo was usually prefaced by "the legendary baseball figure"—even while he was living. After he died, tens of thousands of fans left flowers at Wrigley Field and stood in a line to pay their respects at Holy Name Cathedral during an eight-hour visitation.

Santo signed with the Cubs' organization at age eighteen. He became a nine-time All-Star third baseman, winning five Gold Gloves and setting a long list of major league performance records. On December 5, 2011, Santo was posthumously elected into the Baseball Hall of Fame by the Golden Era Committee.

At age eighteen, he was also diagnosed with juvenile diabetes and given an estimated seven more years to live. Fearing the diagnosis would jeopardize his career, he concealed his Type 1 diabetes. He carried candy bars for blood sugar emergencies—such as the times he was at-bat and seeing two balls coming at him rather than one. After he retired from playing, he talked about his disease and volunteered for three decades, raising more than $60 million for the Juvenile Diabetic Research Foundation. Although both his legs were eventually amputated, he walked with prostheses.

Santo was a WGN-AM sportscaster for twenty years, partnering with play-by-play man Pat Hughes since 1996. Their banter often involved teasing one another: Pat telling about the time Ron's hairpiece caught fire in the broadcast booth; Ron referring to Pat's penny-pinching. In later years, Santo's increasing forgetfulness sometimes led to coaxing player names from Pat during broadcasts. Fans considered this a minor distraction considering the other challenges he coped with daily. In addition to the amputations, a heart attack led to bypass surgery, then cancer

305

led to removal of his bladder. Throughout it all, Santo kept broadcasting;
he died during the offseason at age seventy.

*   This brief tribute by the pastor of Chicago's Holy Name Cathedral de-*
picts the essence of the ever-optimistic Santo, whose hope—for a team that
has not won a World Series in over a century of trying—never wavered.

To you, Vicki, to Ron's children and grandchildren, and to all in your family—I extend the condolences of everybody here in the Cathedral as well as everybody who would like to have been here to pray for Ron and to lift him up to the Lord. If we are lifting Ron to the Lord, let's decide right now to do that lifting with love and to do it with a smile.

I am Monsignor Dan Mayall, the pastor of Holy Name Cathedral. Later on [Cubs owner] Tom Ricketts, [Baseball] Commissioner Bud Selig, and Pat Hughes will talk. All three have an obvious place in this prayer service. A parishioner asked me yesterday, "Monsignor Mayall, how do you fit in?" Let me guess. Is it because I am a Cub fan? I certainly am. Still, that description fits just about everyone here and a few million more. Am I here because my last baseball glove was a Wilson A2170 with Ron Santo's name in the pocket? I don't think I owned the only one of those, although I still have mine. Am I here because every day since I was nineteen years old I have injected myself with insulin in a fight with Type 1 diabetes? That routine certainly bonded me to Ron; but I doubt that I am the only insulin-dependent diabetic here. Then why do I get to preach at Ron Santo's funeral? It's because you're in my church, the most beautiful Church in Chicago, the place where Chicago goes to pray. I am glad Ron's family and the Cubs chose to celebrate Ron at Holy Name Cathedral. If Ron is a Chicago icon, then it is fittingly here that we return him to God from Chicago's most identified church. It's here at Holy Name Cathedral that I get to match the famous Ron Santo to images of faith, images of eternity, divine images.

Let's match Ron with three eternal truths, three virtues. A virtue is a gift from God that makes a person good. They are gifts—you don't buy them, steal them, earn them, or deserve them. Virtues are gifts from God. I think Ron received and cultivated three outstanding virtues.

Try the first virtue—joy. Ron was joyful. Certainly, you heard it in the positive—HELLO, BIG BOY...YES...ALL RIGHT. And you knew it when the joy was missing—OH NO...GEEZ...UN-BELIEVABLE. Joyful is not the same as naïve. "There is a time for everything; a time to be born and a time to die." There even is a time to lose. Ron played on losing teams; he did not always win. His celebrated joy, however, was a virtue that allowed him to expect the best every inning, every day, every season. Joy is a virtue, a gift from God that made Ron Santo good. Ron was joyful.

A second virtue is hope. Hope lets a person see God even when others think he is absent. We exercise hope here declaring that death is never the last word in a Christian's lifetime. "In my Father's house, there are many dwelling places." One of those places has had Ron's name on the door since the day of his baptism. Cub fans breathe hope. Ron was the voice of the Cubs; but he also was the face of hope. No shutout, no blown-save, no strikeout with the bases loaded, no sweep, no illness or disease was ever the last word. Ron Santo was the poster boy for hope. We all hope. "We have fought the good fight. We have run the race." Ron had an overdose of hope.

Third, Ron embodied courage. Courage is the ability to practice all the other virtues—hope, joy, faith, fidelity, honesty, kindness, wisdom, right judgment, reverence—no matter what the circumstances. Ron had courage. He was a good and virtuous man in all kinds of circumstances—after he lost his legs; after he faced death a few years ago; after he met the fight against diabetes; after his last battle with cancer. Ron remained a virtuous man—one who resembled God in the way he exercised God's gifts to him. Ron Santo was a courageous man.

On the day we say goodbye to someone we knew (and did not know); on the day we say goodbye to someone we loved (did you see the fans enter Holy Name Cathedral in a steady stream last night, every other one in real tears?); on the day we say goodbye to someone we will miss (if you think you miss him now, wait until the first pitch from [Cubs' spring training facility in] Mesa), we want to celebrate his life. Ron Santo was the poster boy for joy. Ron Santo had an overdose of hope. Ron Santo lived on courage.

Joy + hope + courage = Ron Santo. Joy, hope, and courage are virtues—gifts from God that make a person good. At the place where Chicago goes to pray, this Cub fan, a diabetic priest with a Ron Santo baseball glove, asks God to receive a joyful, hopeful, courageous Ron Santo to the place reserved for him in heaven. Ron, God bless your soul!

ELIZABETH ANN SETON
IS THE FIRST WHOLLY AMERICAN SAINT!

Homily of Holy Father Paul VI
September 14, 1975
The Vatican

*Prior to the American Revolution and the Declaration of Independence—
and fifteen years before George Washington was inaugurated as the first
president of the United States of America—Elizabeth Ann Bayley Seton
was born in 1774. Her wealthy, Anglican ancestors had been among the
earliest settlers of the colony of New York.*

*After she married William Seton, she was confronted by a series of
crises. William faced bankruptcy during a time when he had also contracted tuberculosis. The family travelled to Italy to seek treatment, but he
died soon after they arrived, leaving the twenty-nine-year-old Elizabeth
a widow with five young children. A Catholic family in Italy took them
in and provided loving support for one year. By the time Elizabeth returned to America, she had decided to convert to Catholicism.*

*She established the first Catholic school and the first religious com-
munity in America, both in Maryland. Elizabeth was thirty-five years
old when she founded The Sisters of Charity of St. Joseph, and dedicated
her new order to caring for America's poorest children. It was 1809, the
year that also saw the birth of Abraham Lincoln.*

*As with her husband, she too died of tuberculosis, just eleven years
after founding her order. By then, her community of eighty-six teaching
sisters had expanded from Baltimore, opening schools in New York and
St. Louis and orphanages in New York and Philadelphia. The Sisters of
Charity eventually grew into independent communities in Ohio, New
York, New Jersey, Pennsylvania, and Canada, all inspired by St. Vincent DePaul and St. Louise de Marillac. These communities went on to
found a college and hospitals to care for the poor in Connecticut, Alaska,*

Massachusetts, Florida, Mississippi, Arizona, North Carolina, Nebraska, Rhode Island, Texas, Virginia, West Virginia, Puerto Rico, and the Virgin Islands. The Mother Seton House in Baltimore is listed in the National Register of Historic Places.

In 2010, as part of their ongoing strategic planning process, the order's members looked back upon two-hundred years of providing life-changing education and care to America's poor. They also stated their commitment to the future: "Our mission calls us to be innovative, inventive, collaborative, and inclusive. We want to do what is best to advocate for the issues of immigration, human trafficking, social injustice, and national health care reform."

The Vatican re-visions too (never quickly, often dramatically) as it did on the day in 1975 when Mother Seton was canonized by Pope Paul VI. Dialogue between the Catholic and Anglican-Episcopal Churches was in its early stages then. Notably, "distinguished Episcopalian dignitaries" accepted invitations to the canonization ceremony. The Pope's recognition that it was the Anglican-Episcopal communion that had "awakened and fostered [Elizabeth Seton's] religious sense," and that she "had preserved all the good things which her membership in the fervent Episcopal community had taught her...." was a landmark step in encouraging dialogue. That ecumenical process had begun in 1963, when Pope John XXIII convened the Second Vatican Council, and continued after his death, when Paul VI, before closing Vatican II, established permanent secretariats for the Promotion of Christian Unity (and also for building relationships with non-Christians and non-believers).

It was a glorious day both for the United States and for worldwide Christianity when Elizabeth Ann Seton was proclaimed the first "wholly American saint."

Yes, Venerable Brothers and beloved sons and daughters! Elizabeth Ann Seton is a Saint! We rejoice and are deeply moved that our apostolic ministry authorizes us to make this solemn declaration before all of you here present, before the holy Catholic Church, before our other Christian brethren in the world, before the entire American people, and before all humanity. Elizabeth Ann Bayley Seton is a Saint! She is the first daughter of the United States of America to be glorified with this incomparable attribute!

But what do we mean when we say: "She is a saint"? We all have some idea of the meaning of this highest title; but it is still difficult for us to make an exact analysis of it. Being a saint means being perfect, with a perfection that attains the highest level that a human being can reach. A saint is a human creature fully conformed to the will of God. A saint is a person in whom all sin—the principle of death—is cancelled out and replaced by the living splendor of divine grace. The analysis of the concept of sanctity brings us to recognize in a soul the mingling of two elements that are entirely different but which come together to produce a single effect: sanctity. One of these elements is the human and moral element, raised to the degree of heroism: heroic virtues are always required by the Church for the recognition of a person's sanctity. The second element is the mystical element, which express the measure and form of divine action in the person chosen by God to realize in herself—always in an original way—the image of Christ (Cfr. Rom. 8, 29).

The science of sanctity is therefore the most interesting, the most varied, the most surprising and the most fascinating of all the studies of that ever mysterious being which is man. The Church has made this study of the life, that is, the interior and exterior history, of Elizabeth Ann Seton. And the Church has exulted with admiration and joy, and has today heard her own charism of truth poured out in the exclamation that we send up to God and announce to the world: She is a saint! We shall not now give a panegyric, that is, the narrative which glorifies the new saint. You already know her life and you will certainly study it further. This will be one of the most valuable fruits of the Canonization of the new saint: to know her, in order to admire in her an outstanding human figure; in order to praise God who is wonderful in his saints; to imitate her example which this ceremony places in a light that will give perennial edification; to invoke her protection, now that we have the certitude of her participation in the exchange of heavenly life in the Mystical Body of Christ, which we call the Communion of Saints and in which we also share, although still belonging to life on earth. We shall not therefore speak of the life of our Saint Elizabeth Ann Seton. This is neither the time nor the place for a fitting commemoration of her.

But at least let us mention the chapters in which such a commemoration should be woven. Saint Elizabeth Ann Seton is an American. All of us say this with spiritual joy, and with the intention of honoring the land and the nation from which she marvelously sprang forth as the first flower in the calendar of the saints. This is the title which, in his original foreword to the excellent work of Father Dirvin, the late Cardinal Spellman, Archbishop of New York, attributed to her as primary and characteristic: "Elizabeth Ann Seton was wholly American!" Rejoice we say to the great nation of the United States of America. Rejoice for your glorious daughter. Be proud of her. And know how to preserve her fruitful heritage. This most beautiful figure of a holy woman presents to the world and to history the affirmation of new and authentic riches that are yours: that religious spirituality which your temporal prosperity seemed to obscure and almost make impossible. Your land too, America, is indeed worthy of receiving into its fertile ground the seed of evangelical holiness. And here is a splendid proof—among many others—of this fact.

May you always be able to cultivate the genuine fruitfulness of evangelical holiness, and ever experience how—far from stunting the flourishing development of your economic, cultural and civic vitality—it will be in its own way the unfailing safeguard of that vitality. Saint Elizabeth Ann Seton was born, brought up and educated in New York in the Episcopalian Communion. To this Church goes the merit of having awakened and fostered the religious sense and Christian sentiment which in the young Elizabeth were naturally predisposed to the most spontaneous and lively manifestations. We willingly recognize this merit, and, knowing well how much it cost Elizabeth to pass over to the Catholic Church, we admire her courage for adhering to the religious truth and divine reality which were manifested to her therein. And we are likewise pleased to see that from this same adherence to the Catholic Church she experienced great peace and security, and found it natural to preserve all the good things which her membership in the fervent Episcopalian community had taught her, in so many beautiful expressions, especially of religious piety, and that she was always faithful in her esteem and affection for those from whom her Catholic profession had sadly separated her.

For us it is a motive of hope and a presage of ever better ecumenical relations to note the presence at this ceremony of distinguished Episcopalian dignitaries, to whom—interpreting as it were the heartfelt sentiments of the new saints—we extend our greeting of devotion and good wishes. And then we must note that Elizabeth Seton was the mother of a family and at the same time the foundress of the first Religious Congregation of women in the United States. Although this social and ecclesial condition of hers is not unique or new (we may recall, for example, Saint Birgitta, Saint Frances of Rome, Saint Jan Frances Fremiot de Chantal, Saint Louise de Marillac), in a particular way it distinguishes Saint Elizabeth Ann Bayley Seton for her complete femininity, so that as we proclaim the supreme exaltation of a woman by the Catholic Church, we are pleased to note that this event coincides with an initiative of the United Nations: International Women's Year. This program aims at promoting an awareness of the obligation incumbent on all to recognize the true role of women in the world and to contribute to their authentic advancement in society. And we rejoice at the bond that is established between this program and today's Canonization, as the Church renders the greatest honor possible to Elizabeth Ann Bayley Seton and extols her personal and extraordinary contribution as a woman, a wife, a mother, a widow, and a religious.

May the dynamism and authenticity of her life be an example

in our day—and for generations to come—of what women can and must accomplish, in the fulfillment of their role, for the good of humanity. And finally we must recall that the most notable characteristic of our saint is the fact that she was, as we said, the foundress of the first Religious Congregation of women in the United States. It was an offspring of the religious family of Saint Vincent de Paul, which later divided into various autonomous branches—five principal ones—now spread throughout the world. And yet all of them recognize their origin in the first group, that of the Sisters of Charity of Saint Joseph's, personally established by Saint Elizabeth Seton at Emmitsburg in the Archdiocese of Baltimore. The apostolate of helping the poor and the running of parochial schools in America had this humble, poor, courageous and glorious beginning. This account, which constitutes the central nucleus of the earthly history and worldwide fame of the work of Mother Seton, would merit a more extended treatment. But we know that her spiritual daughters will take care to portray the work itself as it deserves.

And therefore to these chosen daughters of the saint we direct our special and cordial greeting, with the hope that they may be enabled to be faithful to their providential and holy institution, that their fervor and their numbers may increase, in the constant conviction that they have chosen and followed a sublime vocation that is worthy of being served with the total gift of their heart, the total gift of their lives. And may they always be mindful of the final exhortation of their Foundress Saint those words that she pronounced on her deathbed, like a heavenly testament, on January 2, 1821, "Be children of the Church." And we would add: forever! And to all our beloved sons and daughters in the United States and throughout the entire Church of God we offer, in the name of Christ, the glorious heritage of Elizabeth Ann Seton. It is above all an ecclesial heritage of strong faith and pure love for God and for others—faith and love that are nourished on the Eucharist and on the Word of God. Yes, Brethren, and sons and daughters: the Lord is indeed wonderful in his saints. Blessed be God forever!

CRUCING

FIXED, SOLID, HOLDING A TRUE POSITION: ROBERT F. GRIFFIN, CSC

by Luis R. Gamez
Winter 1999-2000

After the death of their university chaplain, the Reverend Robert F. Griffin, CSC, letters from former students and colleagues poured into Notre Dame Magazine. *It seemed as if everyone had a fond memory or a special story about "Griff" and his ever-present cocker spaniel. He was the consummate priest, many wrote, "a man of great faith and love, a man of total compassion and ferocious smoking habit: a man of old faith and new tolerances."*

Father Griffin became part of the experiment when Notre Dame went coed: The university built a dorm especially for women, and he was assigned to live in it as the dorm's priest. One student recalled that the day Father Griff moved in to the girls' dorm, he received a note from then–Chancellor Father Theodore Hesburgh saying, "Blessed are you among women."

Griff had the appearance of an oversized man even at age nineteen, when he converted to Catholicism. A classmate recalled that his uncharacteristic physical presence set him apart in seminary "as harshly as if he had remained a Baptist." He became "Heavy Griffin" to distinguish him from another seminarian with the same last name. He died at age seventy-four from complications of diabetes and a refusal to allow doctors to begin what he saw as the limb-by-limb amputation process.

Students, friends, and colleagues recall him as "Christ's servant, the steward of God's mysteries."

S earching for the way, trying not to trip in the dark; will we ever get there? It's a cool, drizzly October night in a patch of Michigan woods, all wet leaves and rotting boughs under our flashlights. I'm supposedly night-orienteering with the Boy Scouts, but most of my mind frets anxiously for Griff, who lies dying at Holy Cross House, a hundred miles away. My dear old ghostly father, as I name him, will soon be a ghost himself.

I want to sit beside him, maybe hold his hand and read him some Gerard Manly Hopkins. Perhaps something of my presence will sift down through the fitful, troubled torpor which has settled on him as he strains not to go gentle into that good night.

But first these boys want to show me their stuff. All they have is a compass and a list of numbers to navigate the dark wilderness. But the one landmark, that big rock at the edge of the clearing, is your best friend, because if you can't fix your position at the start then each subsequent bearing will be a little bit off course, and each succeeding step a little more off course, magnifying your error, carrying you further away from your goal.

I suppose that Father Robert Griffin, CSC, was just such a landmark for me and countless other Notre Dame students. He would never actually point out the way, but he was fixed and solid, holding a true position from which I knew the possible coordinates. Griff died on October 20, and I feel as if every step of my adult life was his gift. Now that I'm on my own, can I find the way through the darkness, with only his written words left behind?

> *Death is a bully whose nose should be tweaked, and I hope to be one of the tweakers. I grow weary of fearing death, for myself and for my friends. I become embarrassed for God; death makes such a fool of Him. I want to be present at death's judgment; I want to hear God say that death must die. I want to be present at resurrections that defeat death's victories. I want to see the fallen sparrows renewed in their*

flight. I want to greet death when he comes irresistibly, with insolence and swagger, as though I were a baggy-pants clown to whom the final snickers belong.

He did look clownish, I guess: surely the most awkward man on campus. Large and heavy, baby-faced even when unshaved, unkempt hair escaping from a shabby cap, elephant trousers flecked with cigarette ash, a cocker spaniel named Darby O'Gill yanking its leash between the ankles, Griff would shamble across the North Quad with a wobbly vagueness, a frumpy black-clad reject from the Macy's parade.

He was chaplain of the University for thirty years, but it's almost impossible to identify Griff with any formal organization. His post simply meant that he was the best listener in the world, and he seemed happiest when listening to those on the fringes. He celebrated a Mass for children with mimes and mummers and teddy bear picnics on the altar. He ran a coffee-house-cum-study-hall in the bowels of the student center from midnight until dawn, a haven for insomniacs and the depressed. He spent his summers in the scuzzier part of Manhattan, ministering to alcoholics and druggies and to the prostitutes whom he called joy maidens.

A missionary to the lonely, nobody has ever loved us so much. Griff wrote once, "You cannot sing a night song until the hour before dawn, when the darkness has nearly ended. Then, when loneliness has worn you out, you understand, in an insight as spontaneous as laughter, that God has been keeping watch." Griff taught us to sing night songs of faith in the basement of LaFortune. Even in his last hours of consciousness he insisted on counseling me on my recently failed marriage, as lovingly alert and keenly sympathetic as when I sat at his feet twenty years ago, righting the wrongs of creation with me at midnight over a cup of cocoa. His was the simple but ineluctably vital ministry of being there.

Faith teaches that there is an eternal heartbeat in me that belongs to God; it keeps me from getting weary when I need to care. Yet sometimes the best I can do is give a professional

*attention, wanting to care deeply, yet knowing that in all my
attention there is nothing really personal. Eventually, with
God's help, I touch the place where the nerve ends quiver; I find
the spot where the pain shows through. Then my experience is
like that of Thomas, when he put his finger into the side of
Christ; a personal bond is established because I know how
someone has suffered. Is caring, then, a personal response, a
special cherishing of the person cared for? Sometimes not, I
suppose, but I've never found a person whom I needed to love
whom I couldn't love, if I am patient enough.*

Lovely, Griff. Maybe you shall be missed most as the late Laureate of the Dome, for your golden prose interrogated and enveloped
and chronicled our lives: dozens of columns for *Our Sunday Visitor*,
Scholastic and this magazine, the stuff of journalism awards, essays
collected into two books. But for me your best legacy is the twenty-
five years' worth of weekly "Letters to a Lonely God" that ran in
the Friday *Observer*. How I delight to follow the gentle movement
of your thought, that Senecan amble that takes us to questions and
issues via the roads and by-ways of your singular experience. Your
speculations appear seamlessly to embrace most of writing and culture—the Gospels, Graham Greene, *Saturday Night Fever*, Teilhard
de Chardin, *Henry V*, Jimmy Swaggart, Dr. Seuss—always outlining
a significant argument, but soft-spokenly, glowing with a lucid pe-
riodicity of prose.

Such a lovely stylist, Griff. But what you write! When I was
younger I undervalued you, for you have always wrestled so honestly
for the Truth, and I was mostly charmed by the style. Some years ago,
for instance, you wrote on Tom the gay Catholic, and it's so loving a
response—your critical faculties of discernment are agile and strong,
yet you reach out first, and then utter the truth that you must. You
grasp exactly the psychological and spiritual dimensions of Tom's issues, but when you write you give the impression of listening rather
than that of sternly preaching. Of course my fellow Griff-groupies
and I loved you years ago for this patient attentiveness—but what

awes me now as a reader is how sharp an observer of contemporary life you remain, and how true an ear for the voice of humanity you retain. All this, and preaching the Truth besides. You never shunned the hard, urgent topics—gay Catholics, women wanting the priesthood. Always "with it" and relevant, to be sure: but it's the Gospel you preach, always by reaching out rather than ramming down. Isn't ours the faith that is built upon questions left dangling in the air? You served as our apostle of the unanswered questions, Griff, and, God in heaven, you did a lovely job of it.

> *Death, when it comes unexpectedly, must always seem like a horror. But if death comes when you are waiting for it, hoping for it, it must seem as welcome as a mother's hug. Or if death comes to say: "Not now, not yet. I'll be waiting someplace up the road, but I don't want you to be afraid of going home with a friend"—such a death, comforting as a night sky full of stars, must seem like the dark angel at God's hand, the messenger of his hidden mercies.*

Mercies, yes, but they don't feel like they're for me right now. "When it is a drizzly November in my soul," says Ishmael in *Moby Dick*, "I put out to sea," and we have each one our own solitary, exigent navigations which we must make the best of, howsoever drizzly we feel.

Orienteering is always tough, so very tough. I wish to God I had a better compass and a clearer path. But once, I knew exactly where I was.

ONE WITNESS, POINTING: MARY K. MEYER

by Father Mike Coleman
February 10, 2007
Our Lady and St. Rose of Lima Church, Kansas City, KS

Mary K. Meyer lived her whole life in Kansas, but she travelled the world on behalf of peace and justice. She walked to support nuclear disarmament: from Kansas City to McConnell Air Force Base in Wichita; and in Israel, from Haifa to Bethlehem. She went to Baghdad to bear witness to the suffering of civilian families, and in El Salvador she acted as a human shield for refugees determined to return home from camps in Honduras.

Mostly she worked quietly in her home state. At Manna House in Concordia she offered sanctuary to Central American refugees fleeing persecution. And from 1988 until her death, she worked at Shalom House, a shelter for homeless men in Kansas City.

She discovered her mission at age forty-seven. Prior to that, after graduating with a business degree from Kansas State University, she worked in Chapman, Kansas. For some time, she had felt a growing challenge from Matthew's Gospel imperative to feed the hungry, clothe the naked, welcome the stranger, and visit the prisoner. She later talked about deciding to join Dorothy Day's Catholic Worker Movement: "...It simplifies things. The corporal works of mercy and the spiritual works of mercy are your life. It stretches you.... It's radical."

Above all, that radical work was one of prayer and service to others. Her generosity of spirit extended not only to suffering people but also to those who disagreed with her. She talked of the importance of taking a stance for peace out of love rather than self-righteousness, and of showing sensitivity to and respect for those who thought differently.

After receiving a diagnosis of cancer at age seventy-seven, she expressed gratitude for her opportunity to continue working at Shalom House and for having the time to share memories and say goodbye to the many people who loved her.

During the Second World War when American Marines were retaking the Mariana Islands in the South Pacific from the Japanese, a group landed on one of the islands and encountered a convent of American sisters. The sisters were caring for the displaced, for orphans and for lepers. It was clear that life was very hard on many levels. The Marine captain told the sister in charge: "You couldn't hire me to do this for all the money in the world."

And she quietly said to him: "Me neither." She kind of looked down, then raised her eyes to look at the solider, and smiled, as if sharing a secret, or affirming something the two of them could agree on.

Alejandro had slipped into the United States for many reasons. He was just a kid, a nice young man, as Mary Kay would say, who for the most part was seeking a little adventure. He stayed for a while at Shalom House during the summer, but finally decided that he wanted to be closer to Mexico.

When he left the house to go to the railroad yard, Mary Kay checked to see that he had his money securely concealed in his clothing. And she did two additional things that she had never done with any of the others: she wrote her name and phone number on a piece of paper and gave it to him. "Call me if you get into trouble." And she gave him a kiss. At the time she said she felt very much like his mother. Although she later said she did not know why she had done that, it did become clear in time.

A few days later she received a call from a Sheriff in Louisiana. He said, "Do you know someone named Alejandro? We found the body today at the bottom of a coal car. He apparently had crawled into the car to sleep. And the workers did not know anyone was in the car when they filled it with coal. He had your phone number in his pocket."

In Renaissance paintings coming out of the Catholic Reformation there are many paintings in which we see a person standing in the foreground, and the person is pointing—usually pointing at Christ—and looking at us, just in case we might miss the whole reason why the picture was painted to begin with.

I would like to characterize Mary Kay, and others who think and act as she did, as witnesses who point—whether really or metaphorically.

A witness in this context is a person who is present on God's behalf in the here and now concerning some present condition. A witness may speak aloud, sometimes a witness may actually point, but often the witness simply stands or acts in the scene silently. The purpose of the witnessing is to remind the viewer that there is something here which needs to be paid attention to.

In the Catholic Worker sense of witness, the pointing or the standing is to call attention to the fact that the scene does not conform to right order in the universe. It takes a certain kind of witness who has the guts to raise the question: Why does this condition exist? How much longer must it exist? And can no one fix it?

Archbishop Helder Camara, of Recife in Brazil, said, "When I feed the poor, people say I am a saint; but when I ask why the people are poor, they say I am a communist."

A witness knows fairly well from experience that for all the pointing or being present in the world, the condition is not likely to change. But for the record, for God's record, the situation has been acknowledged and underlined by someone who has pointed out that the situation is not in the interest of God's hopes for the universe.

And so the witness goes to the school of the Americas and points; the witness is arrested for trespassing at a nuclear testing site and is taken away by the MPs; a witness disrupts the talk of a big shot from Washington and is hustled from the room.

A witness is one who says that some human behavior is so awful, so resistant to external forces to change it, that passive resistance is the only tool we have to overcome its power. Some things cannot be "fixed" by external manipulation.

Mary Kay was quoted in the newspaper as saying, "These are not normal times. In the midst of darkness and fear, we need to celebrate the good and the noble deep within us. We need to celebrate the times we have stood up against evil and injustice, and said with our hearts, 'No.'"

And when the hearings are held in the next life, the witness will be summoned to testify: Yes, Lord, I saw it. Yes, I noted it. And yes, I questioned it.

Our Lord said, "I was hungry and naked and homeless, and friendless. And yes, you fed me; you clothed me; you welcomed and befriended me."

There is no middle person here. No illegal, no druggie, no schizophrenic, no someone at the bottom of the food chain.

And by extension Jesus might say, "I was in danger because they taught people in my country refined ways of torture and you gave me asylum; my society, my country was in danger of being destroyed, and you came and walked among us. I had absolutely nothing to give you and you loved me as your own."

If we believe this at all, we believe it more firmly today because of the example of Mary Kay and those of her company.

The witness points to our lips and to our hearts and in effect says, "I hear what your lips say, what does your heart say?"

Perhaps when Mary Kay made the transition to the Light, and met the Light face to face, she kind of looked down, as she was wont to do, then raised her eyes to look at the Lord, and smiled, as if sharing a secret, or affirming something the two of them could agree on. Most likely, she pointed at Jesus, and, not all that surprised, said, "So, you are the one I've been working for all these years, bossing you around, cleaning up after you, taking you to the clinics, putting up with our disruptions, moving you along when the time came, though I have to admit this always saddened me.

"I always found you something of a puzzle on earth—you come in such a variety of flavors and identities."

Then maybe she turned, with a little flick of her ponytail to look around, and here she really pointed. "I see the streets here are not paved with gold. Glad to see that!"

Then turning back to the Lord, she said, "Well, nice place you have here. Anything you need done?"

FROM SLAVE TO PRIEST:
FATHER AUGUSTINE TOLTON

by Deacon Harold Burke-Sivers
Holy Thursday, 2006

Augustine Tolton was born into slavery in Missouri. His father was killed in the Civil War. His mother escaped her owner and made her way in a rowboat with her three children to the free state of Illinois.

In Quincy, Illinois, she and the nine-year-old Augustine found work in a tobacco factory. The Toltons joined St. Boniface Catholic Church where Gospel readings and sermons were spoken in German. Young Augustine retold the Scripture stories to other children in both German and English. The pastor was impressed by the boy's intelligence and placed him in the parish school, at age eleven, during Augustine's three month "off work" period between tobacco seasons. His enrollment triggered threats, vandalism, and a petition demanding the pastor's transfer, driving Mrs. Tolton to put Augustine in the public school. But he ultimately faced rejection there too. Hearing of this injustice, Father Peter McGirr, the Irish pastor of Quincy's St. Peter's Church, enlisted the support of the Sisters of Notre Dame to ensure Augustine a successful enrollment in their parish school.

"As long as I was in that school," Augustine later recalled, "I was safe. Everyone was kind to me. I learned the alphabet, spelling, reading, arithmetic...."

In three months, he also learned Latin and became an altar boy. For many years, the young man enjoyed the continued help of a succession of Franciscan priests who tutored him privately. Hearing of his desire to become a priest, and finding that no American seminary would accept him, the Franciscans arranged for Augustine to enter a seminary in Rome. They even sent him pocket money throughout his six years of study there.

On Easter Sunday, April, 1886, with his friend and mentor

Giovanni Cardinal Simeoni at his side, the newly ordained Father Tolton offered his first Mass in St. Peter's Basilica in Vatican City.

Meanwhile, Father McGirr was planning the kind of "welcome home" celebration Quincy had never seen before. He organized a delegation of Father Tolton's relatives, friends, and priests. He chartered a special railroad car to meet the incoming train in Springfield so they could accompany Father Tolton home. A large crowd, complete with a brass band, met the train in Quincy, cheering as Father Tolton was escorted into a flower-draped carriage drawn by four white horses. Adults and school children lined the streets and waved as the procession made its way to the church. It seemed as if everyone—white and black, Catholic or not—wanted to be a part of the festivities, to congratulate America's first black priest. In a letter to Cardinal Checchi in Rome, Father Tolton wrote:

> *...everyone received me kindly, especially the Negroes but also the white people: Germans, Irish, and all others. I celebrated Mass on July 18, in the Church of Saint Boniface with more than 1,000 whites and 500 colored people present. After the Mass all shouted, "Long live the College in Rome."*

Newspaper coverage of Father Tolton's masses invariably mentioned his stately demeanor and beautiful singing voice, and his early days as pastor of the new Negro Church of St. Joseph in Quincy showed much promise. Altar servers, evening classes, a girls' choir, and the eighty-member women's Altar Society were racially integrated, as were the worshippers at Mass. Many white people who may have come to see a novelty were awed by Father Tolton's sermons and singing. The white worshippers helped defray the costs of maintaining a parish where poverty, illiteracy, and disrupted families were to take a toll on free African-Americans and their progeny.

But this growing congregation also led certain African-American Protestant ministers, as well as a newly appointed pastor in the neighboring German Catholic parish, to view Father Tolton as a competitor for souls. The white priest successfully prevailed upon the Bishop to order Father Tolton to dismiss Caucasians from his church and minister to blacks only.

This harassment led Father Tolton to request a transfer, and he was sent to Chicago in 1889 to establish that city's first black Catholic parish. Within the year, his mother, sister, and nineteen members of St. Joseph parish moved from Quincy to join his Chicago congregation.

By the time the parish had grown to about six-hundred members, the foundation was laid for a new church: St. Monica's. "A Negro architect, Negro contractors, and workmen put up the building, and white Catholics donated liberally." Mother Katharine Drexel (see page 45) was one of the contributors.

As the sole priest for so many families, from baptism to burial, "Good Father Gus" (as he became known) worked tirelessly. But his dedication took its toll. Father Tolton collapsed one day on the street while walking home from the train station during a 105-degree heat wave. He died in 1897 at age forty-three. He is buried at his prior request in Quincy. n February, 2011, as Francis Cardinal George initiated the cause for Father Tolton's canonization, he said, "The introduction of his Cause now gives the Church...the opportunity to affirm his courage and enable him, long after his death, to take his place in our history and our prayers."

His death was the beginning of the end for St. Monica's parish. Although a new pastor came and even initiated a school, the church was never completed. In 1924, the St. Monica congregation was consolidated with St. Elizabeth Church and became the center of Chicago's black Roman Catholic community. Mother Drexel's Sisters of the Blessed Sacrament moved to the parish to serve with the sisters of Mercy already at St. Elizabeth School.

Today, this parish is served by Rev. Richard Andrus, SVD, pastor; the Daughters of Divine Love (DDL); an active men's club; a staff of twenty-five; and many volunteers. School and preschool enrollment is 255 students, who also enjoy after-school activities. The Drexel Community Center and a Parish Center feed an average of one hundred hungry people a month, and provide a credit union; an outreach to shut-ins; bible study; marriage preparation; addiction counseling; and all the other services of a busy congregation.

The parish website tells of a landmark event in the spring of 2005: A United States Senator from Illinois visited St. Elizabeth School and spoke to the parents and children. His name was Barack Obama.

Father Augustine Tolton's life is a poignant reminder that with God all things are possible.... Confronted with a succession of seemingly indomitable challenges (a narrow escape from slavery, his father's death, abject poverty, exclusion from American seminaries), Father Tolton's fervent desire to study Catholicism, his intense longing for the priesthood and his mother's loving support were the wellsprings from which he drew the strength to persevere.

Father Tolton knew that unconditional trust in God meant that he must become completely vulnerable before the God who made him. Father Tolton...confidently [exposed] the deepest parts of his soul before God who gave him the strength to exercise his priestly ministry under the weighty yoke of racism. He was a beacon of hope to black Catholics in the nineteenth century who were trying to find a home in the American Church. Father Tolton in his abiding faith and selfless charity, was the instrument through which God's love shone brightly. The resplendent chorus, "I have come... not to do my own will, but the will of him who sent me" (John 6:38) echoed majestically throughout Father Tolton's brief life.

Despite the oppressive hardships placed upon Father Tolton by a culture firmly rooted in the arid soil of hatred and malevolence, God brought him out of the heart of darkness and used him as an instrument of grace. Father Tolton was a tireless messenger of the Gospel and "was not afraid to go into the deep South, where racial hatreds had reached a high pitch and where segregation was decreed by harsh laws." Despite the novelty of being the only black priest in an all-white clergy, the gifted Father Tolton was able effectively to convey the richness, beauty, and truth of the Catholic faith, which penetrated even the hardest hearts. ("Wherever he went, he was respected and honored")....

Father Tolton, a former slave become Catholic priest...endured years of frustration, humiliation, and rejection in a country boasting openness to religious freedom and tolerance. Despite the fact that slaves were "free," they were far from liberated. In Father Tolton's own words: "We are only a class—a class of dehumanized, brutalized, depersonalized beings." The nation failed the "freedom" litmus test rooted in its own Declaration of Independence, while the Catholic Church in America failed to live up to the tenets of her own creed and gospel by not recognizing that genuine liberation means freedom from the bondage of iniquity and sin.

With the assistance and support of several very persistent and undaunted priests, Father Tolton was finally accepted by the Catholic Church—in Rome! He thrived in the Eternal City where his priestly vocation was nurtured and where his gifts and talents were recognized, prompting even the prefect of the Sacred Congregation *de Propaganda Fide* to note what the American Church failed to appreciate: "Father Tolton is a good priest, reliable, worthy and capable. You will discover that he is deeply spiritual and dedicated." For his part, Father Tolton acknowledged the great gift of his Catholic faith and, despite bitter trials and turmoil, remained faithful to the teachings of the Church. He was a visionary who saw far beyond race and politics, looking inward—into the heart of the Church herself. He taught, "The Catholic Church deplores a double slavery—that of the mind and that of the body. She endeavors to free us of both.... She is the Church for our people."

The life of Father Tolton is a study in faithful obedience. When the Vatican assigned Father Tolton to serve as a missionary priest in the United States, where he was "a slave, an outcast, a hated black," he obeyed in faith. His was not the faith of blind obedience, like that of an automaton or domesticated animal, but a spirit of faith that, as a child of our Heavenly Father—in complete humility and generosity—he continually strove to discern and fulfill the will of God under the loving guidance and direction of the Holy Spirit. It is precisely *duc et altum*—into the void, the unknown—that Father Tolton received his mission to be a fisher of men.

The greatest legacy of Father Augustine Tolton does not lie in the fact that he was a pioneer, the first black American priest in the

United States. Yes, he was that—but he was so much more! Father Tolton loved and served the Lord with great fervor and intensity. He knew that God's love is so immense, its power so limitless, its embrace so tender and intimate, that Love Himself brings forth life. Father Tolton was a living testimony to God's creative, life-giving work.

Father Tolton serves as a role model for those who seek to be configured more perfectly to Christ. Amid great persecution, Father Tolton showed us that being configured to Christ means emptying ourselves so that God can fill us; it means exposing the weakest parts of who we are so that God can make us strong; it means becoming blind to the ways of this world so that Christ can lead us; it means dying to ourselves so that we can rise with Christ.

I pray that everyone…will be inspired by Father Augustine Tolton, who, guided by the Holy Spirit, became a living example of what it means to be fully alive in our Catholic faith.

VII. WE REMEMBER

with Poetry

GAME CALLED: BABE RUTH IS GONE

by Grantland Rice
August 17, 1948

His parents put George Herman Ruth, Jr., age seven, into a reform school-orphanage. They signed over custody to the Xaverian Brothers, the Jesuit Missionaries who ran the facility. Ruth spent the next twelve years there, never visited by relatives on Sundays or holidays. He was labeled "incorrigible," but one administrator, Brother Matthias, took a special interest in him, and provided the guidance and support the boy needed. Brother Matthias also discovered and nurtured Ruth's talent for baseball.

In 1914, Ruth, age nineteen, signed with the Boston Red Sox, where his boyish face led his teammates to nickname him "Babe." Grantland Rice once noted that during his entire career, Ruth was especially fond of his youngest fans, always making himself available to children seeking autographs at the ballpark, visiting orphanages and children's hospitals, and even sometimes paying children's doctor bills. He also did a lot to help the Xaverian Brothers and his alma mater.

During his career, mostly with the New York Yankees, Ruth set or tied seventy-six baseball records. His popularity is often credited with "saving" baseball after the Chicago "Black Sox" scandal of 1919. In 1920, the Yankees became the first team in history to draw more than one-million fans in a season, and Yankee Stadium became known as "the house that Ruth built." Ruth also drew standing-room-only crowds on the road.

After Ruth died in 1948, his body lay in state for two days at the entrance to Yankee Stadium. Hundreds of thousands of fans came to pay their respects. Rice rewrote a popular poem (originally published in 1910) into this eulogy.

"Some twenty years ago," said baseball writer Tommy Holmes, "I stopped talking about the Babe for the simple reason that I realized that those who had never seen him didn't believe me."

GAME CALLED

Game Called by darkness—let the curtain fall.
No more remembered thunder sweeps the field.
No more the ancient echoes hear the call
To one who wore so well both sword and shield:
The Big Guy's left us with the night to face
And there is no one who can take his place.

Game Called—and silence settles on the plain.
Where is the crash of ash against the sphere?
Where is the mighty music, the refrain
That once brought joy to every waiting ear?
The Big Guy's left us lonely in the dark
Forever waiting for the flaming spark.

Game Called—what more is there for us to say?
How dull and drab the field looks to the eye
For one who rules it in a golden day
Has waved his cap to bid us all good-bye.
The Big Guy's gone—by land or sea or foam
May the Great Umpire call him "safe at home."

QUID PRO QUO: ON LOSING A CHILD

by Paul Mariani
1996

There's a whole world in this brief, ironic exchange—one father to Another—about losing a child: anger and awe; desolate and holy places; signs and wonders.

QUID PRO QUO

Just after my wife's miscarriage (her second
in four months), I was sitting in an empty
classroom exchanging notes with my friend,
a budding Joyce scholar with steelrimmed
glasses, when, lapsed Irish Catholic that he was,
he surprised me by asking what I thought now
of God's ways toward man. It was spring,

such spring as came to the flintbacked Chenango
Valley thirty years ago, the full force of Siberia
behind each blast of wind. Once more my poor wife
was in the local four-room hospital, recovering.
The sun was going down, the room's pinewood panels
all but swallowing the gelid light, when, suddenly,
I surprised not only myself but my colleague

by raising my middle finger up to heaven, *quid
pro quo*, the hardly grand defiant gesture a variant
on Vanni Fucci's figs, shocking not only my friend
but in truth the gesture's perpetrator too. I was 24,
and, in spite of having pored over the *Confessions*
& that Catholic Tractate called the *Summa*, was sure
I'd seen enough of God's erstwhile ways toward man.

That summer, under a pulsing midnight sky
shimmering with Van Gogh stars, in a creaking,
cedarscented cabin off Lake George, having lied
to the gentrified owner of the boys' camp
that indeed I knew wilderness & lakes and could,
if need be, lead a whole fleet of canoes down
the turbulent whitewater passages of the Fulton Chain

(I who had last been in a rowboat with my parents
at the age of six), my wife and I made love, trying
not to disturb whosoever headboard & waterglass
lie just beyond the paperthin partition at our feet.
In the great black Adirondack stillness, as we lay
there on our sagging mattress, my wife & I gazed out
through the broken roof into a sky that seemed

somehow to look back down on us, and in that place,
that holy place, she must have conceived again,
for nine months later in a New York hospital she
brought forth a son, a little buddha-bellied
rumplestiltskin runt of a man who burned
to face the sun, the fact of his being there
both terrifying & lifting me at once, this son,

this gift, whom I still look upon with joy & awe, Worst,
best, just last year, this same son, grown
to manhood now, knelt before a marble altar to vow
everything he had to the same God I had had my own
erstwhile dealings with. How does one bargain
with a God like this, who, *quid pro quo,* ups
the ante each time He answers one sign with another?

HIS TOOLS, FOR MY FATHER

by Michael Fleming
October, 2004

Michael Fleming wrote this tribute to his father, Paul William Fleming, whose funeral was June 2, 2003, at St. Anthony's Church in Casper, Wyoming. Michael's poetic catalog of his father's "tools" reveals a dentist, a hunter, and a fisherman; a flutist and performer in local Gilbert and Sullivan productions; a husband and father with a messy workshop full of would-be "fix it" appliances (with all their useful parts missing); and the driver of a beat-up car that took him everywhere he needed to go.

But Michael's reflection is much more than a laundry list. Laid out with affectionate humor and gratitude for the life these "tools" represent, the list reveals both the love between father and son and the loss felt over the death of a simple, humble, optimistic dad.

At the funeral, Michael read passages from his father's favorite book, The Imitation of Christ *by Thomas à Kempis, which counsels readers "to take no account of oneself, but always to think well and highly of others." Michael said that striving to follow this advice led his father to "an absolutely triumphant life."*

HIS TOOLS, FOR MY FATHER

His instruments:
cunningly arrayed, the picks and probes, the nippers and syringes;
the darkroom, with its burgundy gloom and chemical tang; the treasure
chest; the spit sucker, connected to an ordinary vacuum cleaner down,
down in the crawl space, where he would dispatch me at night to open
its carapace and wring out the brainlike sponge inside, sopping
with the spit and blood and toothgrit of a thousand strangers.

His tackle:
the tangle of cowbells and leaders; treble hooks embedded in petrified
velveeta years after the last gingerly trip onto the ice; the stinking, slime-
crusted creel, flecked with the tiny mirrors of trout scales; the boat, battered
aluminum, the bailer roughly cut from a clorox bottle, the stubborn
outboard motor and its sock-scarred propeller, the paddle, the trolling
rods with black reels like spaceships; the net.

His guns:
the Savage .250, always cleaned, always oiled, and the scope, carefully
calibrated every September; the boxes of shells, brass casings with steel-
jacketed points fatal to antelope and deer and elk by the freezerful;
the pistol I shot just that one time; into a steaming heap of antelope
guts that bled what looked like mustard and stank of sage, while the dads
wiped their knives on their pants and laughed.

His woodshop:
ball-peen hammers, sewer snakes, keyhole saws, wire-strippers, friction
tape, files, rasps; the vise; the mighty Shopsmith with its screaming
blades, its motor that made the lights go brown; the rubber mallet ("General
Anesthetic"); the all-in-one solutions he was such a sucker for—pliers
with wrenches for grips, nests of screwdrivers, splays of allen keys like fingers;
the paint-spattered drill, the plastic packs of bits; all the useful sizes missing.

His flute:
the touch-burnished keys, lip-plate left with the brass impression
of his mouth that softly, gradually kissed away the silver from under
the embouchure hole, seventy years of school band, army band, city band,
orchestra, of weddings and funerals, of weekly rehearsals and Sunday
Mass, of Bach and Mozart and Sousa and Anon.; the case, an elegant blue-
velvet-lined coffin; and his piccolo: sweet miniature, a toy.

His car:
dented and scratched after decades of trips to the office, lumber yard, wild
goose chases; to Alcova, Pathfinder, Casper Mountain; to band practice, choir
practice, Gilbert & Sullivan; to Saint Anthony's, Fatima, Saint Pat's, the Knights
of Columbus, the ADA, the National Guard, the Lions and the Elks; to poker
and to Frosty's; and his keys, dangling from a souvenir keyring of a bank long
defunct, hanging next to so many other keys that don't open anything anymore.

TO MOTHER MARIANNE

by Robert Louis Stevenson
1896

Catholic students of the twentieth century heard the tale of "Father Damien, the leper priest" who served in Moloka'i and ultimately contracted leprosy. But few have heard of the nuns who also went to the Kingdom of Hawaii to care for victims of a disease that had terrified people from Biblical times down through the centuries. Now called Hansen's disease, its victims suffered a social stigma every bit as painful as its physical disfigurement and progressively disabling symptoms. Because the disease was thought to be highly contagious, and because there was no remedy, its victims were removed from their homes—many snatched as children by government officials—and sent to isolated islands to be quarantined until their death.

Mother Marianne Cope was one of the brave women who answered a call to help these patients. She was forty-five years old when a priest emissary wrote on behalf of the King and Queen to ask for her help managing hospitals and schools that served lepers in the Hawaiian Islands. On that day in 1883 when she received the letter, she was a Provincial Mother of the Sisters of St. Francis in Syracuse, New York. She had been a school teacher and principal and participated in the establishment of two of the first hospitals in the central New York area, one of which she was then serving as the head administrator.

The priest's plea touched her deeply, and she and six of her sisters went to work at the leprosy hospital in Kaka'ako. She soon founded a home inside the hospital grounds to care for healthy daughters born to the patients. Father Damien (now St. Damien) seemed in good health when they arrived, but by 1886 he was disfigured with the disease. Mother Marianne assured him that her sisters would carry on his work (which included running his home for males), especially for those with leprosy.

A new government later closed the hospital at Kaka'ako. Mother Marianne and her sisters accompanied the girls and women from there to Moloka'i in 1888. Father Damien died knowing that his work was in good hands.

Mother Marianne never contracted the disease and never returned to New York. She died in 1918 in Hawaii at age eighty. When she was beatified in 2005, many joyful Hawaiians attended the ceremony, and a Franciscan sister gave the Pope Benedict XVI the first lei of his papacy. She was beatified by the same pope on October 21, 2012, becoming the eleventh American saint.

Honolulu's 1988 centennial celebration of the Franciscan Mission at Moloka'i honored Mother Marianne, as Hawaiians had frequently done during her years of active service. In 1948, she was the first woman named to the Oneida County Hall of Fame in Utica, New York, and she was inducted into the National Women's Hall of Fame in Seneca Falls, New York, in 2005.

Her admirer, the famed Scottish poet Robert Louis Stevenson, remains one of the most translated writers in the world today, ranking ahead of his contemporaries Charles Dickens, Edgar Allen Poe, and Oscar Wilde. His widow wrote that while visiting Moloka'i in 1889 and seeing the sisters at their demanding work, Stevenson presented this poem to Mother Marianne before his departure.

TO MOTHER MARIANNE

To see the infinite pity of this place,
The mangled limb, the devastated face,
The innocent sufferer smiling at the rod—
A fool were tempted to deny his God.
He sees, he shrinks. But if he gaze again,
Lo, beauty springing from the breast of pain!
He marks the sisters on the mournful shores;
And even a fool is silent and adores.

TO KOŚCIUSZKO

by John Keats
December, 1816

The Continental Army, led by General George Washington, revered Thaddeus Kościuszko. Thomas Jefferson was one of his closest friends. In recognition of his dedicated service to America during the Revolutionary War, this Polish hero was brevetted by the Continental Congress to the rank of brigadier general and designated a naturalized citizen of the United States, so he could be recognized as an American hero too.

In 1798, on a return visit to America, Kościuszko drafted a will extraordinary for the era. The document authorized Jefferson to employ all of the money "in purchasing Negroes from among his own or any others and giving them Liberty in my name, in giving them an education in trades or otherwise and in having them instructed for their new condition in the duties of morality which may make them good neighbors, good fathers or mothers, husbands or wives and in their duties as citizens teaching them to be defenders of their Liberty and Country and of the good order of society and in whatsoever may make them happy and useful. ..."

Kościuszko was born in Poland on February 12, 1746. Taught in his early years by his mother and by the Piarist Fathers, he graduated in the first class of a new military academy in Warsaw. He went out into the world—as he wrote in a letter to a friend—with a belief that "the will of God is identical with character, justice, and the humanistic conduct of man."

After the wealthy father of his bride-to-be subverted their plans to elope, the heartbroken young man borrowed money to go abroad, seeing no opportunities to advance amid the political turmoil then in Poland. In 1776, he arrived on the shores of another land in great political upheaval: the American colonies.

But in that new place and time, Kościuszko was exactly what Gen-

eral Washington needed. The Polish volunteer possessed engineering and military skills that were sorely lacking among the farmers-turned-soldiers now fighting the highly trained British army. He distinguished himself on the battlefield in strategic planning and by impeding invasions. He built fortresses, repaired bridges, and designed ways to procure supplies. After Jefferson was elected president, Kościuszko wrote to congratulate him and suggested he establish an American military academy that would educate young men to love and defend democracy. Jefferson agreed, signing legislation to establish the United States Military Academy at West Point. A statue of Kościuszko stands on its grounds today.

By 1781, Kościuszko returned to his native land to help its army protect Poland's independence from Russia. He brought back from America, one biographer said, "a deepened love of freedom and democracy and the consciousness that even an undisciplined and ragged citizen army, if fired with zeal for a sacred cause, can win victories against a powerful nation." He continued fighting in various Polish revolts against Russian occupation. He was defeated as the leader of an uprising in 1794, imprisoned, and eventually freed to live the rest of his life in émigré communities throughout Europe.

On a later visit to America—which he called "my second country"—his friendship with then-Vice President Thomas Jefferson deepened. Jefferson wrote Major General Horatio Gates that: "I see him often and with great pleasure mixed with commiseration. He is as pure a son of liberty as I have ever known." During his visit in 1798, Kościuszko asked Jefferson's help in putting his will into proper English, and it was witnessed and signed.

He returned abroad, and was eventually exiled to Switzerland. Later in life, he enjoyed several happy weeks during a visit from the first woman he had ever loved (who had pleased her father by marrying a prince). He died shortly after.

At Kościuszko's request, a group of orphaned children led his funeral procession. His simple coffin was carried by six poor men to a Jesuit sanctuary. Within a few months, his body was moved to the Cathedral in Krakow to lie among the royalty of Polish history.

Jefferson wrote to the mutual friend who had informed him of Kościuszko's death: "To no country could that event be more afflicting nor

to any individual more than to myself. I had enjoyed his intimate friend-
ship and confidence for the last twenty years, and during the portion of
that time which he past in this country, I had daily opportunities of ob-
serving personally of his virtue. ..."

Referring to Kościuszko's will, the aging Jefferson added, "I am...
taking measures to have it placed in such hands as will ensure a faithful
discharge of his philanthropic views."

That faithful discharge of Kościuszko's desires was never realized.
After forty-five years of jurisdictional and legal challenges, the Supreme
Court finally awarded Kościuszko's American estate to his relatives in
Poland.

TO KOSCIUSKO
by John Keats

Good Kosciusko, thy great name alone
Is a full harvest whence to reap high feeling;
It comes upon us like the glorious pealing
Of the wide sphere—an everlasting tone.
And now it tells me, that in words unknown,
The names of heroes, burst from clouds concealing,
And changed to harmonies, for ever stealing
Through cloudless blue, and round each silver throne.
It tells me too, that on a happy day,
When some good spirit walks upon the earth,
Thy name with Alfred's, and the great of yore
Gently commingling, gives tremendous birth
To a loud hymn, that sounds far, far away
To where the great God lives for evermore.

ATONEMENT: JOYCE KILMER R. I. P.

by Aline Kilmer
1921

Aline Murray Kilmer was the daughter of poet Ada Foster Murray and the wife of poet Joyce Kilmer. Joyce and Aline's second child, Rose, contracted polio shortly after her birth in 1912. The couple turned to prayer for their paralyzed daughter and began to explore the Catholic faith at the Church of the Holy Innocents in New York City. They were received into the Church in 1913, the same year that Joyce's popular poem, "Trees," launched his writing career. In that era, Joyce became widely regarded as the poet laureate of the Catholic Church in America.

Within a few days after America entered World War I in 1917, Joyce enlisted in the Army. Before he was deployed, Rose died. Twelve days later, their fifth child, Christopher, was born.

Ten months later, Joyce was killed in action just two days before Aline's thirtieth birthday. He was thirty-one.

This widow's lament appeared in a collection of Aline Kilmer's poems, called Vigils, *published in 1921.*

ATONEMENT
by Aline Kilmer

When a storm comes up at night and the wind is crying,
    When the trees are moaning like masts on laboring ships,
I wake in fear and put out my hand to find you
    With your name on my lips.

No pain that the heart can hold is like to this one—
    To call, forgetting, into aching space,
To reach out confident hands and find beside you
    Only an empty place.

This should atone for the hours when I forget you.
    Take then my offering, clean and sharp and sweet,
An agony brighter than years of dull remembrance,
    I lay it at your feet.

TO PHILIP

by Daniel Berrigan, SJ

Eulogist Daniel Berrigan and his brother Philip were two of six sons born to working class, Irish-German parents in Minnesota. Philip served as an infantry and artillery officer in World War II, where he fought in the Battle of the Bulge. Discharged after the bombing of Japan, he entered college and later, seminary. He was ordained in 1955 as a priest of the Society of St. Joseph, an order formed during Reconstruction to serve African-Americans in the deep south. During his first assignment as a teacher in New Orleans, he became aware of a pervasive racism that damaged both its victims and its perpetrators.

Phillip began what was to become a lifelong commitment to activism. He marched for civil rights in the 1960s; he was the first Roman Catholic priest to be imprisoned for political reasons in the United States for his non-violent protests against the Vietnam War. In total, he would spend about eleven years of his life in prison.

He eventually left the priesthood and married Elizabeth McAlister. They had three children. He is the founder of the international Plowshares Movement for nuclear disarmament, and Jonah House, a sustainable community in Baltimore with a commitment to peace, where he and his wife lived until his death in 2002. He died at age seventy-nine, surrounded by friends and family, and is buried at Jonah House.

Daniel Berrigan, now eighty-nine-years old, has been a Jesuit priest since 1939. He joined his brother Philip and seven other Catholics who destroyed draft records in Catonsville, Maryland, in 1968, as a demonstration against the Vietnam War. Philip was sentenced to seven years for that activism; Daniel and the others served three years.

Father Berrigan has preferred to express his convictions as a writer in more than fifty published books. In 1972, his award-winning play, The Trial of the Catonsville Nine, *was turned into a film produced by*

Gregory Peck. The drama has been revived in recent years as a series of public readings by the Actors Gang, a non-profit arts group based in Los Angeles. After a star-studded opening in August of 2007, with actors Tim Robbins portraying Philip and Martin Sheen as Daniel, the new version has since been performed throughout America and Australia.

TO PHILIP
by Daniel Berrigan, SJ

Dimidium animae meae; the half
of my soul, Augustine wrote.

Death keep you intact, dear brother.
Death's finger cross your lips –
not a word, a syllable, a sigh
escape.
   I mourn,
I accede, the absolute
dictum; chafed bones,
skull put to silence, the slow
diurnal surrender of flesh to earth.

'Don't be,' your law of being
elsewhere. Your 'No,' a not to be –
absolute, unbribeable by tears.

Faith, a huge boulder, rolls
athwart the cave named (alas for lack) -
twilight, memory.

THE INNOCENTS: MARY SURRATT AND OTHERS

by Al Rocheleau

To those who knew her, Mary Surratt was a faithful and compassionate Catholic. But she is known to history as the first woman to be executed by the United States government.

Born in 1823 into an Anglican family, Mary attended a Catholic school in the Washington, D.C., area, where she was taught by the Daughters of Charity, the order founded by Elizabeth Ann Seton (see page 321). Mary converted to Catholicism sometime before she turned sixteen, when she met her husband-to-be John Surratt, who was then twenty-six years old.

They eventually married and had three children: Isaac, Elizabeth ("Anna"), and John, Jr. At age twenty-four, Mary was actively soliciting funds for the construction of a church in nearby Oxon Hill, Maryland. The cornerstone for St. Ignatius Catholic Church was laid in 1849. By the time the church was completed, John Surratt, Sr., was in debt, showing signs of alcoholism, and a fire had destroyed their home. To Mary's distress, her husband borrowed even more money to open a tavern.

As her husband's drinking grew worse, Mary became an innkeeper catering to wayside travelers. The Surratt Tavern was frequented by Union troops as a place to eat, and it served both North and South as a postal center. With the financial assistance of clergymen friends, the Surratt children went to Catholic schools, and their sometimes difficult son John, Jr. began his studies for the priesthood at age fifteen. He did well in the strict environment of the seminary, where he met a friend, Louis Weichmann.

When John, Sr., died in 1862, he left Mary deeply in debt. Young John quit the seminary and returned home. Mary leased the tavern to John Lloyd and moved her family to a Washington home, where she began taking in long-term residents. She also hoped the move would distance

John from what she suspected was his involvement in dangerous courier activity on behalf of the Confederacy.

By late 1864, John's seminary friend Louis Weichmann had moved into the Surratt House and was employed by the War Department. The two men were introduced to the celebrity actor John Wilkes Booth by Dr. Samuel Mudd. Historians have no doubt that John Surratt was part of Booth's early plan to kidnap President Lincoln, hoping to exchange him for Confederate POWs. But by April 12, 1865, Confederate General Lee surrendered to Ulysses Grant, and the war was nearly over.

President Lincoln was assassinated just two days later, on Good Friday. While historians may disagree on the extent of Mary's involvement in the events surrounding the assassination of President Lincoln, Mary's activities during Holy Week are of interest to Catholics, as they are either not mentioned or deemphasized in many books examining the case—even those advocating her innocence.

On Holy Thursday, April 13, Mary went to confession at St. Patrick's Catholic Church. The following morning, Mary and Lou Weichmann walked to St. Patrick's together to attend a Good Friday service. That evening—a little before the President was fatally shot in the Ford Theater—Mary and her boarder Eliza Holohan were walking to church, but the weather became so bad that they turned back and went home. At 2:30 a.m. detectives woke everyone at the Surratt House to search for John Surratt and John Wilkes Booth. The police believed that it was John Surratt who had attacked Secretary of State William Seward at his home, while Booth took the life of the President in the theater. Mrs. Surratt told the detectives that John was away. For two weeks she had been receiving letters from him; the one she received that day had come from Canada.

By Easter Monday all the men from the Surratt boarding house were in custody, and the authorities came to arrest Mary. John T. Ford, the theater owner, and all of his employees had also been incarcerated.

Most histories examining Mary Surratt's case have focused on various miscarriages of justice, including both legal and law enforcement procedures that were carried out in an atmosphere of grief, fear, vindictiveness, and fury over both Booth and John Surratt evading capture. One of those arrested was John Lloyd, who leased Mary's tavern. When

Lloyd refused to implicate her, he was hanged by his thumbs. Later in prison, Lloyd told John Ford that he had perjured himself against his landlady because of the torture. His testimony did much to build the case against Mary Surratt.

Also in prison, Louis Weichmann told John Ford that "Mrs. Surratt was an exemplary Christian woman. To him she had fully filled the place of mother, and in every relation of life she was eminently a consistent, pious lady." But Weichmann was soon intimidated. After placing a rope around Weichmann's neck, Secretary of War Edwin Stanton told him that if he didn't testify as the government wished, he would be hanged. Weichmann's trial testimony for the prosecution put sinister implications on what he knew were Mrs. Surratt's innocent activities.

On April 26, Booth was shot and killed, and Dr. Samuel Mudd, who had treated Booth's broken leg when he had been a fugitive, was arrested.

Mary was named, along with Dr. Mudd, as two of eighteen alleged co-conspirators in the assassination of Abraham Lincoln. They faced a military trial in which military officers acted as judge and jury. Designed for a speedy inquisition of the enemy during wartime, such trials do not satisfy most protections (presumed innocence, due process, etc.) guaranteed by the U. S. Bill of Rights.

After Mary was judged guilty, an Army colonel questioned her pastor, Father Jacob A. Walter, about his public statements that Mrs. Surratt was innocent. The priest concluded he would have to remain silent if he wanted to administer sacraments to her. Many historians believe that Mrs. Surratt was charged in hopes that putting her on trial would flush John out of hiding, that to save his mother he would admit his part in the conspiracy. This did not happen.

Lewis Powell (aka Payne), a friend who sometimes came to the Surratt House to see John, was charged with the attack on Seward, found guilty, and sentenced to death. The night before the execution, Powell declared Mrs. Surratt innocent, saying his testimony was largely responsible for her persecution, and that he would gladly suffer death twice if it would save her from hanging.

Mrs. Surratt was alone in her cell when told that she was to be *hanged the next day. On the morning of her execution, Father Walter heard her confession and—convinced of her innocence—rushed with Anna Surratt to the White House to see President Andrew Johnson. In a final attempt to save Mary from the gallows, former Pennsylvania Congressman Thomas Florence, John Ford (now freed), and Mrs. Stephen A. Douglas (wife of the man who had run against Lincoln for the presidency), joined their plea for clemency. But the president refused to become involved.*

Defeated, Father Walter returned to prison to administer Holy Communion to Mrs. Surratt. Spent and barely articulate, she asked her friend John Holohan, "Please stay with Annie today. God knows I am innocent but for some cause, I must suffer today. Goodbye. God bless you." Her final request was that, someday after passions had cooled, attempts be made to clear her name. While an absolute answer to her innocence or guilt cannot be determined, most historians agree that her trial was a miscarriage of justice.

At the gallows, facing his own imminent death, Powell again pleaded for Mary: "She does not deserve to die with us." Father Walter accompanied her to the hanging platform, and stayed until she and the three others who had been found guilty were hanged.

Anna later begged for the body of her mother so that she could bury it properly. Almost four years later, President Johnson finally allowed the remains to be taken from the penitentiary grounds to Mt. Olivet Cemetery in Washington, D.C.

John Surratt, Jr. evaded capture by going abroad. Two years later, he was arrested in Egypt and extradited to the United States to stand trial for treason. The jury did not reach a verdict. Further delays exceeded the statute of limitations pertaining to extradition, and John was eventually freed.

Louis Weichmann spent most of the rest of his life begging favors from the trial judge and War Secretary Edwin Stanton. He wrote a book about the trial, attempting to vindicate himself, but out of fear for his life it was not published until after his death.

Dr. Mudd's defending attorney at the trial was the highly respected Thomas Ewing, step-father of General William T. Sherman (see page

55). Mudd was spared hanging but spent seven years in jail.

In 1891, in a presentation before the United States Catholic His-torical Society, Father Walter reflected on the unlikelihood of a devout Catholic woman going to confession on Holy Thursday and being com-plicit in a murder on Good Friday. He testified that Mary Surratt's last statement to him was, "I am innocent," and that, "These words were ut-tered whilst she stood on the verge of eternity, and were the last confession of an innocent woman."

Anna died at age sixty-one. She is buried beside her mother. She spent the rest of her life trying to clear her mother's name.

Even today, legislators see no advantage in reopening a case per-taining to the murder of America's most beloved president. The govern-ment in Washington finds no reason to question if justice was served by hanging Mary Surratt. Hollywood, however, does.

At this writing, Robert Redford is coproducing and directing a film in Savannah, Georgia, tentatively titled The Conspirator. *Robin Wright Penn is cast as Mary Surratt, and Kevin Kline plays Secretary of War Stanton (rumored to be the screenplay's villain). Advisors to the production include James McPherson, a Pulitzer-Prize-winning Civil War historian, and Thomas Turner and U. S. Army regimental historian Colonel Fred Borch, both Lincoln assassination experts. The project is af-filiated with* The American Film Company, *whose CEO has said that "Mary Surratt's trial is a powerful, relevant story."*

THE INNOCENTS: MARY SURRATT AND OTHERS
by Al Rocheleau

Mary Surratt
guilty of innkeeping
fell
like a hundred pounds of millet

through a hole in the
universe,
her parlor undusted
in July heat

> as the fight for Lincoln's body
> raged in Springfield
> and Mary Todd's
> clairvoyant saw pigeons
> roosting in a fat eave,
> which meant to Mary

> it was right to grieve
> it was right to grieve

and while Samuel Mudd
boarded a skiff
for the ride to
Tortuga,
catching a nail on his striped sleeve

> Edwin Booth
> dodged rocks and turnips
> on a Baltimore street
> thinking of Lear, Prospero,
> the Fates, and Corinth

> under seige.

VII. WE REMEMBER
the Unknown Child

RESTORING DIGNITY
TO ABANDONED CHILDREN:
REST IN HIS ARMS

In August, 2005, Susan Walker came upon a story tucked away in the back of the *Chicago Tribune*: A baby had been found dead in a landfill in Grayslake, Illinois. While her twenty-month-old daughter, Gracie, played at her feet, Walker felt suddenly sickened—the child had literally been thrown in the trash.

She clipped the article out of the newspaper and carried it around with her for days. She felt God leading her, but she wasn't sure what she was to do. Finally, it became clear: The dead baby needed a proper burial. He deserved a proper burial. Even if his family had forgotten him, there needed to be at least one person in the world who had not.

Walker called the Lake County coroner's office, which referred her to the sheriff's department. The way she tells it, she's not even certain of the words that came out of her mouth, but "I was convinced everyone thought I was nuts." She asked if she could give the dead child a Christian funeral. Not having heard such a request before, the sheriff's department found the request suspicious and investigated her to make certain she wasn't the child's mother.

Eventually though, the child's body was released for burial. Feeling that naming the child restored a large portion of the dignity that had been stolen from him, Walker named him Baby Michael Gerard.

Walker helped arrange the infant's funeral with the help of Kathy Needham and other newfound friends at the coroner's office. To her surprise, although there had been only a small notice in the suburban newspaper, along with a few email announcements that Walker sent to family and friends, nearly one-hundred people came to the funeral. It was then she knew her calling, she says: "From that point on, everything came together too easily for this endeavor to be anything other than divinely inspired."

Shortly after the funeral, Walker learned of two other abandoned children who deserved the same consideration that she and a hundred others had shown to Baby Michael Gerard. It was as if she were suddenly aware of a great injustice that needed to be made right. If she wouldn't recognize these forsaken lives, given up and sometimes murdered by the very people who had brought them into the world, who would?

That fall, Walker and another like-minded mother, Judi Seguy, founded Rest in His Arms. It was incorporated as a 501c3 non-profit in February, 2006. Walker says this work has made her "a spiritual mother to eighteen little angels" over the past five years.

According to its mission statement, Rest in His Arms proclaims, "These children are precious—even if they only lived for one minute." Volunteers make all the arrangements, including a priest, flowers, and music as part of a funeral Mass, and they host each service. Every funeral is open to other concerned persons who wish to pay their respects.

Their work also relies upon the generosity of countless others. Father Pat Pollard, Pastor of Christ the King Parish and Priest Director of Catholic Cemeteries, was a force behind The Archdiocese of Chicago and Catholic Cemeteries' donation of forty-eight cemetery plots at All Saints Cemetery in Des Plaines, Illinois. This donation allows all of the unknown children to be buried side by side, each with his or her own headstone, ending the county's former practice of burying them in a potter's field with the unclaimed bodies of adults.

Another mom whom Walker met online hand-sews and donates all of the burial gowns. Other moms have donated baby blankets, booties, teddy bears, and child-sized rosaries.

Bevel Granite Company, Inc., in Merrionette Park, Illinois, donated all past, present, and future monuments—even cutting an identical design into each headstone so the graves can be easily identified. Glueckert's Funeral Home in Arlington Heights and Strang's Funeral Home in Grayslake are also significant donors. The Worsham Mortuary School in Wheeling has helped to prepare children's bodies for burial at no cost, and its students serve as pallbearers. The Knights of Columbus always provide the color guard. A brief homily at each funeral is offered by Father Dennis Conway, MCCJ, or Father Steve Dombrowski, such as the following:

> *We are here today because this is our child. Although abandoned by her biological parents, she has been claimed by us as ours. It is important to show the world that all life has value; we believe it and so we profess it by our presence.*

> *God didn't have to make this little one. He was under no obligation whatsoever. And He knew exactly what He would get if He did decide to create her. With that knowledge and freedom, God decided that His world and His life would be better if this little one was part of it. [She] had a very short earthly life, but God granted her an eternal spirit and so this little one will live on forever with God, which is what God's dream was all about anyway.*

Still, Rest in His Arms hopes to go out of business eventually —Walker and the other board members (Judi Seguy, Deacon Jim Pauwels, and Rosalyn Popham) look forward to a day when their services are no longer needed because no more children are abandoned.

Toward this goal, the organization has teamed with the Save Abandoned Babies Foundation to build awareness of the Illinois Abandoned Newborn Infant Protection Act. Often referred to as "the Safe Haven Law," it allows parents to leave infants up to thirty days old with the staff at any fire or police station, hospital, or emergency medical center. Provided that the child has not been harmed, parents cannot be prosecuted for abandonment and no questions will be asked. Despite this law, approximately twenty babies are still illegally abandoned each year in Illinois.

While there are a few similar groups elsewhere in the country, Rest in His Arms is trying to discern if it might have a role in other states. Meanwhile, Walker believes the future of her organization may lie in helping bury deceased children whose parents cannot afford funeral and burial expenses.

"It's important to remember all of these children," Walker says, "not only for their dignity, but for our own, as Catholics and as Americans." Each child is commemorated yearly on the anniversary of his or her death, at a Mass in St. Edna Catholic Church in Arlington Heights, Illinois. When the date of death is unknown—as it was for Baby Michael Gerard—Mass is said on the date the child's body was discovered.

These children are:

Child	Death Date
Baby Rosa	01/12/02
Baby Theresa Anne	01/15/06
Child Joseph "The Naperville Boy"	03/19/05
Baby Gabriel	03/21/08
Baby Thomas	04/01/08
Baby Andreas	06/22/08
Baby Morales	07/10/05
Baby Jasmine	07/10/08
Baby Jalin	07/10/08
Baby Kinzie Marie	07/21/06
Baby Johnita Monique	08/04/07
Baby Michael Gerard	08/16/05
Baby David	08/26/01
Baby Lexi Elizabeth	09/13/06
Baby Hope	10/26/06
Baby Angel	12/01/07
Baby Ajanni	12/26/08
Child Vansh Kumar	12/30/07

NOTES

Introduction

p. 16 (first full paragraph) Hennesy, James J., *American Catholics: A History of the Roman Catholic Community in the United States*, (New York 1981), p. 191, cited in Valenti, Patricia Dunlavy, *To Myself a Stranger: A Biography of Rose Hawthorne Lathrop*, (Louisiana State University Press, Baton Rouge, Louisiana: 1991) p. 123.

p. 16 (fourth paragraph) www.stratfordhall.org./learn/teacher/medicine.php.

p. 16 (first full paragraph) www.digitalhistory.uh.edu/historyonline/usdeath.

p. 17 (first paragraph) "At Joyce Kilmer's Grave in France; Comrade of *New York Times* Staff Describes Visit to Poet-Soldier's Last Resting Place," *The New York Times*, August 25, 1918.

The Happiest Man on Earth: Chaplain Mychal Judge, NYFD

p. 23 (first paragraph) www.september11news.com.

An American Original: Mother Katharine Drexel

p. 33 (third paragraph) Sisters of Blessed Sacrament. Annals, 3-16, as quoted in *Katharine Drexel: A Biography*, by Sister Consuela Marie Duffy, S. B. S. (Mother Katharine Drexel Guild: The Sisters of the Blessed Sacrament, Cornwells Heights, PA 19020, 2nd printing 1972).

p. 34 (fifth full paragraph) Burton, Katherine. *The Golden Door: The Life of Katharine Drexel* (P. J. Kenedy & Sons, New York, 1957).

A Hero's Last March: General William Tecumseh Sherman

p. 44 (second full paragraph) Hirshson, Stanley P. *The White Tecumseh: A Biography of William T. Sherman* (John Wiley & Sons, Inc., New York, 1997). pp. 386-7.

Biographical material cited in the preface comes from the Notre Dame University collection of Sherman papers and the following sources:

- Sherman, W. T. *The Memoirs of General W. T. Sherman*, by William Tecumseh Sherman. (Library of America, October 1, 1990);

- Winik, Jay. *April 1865: The Month That Saved America*. (Harper Perennial by HarperCollins Publishers, 2001);

- Lewis, Lloyd, *Sherman: Fighting Prophet*. (Harcourt Brace and Company, New York, 1932, 1958 Edition)

- Marszalek, John F. *Sherman: A Soldiers' Passion for Order*. (The Free Press, 1993).

The "Opposing General's" Valor: President John Fitzgerald Kennedy

p. 51 (third paragraph) Noonan, Peggy, "The Reagans and the Kennedys," (*Wall Street Journal*, August 29-30, 2009).

A Saint for Our Age: Dorothy Day

p. 57 Many websites advocate the canonization of Dorothy Day. For a prayer for her canonization, see www.dorothydayguild.org.

A Eulogy to Whitefeather of the Ojibway: Larry Cloud-Morgan

p. 71 An expansion on material in the preface can be found at www.whitefeatherpeace.org.

Remembering Pup: William F. Buckley, Jr.

p. 85 (third paragraph) Ponte, Lowell, "Memories of William F. Buckley, Jr." (Newsmax: 02-28-2008).

p. 86 (first paragraph) Tanenhaus, Sam, "On William F. Buckley, Jr." Paper Cuts blog at www.newyorktimes.com, 2/27/08.

p. 86 (first full paragraph) Buckley, William F. Jr. "My Smoking Confessional" (United Press Syndicated: 12/ 3/07).

Coming Home to St. Pat's: Rosemary Clooney

pp. 125-6 Carol DeChant is indebted to www.rosemaryclooney.com for biographical information.

What You Can Expect from the Son of a Bookmaker: Wellington T. Mara

p. 129 (first paragraph) Myers, Gary. "New York Giants Co-Owner John Mara Remembers the Stadium His Father Built in the Meadowlands." The New York *Daily News*. December 27, 2009.

p. 129 (first paragraph) Goldstein, Richard. "Wellington Mara, the Patriarch of the NFL, Dies at 89." *The New York Times*. October 26, 2005.

p. 129 (second paragraph) "Wellington T. Mara (1916-2005)." www.giants.com.

p. 130 (first paragraph) Burke, Monte. "Influential Football Owner Wellington Mara Dies." www.forbes.com. October 25, 2005.

Eulogy for a Baby Who Dies After Baptism

p. 137 (second paragraph) Lynch, Thomas *The Undertaking: Life Studies of the Dismal Trade* (W. W. Norton & Company; reprint edition, June 22, 2009).

The Cardinal's Epistle to the Jews: John Cardinal O'Connor

p. 169 (second paragraph) Boys, Mary C. "Does the Catholic Church Have a Mission 'with' Jews or 'to' Jews?" (Studies in Christian-Jewish Relations, Vol 3, 2008) http://escholarship.bd.edu/scjr/vol 3

p. 169 (fourth paragraph) Jacobson, Kenneth "Pope John Paul II: An Appreciation: A Visionary Remembered" (2 April, 2005, ADL)

Remembering My Friend Tim Russert

p. 165 For more about Tim Russert's Catholic activities, go to www.catholicnews.com/data/stories/cns/0803173.htm.

Eulogy for Andy Warhol

p. 183 Professor of Religious Studies cited in preface to eulogy is Cliff Edwards, whose article appeared in *Christian Century*, March 10, 1999.

Danny's Promise: In Memory of Danny Thomas

p. 188 (first full paragraph) Historical material in the preface is taken from the autobiography, *Make Room for Danny* by Danny Thomas with Bill Davidson pp. 40, 78, 203-205, and 300. (G. P. Putnam's Sons, New York, 1991).

p. 188 (second paragraph) *From His Promise: The Story of St Jude Children's Research Hospital & American Lebanese Syrian Associated Charities. In Memory of Danny Thomas.* Afterword, p. 206. Written and compiled by Palmer Thomason Jones. Editor and publisher Randall Bedwell. (Guild Bindery Press, Inc., Memphis TN, 1996).

p. 188 (second full paragraph) See "Quick Facts about St. Jude" at www.stjude.org.

p. 189 (second full paragraph) Thomas, *op. cit.*, Danny's autobiography tells that this phrase signaled a promise from his children: When they said "honor bright" it meant they were telling the absolute truth—no little white lies permitted. p. 175.

The Angels of Patricia Neal

p. 191 (third paragraph) "Actress Patricia Neal Died Sunday at 84," *The Martha's Vineyard Times* (August 11, 2010).

Wit and Wisdom on the Refrigerator Door: Erma Bombeck

p. 209 (second paragraph) Quoted by Palmatary, Donna, in "For the Love of Erma," *St. Anthony Messenger* (January, 2001).

p. 210 (first full paragraph) Martin, Donna and McDermott, Alan, in *Foreword to Forever Erma: Best-Loved Writing from America's Favorite Humorist* (Andrews & McMeel, Kansas City: Missouri 1996).

The Invisible Artist: Sculptor Frederick Hart

p. 217 (first paragraph) Smith, Edward C., from "Couriers of the Spirit: Frederick Hart's Daughters of Odessa," 1998, cited in *Frederick Hart: Changing Tides*, Mary Yakush, Ed. (Hudson Hills Press: New York and Manchester, Vermont, 2005) p. 57.

p. 217 (first paragraph) At the presentation of the cross to the Holy Father, May 17, 1997, *op. cit.*, p. 84.

p. 217 (first paragraph) Bergman, Ingmar, in the Introduction to *Four Screenplays by Ingmar Bergman*, (Simon & Schuster, 1960). Bergman himself was a person of no faith, who eschewed the usual labels for that mindset. The son of a Lutheran minister, he has often been quoted as saying, "I hope I never get so old I get religious."

p. 217 (third paragraph) Smith, *op. cit.*, p. 58.

p. 217 (third paragraph) Hart, Frederick. Late 1980s. *op. cit.*, p. 71.

p. 218 (first paragraph) *ibid.*, Hart explaining his subtitle *Martyrs of Modernism* to his *Daughters of Odessa*, a tribute in bronze to the innocent victims of war and repression of the twentieth century, p. 54.

p. 218 (third paragraph) Lufkin, Martha "Moral rights; a US case history," *The Art Newspaper, International Edition*, April, 1998, cited in *Frederick Hart: Changing Tides, op. cit.*, pp. 86-7.

p. 218 (fourth paragraph) Hart, in 1989. *Frederick Hart: Changing Tides, op. cit.*, p. 183.

p. 218 (fifth paragraph) Wolfe's many books include the novel *Bonfire of the Vanities* and *The Right Stuff*, a character study of America's test pilots and astronauts during the mid-twentieth century.

p. 218 (fifth) Bergman, Ingmar, *op. cit.*

Servant of Incurable Cancer Patients: Rose Hawthorne Lathrop

p. 231 (third paragraph) Valenti, Patricia Dunlavy, *To Myself A Stranger: A Biography of Rose Hawthorne Lathrop*, pp. 100-102 (Louisiana State University Press: 1991).

p. 231 (fourth paragraph) Hapenney, Alberta, *A Legacy of Love: A Biography of Rose Hawthorne Lathrop in Three Parts*, Dorrance Publishing Co., Inc., Pittsburgh, Pennsylvania: 1999.

p. 232 (first paragraph) "Rose who had long been...cancer) Three of Mother Alphonsa's biographers had access to the vast Hawthorne-Lathrop families' correspondence in her order's archives, yet emphasize different reasons for the separation. Theodore Maynard (*A Fire Was Lighted: The Life of Rose Hawthorne Lathrop*, The Bruce Publishing Company, Milwaukee: 1948, pp. 250-251) speculated that George's drinking was a big factor; Hapenney, (*op. cit.*, p. 56) calls it George's "alcoholism." Valenti (*op. cit.*, pp. 147-8) claims that his alcoholism was never substantiated, and seems doubtful. All agree that the couple's basic incompatibility was the central problem.

In a letter, Rose wrote that she moved out to lead a religious life; in another letter written during an earlier separation, she said that she had no plans to divorce. Obviously, she had discussed matters with her spiritual advisor: she asked for and received the sanction of the Church for this separation.

p. 232 (first full paragraph) www.hawthorne-dominicans.org.

p. 232 (second full paragraph) www.miningswindles.com/html/julian_hawthorne.html.

p. 232 (second full paragraph) Valenti, *op. cit.*, p. 176.

The Angel of AA: Sister Mary Ignatia

p. 260 (third full paragraph) Darrah, Mary C., *Sister Ignatia: Angel of Alcoholics Anonymous*, 2nd Ed. (Hazelden, Center City, MN: 2001)

p. 261 (first full paragraph) Anonymous recovering alcoholic priest, cited in Darrah, *op. cit.*, p. 229 in interview with the author, July 15, 1985.

p. 273 (first full paragraph) Edward Dowling, S. J. at the 1953 Clergy Conference, in Darrah, *op. cit.*, p. 211. (Father Dowling was not an alcoholic, but in ministering to them he became convinced that AA offered the only hope for them.)

p. 261 (third full paragraph) Fisher, Ed. WJW-AM, April, 4 1966.

p. 262 (first paragraph) Tape recorded oral history of Dan K., Alcoholics Anonymous Archives, New York, NY, in Darrah, *op. cit.*, p. 145.

Thank God for the Life of Elly Chovel!

p. 271 (second paragraph) "About Us" and "History" www.pedropan.org.

p. 271 (third paragraph) Fields-Meyer, Thomas, "To Cuba, With Love," *People* magazine, February 09, 1998. Vol 49. No. 5.

p. 271 (third paragraph) Yanez, Luisa, "Pedro Pan was Born of Fear, Human Instinct to Protect Children," (*The Miami Herald*) May 16, 2009, (incorporating a correction by Elly Chovel daughter Brigid Prio).

p. 271 (fourth paragraph). "Who We Are," Catholic Charities of the Archdiocese of Miami, Inc.

p. 272 (first paragraph) www.catholiccharitiesadm.org/who_we_are.htm.

p. 272 (first paragraph) www.pedropan.org, *op. cit.*

p. 272 (second full paragraph) Yanez, *op. cit.*

p. 272 (third paragraph) Fields-Meyer, Thomas, *op. cit.*

In the Irish Tradition: Daniel Patrick Moynihan

p. 275 (third paragraph) Hodgson, Godfrey. *The Gentleman from New York: Daniel Patrick Moynihan, A Biography*, p. 20. (Houghton Mifflin Company, Boston. New York, 2000).

p. 275 (fourth paragraph) *ibid.*, p. 31.

p. 276 (first paragraph) *ibid.*, pp. 99-100.

p. 276 (first full paragraph) Faxx, Israel. "Pope Apologizes to Jews." Electronic World Communications Inc. 2002. *HighBeam Research.* 18 November 2009. http://www.highbeam.com.

p. 276 (second full paragraph) cited in Mark Feeney, *Globe.* "Daniel Patrick Moynihan, 76, Leading Intellect of U.S. Politics." *The Boston Globe* (Boston, MA). McClatchy-Tribune Information Services. 2003. *HighBeam Research.* 4 Nov. 2009 http://www.highbeam.com.

p. 276 (second full paragraph) http://townhall.com/columnists/GeorgeWill/2003/03/27/pat_moynihan,_rip.

p. 276 (third full paragraph) James Q. Wilson, quoted in Hodgson, *op. cit.*, p. 404.

The Poster Boy for Hope: Ron Santo

p. 305, Biographical material from Sherman, Ed. "Ron Santo Dead at 70," *Crain's Chicago Business*, posted 12/3/2010 at www.chicagobusiness.comsection/blogs.

Elizabeth Ann Seton Is the First Wholly American Saint!

p. 310 (first full paragraph) "Visioning for the Mission Unites the Daughters of Charity" paper, January 13, 2010, Sister Claire Debes, D. C., Provincial Superior, Emmitsburg, MD.

Fixed and Solid, Holding a True Position: Robert F. Griffin, CSC

p. 315 (fourth paragraph) Memories of Father Griff shared by Michael Molinelli '82 and Reverend James Tunstead Burtchaell, C.S.C., in *Notre Dame Magazine*, Winter 1999-2000 issue.

One Witness, Pointing: Mary K. Meyer

p. 321 Material taken from an interview with Mary K. Meyer by Michael Humphrey, and a eulogy by Brad Grabs at www.kcolivebranch.org.

From Slave to Priest: Father Augustine Tolton

p. 327 (second paragraph) Hemesath, Caroline, SSF *From Slave to Priest: A Biography of the Reverend Augustine Tolton (1854-1897) First Black American Priest of the United States* p. 39. (Ignatius Press: San Francisco 2006).

Father Tolton's African heritage from both parents is the basis of Caroline Hemesath's claim that he was the first "black" priest in America. Her preface to the 1973 edition of his biography distinguishes between his full-blooded ancestry and that of three mixed-blood sons of an Irishman with an African woman who became Catholic priests, also in that era. One of them was ordained in the year of Father Tolton's birth, and later named bishop of Portland, Maine. pp. 13-15.

p. 327 (third paragraph) *ibid.*, p. 51.

p. 329 (second paragraph) *ibid.*, p. 166.

p. 329 (second paragraph) Zimmerman, Father A., SVD, in *The Beginning of an Era* cited in Hemesath, *ibid.*

p. 329 (sixth paragraph) www.stelizabethchicago.org.

Game Called: Babe Ruth Is Gone

p. 335 (first paragraph) http://www.baberuth.com/about/biography.html.

p. 335 (second paragraph) *The Babe Ruth Times* "The Babe is Born," http://xroads.virginia.edu/%7EUG02/yeung/Baberuth/born.html.

p. 335 (third paragraph) *The Babe Ruth Times, op. cit.,* "A Hero to Save the Game."

p. 335 (fourth paragraph) *ibid.,* "The Babe is Born."

p. 335 (fifth paragraph) Smith, Phyllis W. quoting Tommy Holmes in *Red Smith on Baseball: The Game's Greatest Writer on the Game's Greatest Years* (Ivan R. Dee Publishers, Chicago, IL, 2000).

To Mother Marianne

p. 346 (second paragraph) www.blessedmariannecope.org.

p. 346 (fourth paragraph) Index Translationum, UNESCO database.

p. 346 (fourth paragraph) Stevenson, Mrs. R. L., *The Cruise of the Janet Nichol Among the South Sea Islands* (Chatto & Windus London: 1915).

To Kościuszko

p. 349 (second paragraph) "Armstrong v. Lear, Administrator of
Kościuszko," in Henry Wheaton, ed., *Reports of Cases Argued and
Adjudged in the Supreme Court of the United States, in January Term, 1827,*
(Rochester, NY: Lawyer's Co-operative Publishing Company, 1918), Vol.
12, 590, cited by Pula, James S. in *Thaddeus Kościuszko: The Purest Son of
Liberty* (Hippocrene Books, New York, 1999).

p. 349 (second paragraph) In a letter to Prince Adam Kazimierz
Czartoryski, quoted by Józef Żuraw, in *Tadeusz Kościuszko—The Polish
Enlightenment Thinker,* cited by Pula, *op. cit.*

p. 350 (first full paragraph) Mizwa, Stephen P. "Tadeusz Kościuszko," in
Great Men and Women of Poland (New York: Macmillan Company, 1942),
Pula, *op. cit.*

p. 350 (second full paragraph) Jefferson to Gates, February 28, 1798,
Jefferson Papers, Library of Congress, Pula, *op. cit.*

p. 351 (first full paragraph) Jefferson to Francis Zeltner, July 23, 1818,
in Haiman, Mieczyslaw, Jefferson: Leader and Exile, (New York: Polish
Institute of Arts and Sciences in America, 1946), Pula, *op. cit.*

p. 351 (second full paragraph) From *Friends of Liberty,* by Graham
Russell, Gao Hodges and Gary Nash. (Basic Books, 2008) cited in "Why
We Should All Regret Jefferson's Broken Promise to Kościuszko," at
www.hnn.us/articles/48794.html.

p. 351 (Keat's poem) English poet John Keats has written a Petrarchan
sonnet, with an intricate rhyme scheme: ABBAABBACDEDCE. He
was one of several prominent poets of his era who wrote tributes to
Kościusko. Poem is at www.bartleby.com/126/29.html.

Atonement: Joyce Kilmer, R.I.P.

p. 353 The sequence of events in the Kilmers' life and careers is from
John Hillis, in *Joyce Kilmer: A Bio-Biography.* Master of Science (Library
Science) Thesis. (Catholic University of America. Washington, DC)
cited by Robert Cortes Halliday, Editor, in *Joyce Kilmer: Poems, Essays and
Letters, 2 Volumes* (George H. Doran Company, New York, 1918), both on
www.wikipedia.com.

To Philip

p. 355 (third paragraph) Berrigan, Jerome "Philip Berrigan and the Plowshares Movement," December 9, 2004. www.jonahhouse.org/phil. htm.

p. 355 (fourth paragraph) "Profile: Fr. Daniel Berrigan, S.J." Printed in *Here and Abroad*, (New York, Province of the Society of Jesus, May, 2004) www.jonahhouse.org/danProfile.htm.

p. 356 (first paragraph) www.theactorsgang.com/news/news73.htm.

The Innocents: Mary Surratt and Others

p. 357 (third paragraph) Trindal, Elizabeth Steger, *Mary Surratt: An American Tragedy* (Pelican Publishing Company: Gretna, Louisiana: 1996) p. 29.

p. 358 (first full paragraph) Weichmann, Louis, J. *The True History of the Assassination of Abraham Lincoln and of the Conspiracy of 1865* (New York: Alfred A. Knopf, Inc., 1975) p. 25, in Trindal, *op. cit.*, p. 86.

p. 358 (second full paragraph) DeWitt, David Miller *The Judicial Murder of Mary E. Surratt*, an 1894 book, thoroughly examines the trial, pointing out that it was unconstitutional, illegal, that evidence was suppressed and witnesses bought, and concluding that Mrs. Surratt's execution was "the foulest blot on [America's] history." DeWitt never uses the word "Catholic" in his entire book, even in the one brief paragraph about priests' testimony affirming her character as "a lady and a Christian." (Newer edition by Bibliolife, Charleston, South Carolina, which reprints books in the public domain.) Perhaps what seems to be an obvious avoidance of acknowledging Mrs. Surratt as Catholic by this advocate was his nod to the anti-Catholic "Know Nothing" party sentiment. Although that movement had split over slavery, the animosity towards Catholics remained, and was reorganized in the year of the trial by six Confederate veterans into the Ku Klux Klan. Initially, it's goal was to terrorize freed African-Americans, but the KKK eventually broadened its focus to include terrorizing Catholics and Jews also.

p. 358 (third full paragraph) Trindal, *op. cit.*, p. 116.

p. 358 (third full paragraph) *ibid.*, p. 117-121.

p. 358 (third full paragraph) *ibid.*, *The Trial of John H. Surratt in the Criminal Court for the District of Columbia*, (Washington, DC: Government Printing Office, 1867) p. 698, testimony of [Detective] John

Clarvoe, in Trindal, p. 120.

p. 358 (fourth full paragraph) DeWitt, *op. cit.*, p. 8.

p. 359 (first paragraph) Barbee, David Rankin, "The Murder of Mrs. Surratt," a paper presented at the Emerson Institute, 25 February 1950. The David Rankin Barbee Collection, Georgetown University Library, Washington, DC, in Trindal, *op. cit.*, p. 133.

p. 359 (first full paragraph) *ibid.*, p. 17, in Trindal, *op. cit.*, p. 139.

p. 359 (third full paragraph) Dewitt, *op. cit.*, p. 35. Jefferson Davis, President of the Confederate States of America. was one of those named as co-conspirator.

p. 359 (fourth full paragraph) Walter, The Reverend J. A., "The Surratt Case," *Church News*, Washington, DC, 16 August 1891, also read before the U. S. Catholic Historical Society, 25 May 1891. Ref: Tonry Collection, E 457.5 .S985 No. 1, Surratt Society Archives, Clinton, MD, in Trindal, *op. cit.*, p. 207.

p. 359 (fifth full paragraph) Pittman, Benn, *The Assassination of President Lincoln and the Trial of the Conspirators*, Facsimile Edition (New York: Funk and Wagnalls, reprint 1954, by Philip Van Doren Stern), p. 132, testimony of Honora Fitzpatrick for the defense, in Trindal, *op. cit.*, p. 210.

p. 360 (first full paragraph) The dialogue was taken from an alleged note that Mrs. Surratt possibly wrote either to Eliza Holohan or Eliza Wildman Queen. Due to ink blots and a poor pen, the note is barely legible. Ref: Manuscript Division, Library of Congress, AC.2670. In Trindal, *op. cit.*, p. 218.

p. 360 (first full paragraph) Guy W. Moore, *The Case of Mrs. Surratt* (Norman: University of Oklahoma Press, 1954). p. 70. In Trindal, *op. cit.*, p. 220.

p. 360 (second full paragraph) John Brody's affidavit, Washington Constitutional Union, 11 July 1865, in Trindal, *op. cit.* p. 222.

p. 360 (fifth full paragraph) Trindal, *op. cit.*, pp. 233-234.

p. 361 (first paragraph) 18 Walter, J.A., in Trindal, *op. cit.*

p. 361 (fourth paragraph) Daily Variety at http://www.variety.com/article/VR1118007406.htm.

Restoring Dignity to Abandoned Children: Rest in His Arms

p. 365 Rest in His Arms accepts donations through their website, RestinHisArms.org, or in care of Harris Bank in Buffalo Grove, IL.

CREDITS AND PERMISSIONS

I. WE REMEMBER OUR HEROES

Plain-Spoken, Practical, Taking Care of Business: Major David G. Taylor by John Taylor courtesy of John Taylor (originally delivered at the funeral, October 28, 2006)

II. WE REMEMBER FAMILY

Aloise Steiner Buckley, R. I. P. by William F. Buckley, Jr. courtesy of © National Review, Inc., 215 Lexington Avenue, New York, NY 10016. Reprinted by Permission (originally appeared as "Aloise Steiner Buckley, R.I.P." in *National Review*, April. 19, 1985 pp. 20-21)

Remembering Pup: William F. Buckley, Jr. by Christopher Buckley courtesy of International Creative Management, Inc. © March, 2008 by Christopher Buckley (originally appeared as "Remembering Pup: William F. Buckley, Jr." on TheDailyBeast.com, March, 2008)

Every Gift but Length of Years: John F. Kennedy, Jr., by Senator Edward Kennedy (originally delivered as "Tribute to John F. Kennedy Jr." in Church of St. Thomas More, New York, NY, July 23, 1999. It is reprinted from www.historyplace.com/speeches/ted-kennedy-jfk-jr.htm)

The Golfatorium: Meditation on a Mother Dying by Thomas Lynch courtesy of W.W. Norton & Company, Inc. (originally appeared as "The Golfatorium" in *The Undertaking: Life Studies from the Dismal Trade* by Thomas Lynch, copyright © 1997 by Thomas Lynch)

Coming Home to St. Pat's: Rosemary Clooney by Nick Clooney courtesy of Nicholas Clooney (originally appeared as "Coming Home to Maysville: Rosemary Clooney" in *The Cincinnati Post*, July 5, 2002)

What You Can Expect from the Son of a Bookmaker: Wellington T. Mara by John K. Mara courtesy of John K. Mara and the New York Giants (originally delivered as "Eulogy to His Father Wellington Mara" October 28, 2005)

Eulogy for a Baby Who Dies after Baptism, by his father courtesy of http://www.transporter.com/FatherPeffley/Family/eulogy.html

III: WE REMEMBER OUR FRIENDS

Leaving a Legacy of Kindness: Phil Rizzuto by Bob Klapisch courtesy of The Record (Bergen County, N.J.), 2007 (originally appeared as "Yankees Legend Leaves a Legacy of Kindness: Remembering Phil Rizzuto" in The Bergen New Jersey *Record*, August 2007)

Sissies Anonymous: Andre Dubus by Tobias Wolff courtesy of the Xavier Review Press (originally appeared as Afterword in *Andre Dubus: Tributes*, Xavier Review Press, New Orleans, 2001)

My Closest Friend for Sixty Years: Remembering Walker Percy by Shelby Foote, Jr. courtesy of the Estate of Shelby Foote (originally appeared in *Walker Percy: 1916-1990*, © Farrar, Straus and Giroux, Inc. 1991)

Enemy of the Passive Voice, Who Rocked Some Jaunty Hats: Liz Christman by Melinda Henneberger courtesy of Melinda Henneberger (originally appeared on PoliticsDaily.com, February 8, 2010)

A Friend of the Family: Mr. O'Connell Is Dead by Dorothy Day courtesy of CatholicWorker.org (originally appeared as "A Friend of the Family: Mr. O'Connell Is Dead" in *The Catholic Worker*, March, 1952, 1, 6. Document #603. It is reprinted from "Dorothy Day Library on the Web" at www.catholicworker.org/dorothyday).

The Cardinal's Epistle to the Jews: John Cardinal O'Connor by Rabbi Haskel Lookstein courtesy of Rabbi Haskel Lookstein (originally appeared as "The Cardinal's Epistle to the Jews" in *The Jewish Week*, May 12, 2000)

Remembering My Friend Tim Russert by Maria Shriver courtesy of The Huffington Post (www.huffingtonpost.com) (originally delivered at Tim Russert Memorial Service, The John F. Kennedy Center for the Performing Arts, June 18, 2008 and originally appeared in print on www. huffingtonpost.com/2008/06/18/tim-russet-memorial-frie_n_107949. html)

IV. WE REMEMBER OUR ARTISTS

Eulogy for Andy Warhol by John Richardson courtesy of *The Religious Art of Andy Warhol* by Jane Daggett Dillenberger, copyright © 2001. Reprinted by permission of the Continuum International Publishing Group.

Danny's Promise: In Memory of Danny Thomas by Phil Donahue courtesy of Phil Donahue and Marlo Thomas (originally delivered at Church of the Good Shepherd, Beverly Hills, CA, February 8, 1991)

The Angels of Patricia Neal by Terry Mattingly courtesy of Terry Mattingly (originally appeared as "The Angels of Patricia Neal" for Scripps-Howard News Service, August 21, 2010)

He's Comin'Through: Milton Batiste by Jason Berry courtesy of National Catholic Reporter, 115 E. Armour Blvd., Kansas City, MO 64111 www.ncronline.org (originally appeared as "He's Comin'Through" in *National Catholic Reporter*, May 18, 2001)

Wit and Wisdom on the Refrigerator Door: Erma Bombeck by D. L. Stewart and Anne Gasior courtesy of The Dayton *Daily News* (originally appeared as "Erma Bombeck 1927-1996: A Wonderful Friend" in the Dayton *Daily News*, April 23, 1996)

An Unwieldy Radiance of Spirit: Flannery O'Connor by Katherine Anne Porter courtesy of The University of Scranton Press, Scranton, PA (originally appeared as "Gracious Greatness" in *Flannery O'Connor: A Memorial*, J.J. Quinn, SJ ed., 1996)

The Invisible Artist: Sculptor Frederick Hart by Tom Wolfe (originally appeared as "The Invisible Artist" in Hooking Up by Tom Wolfe. Copyright © 2000 by Tom Wolfe. Reprinted by permission of Farrar, Straus and Giroux, LLC)

V. WE REMEMBER THOSE WHO SERVED US

Servant of Incurable Cancer Patients: Rose Hawthorne Lathrop by Julian Hawthorne (originally appeared as "A Daughter of Hawthorne" in the *Atlantic Monthly*, September, 1928)

Imperiled Men: Mourning CAG by Andre Dubus courtesy of the Andre Dubus Estate (appears as "Imperiled Men" in *Meditations from a Movable Chair* by Andre Dubus, Vintage 1999, pp. 33-44)

The Great Heart of Thomas P. "Tip" O'Neill by Thomas O'Neill III (originally delivered at funeral, January, 1994. This eulogy was furnished by the eulogist Tip O'Neill III and printed by the authority of H. Res. 328. 103d Congress HOUSE DOCUMENT 103-340 US Government Printing Office, Washington, DC, 1995)

The Angel of AA: Sister Mary Ignatia by "Bill W." originally appeared as "For Sister Igantia: Our Everlasting Gratitude" Copyright © the *AA Grapevine*, (August, 1966). Reprinted with permission. Permission to reprint the AA Grapevine, Inc., copyrighted material in *Great American Catholic Eulogies* does not in any way imply affiliation with or endorsement by either Alcoholics Anonymous or The Grapevine, Inc.

Thank God for the Life of Elly Chovel! by Reverend George A. Garcia courtesy of Reverend George A. Garcia (originally delivered at St. Hugh Catholic Church in Coconut Grove, FL, September 4, 2007)

In the Irish Tradition: Daniel Patrick Moynihan by Lawrence J. McCaffrey courtesy of *The Irish Literary Supplement* and Lawrence J. McCaffrey (originally appeared as "In the Irish Tradition: Daniel Patrick Moynihan" in *The Irish Literary Supplement*, September 22, 2003)

VI. WE REMEMBER THOSE WHO SHOWED US THE WAY

Didn't He Show Us the Way?: Joseph Cardinal Bernardin Homily of Msgr. Kenneth Velo courtesy of *National Catholic Reporter*, 115 E. Armour Blvd., Kansas City, MO 64111 www.ncronline.org (originally appeared as "Didn't He Show Us the Way?" in *National Catholic Reporter*, December 6, 1996)

The Work of Democracy: César Chávez by Mario T. Garcia courtesy of Sheed & Ward, a member of the Rowman Littlefield Publishing Group (originally appeared as the Introduction to *The Gospel of César Chávez: My Faith in Action*, Mario T. Garcia, Editor, 2007 pp. 1-23)

"The Poster Boy for Hope: Ron Santo." Homily by Monsignor Dan Mayall, courtesy of Monsignor Mayall. (originally delivered as the homily at the funeral of Ron Santo, Holy Name Cathedral, Chicago. December 10, 2010)

Elizabeth Ann Seton Is the First Wholly American Saint! Homily of the Holy Father Paul VI courtesy of the Libreria Editrice Vaticana (originally delivered at Canonization of Elizabeth Ann Seton, September 14, 1975, © Libreria Editrice Vaticana)

Fixed, Solid, Holding a True Position: Rev. Robert F. Griffin, CSC by Luis R. Gamez courtesy of Luis R. Gamez (originally appeared as "Robert F. Griffin, CSC: 1925-1999" in *Notre Dame Magazine*, Winter, 1999-2000)

One Witness, Pointing: Mary K. Meyer Homily of Father Mike Coleman courtesy of The Olive Branch, Kansas City, KS (originally delivered as the homily for the Funeral Mass of Mary K. Meyer, Our Lady and St. Rose of Lima Church, February 14, 2007. It is reprinted from http://kcob.wordpress.com/2007/02/14/homily-for-the-funeral-mass-of-mary-k-meyer/

From Slave to Priest: Father Augustine Tolton by Deacon Harold Burke-Sivers (appears as a Foreword to *From Slave to Priest: A Biography of the Reverend Augustine Tolton (1854-1897)* First Black American Priest of the United States by Sister Caroline Hemesath, SSF © Ignatius Press, San Francisco, 2006, pp. 9-12)

VII. WE REMEMBER WITH POETRY

Game Called: Babe Ruth Is Gone by Grantland Rice (as it appeared as "Game Called" in The New York *Sun*, 1948)

Quid Pro Quo: On Losing a Child by Paul Mariani courtesy of W.W. Norton & Company, Inc. (originally appeared as "Quid Pro Quo" in *The Great Wheel* by Paul Mariani, copyright © 1996 by Paul Mariani)

His Tools, for My Father by Michael Fleming courtesy of Michael Fleming (appears on http://www.dutchgirl.com/foxpaws/poems/longer%20poems/histools.html)

To Mother Marianne by Robert Louis Stevenson (originally appeared in *Songs of Travel* by Robert Louis Stevenson, 1896)

To Kościuszko by John Keats (originally appeared in *The Poetical Works of John Keats*, 1884)

Atonement: Joyce Kilmer, R.I.P. by Aline Kilmer (originally appeared in *Vigils* by Aline Kilmer, 1921)

To Philip by Daniel Berrigan, SJ courtesy of Daniel Berrigan, SJ (appears on http://www.JonahHouse.org)

The Innocents: Mary Surratt and Others by Al Rocheleau appears on http://www.poetrymagazine.com and http://www.surratt.org

VIII. WE REMEMBER THE UNKNOWN CHILD

Homily courtesy of Reverend Dennis Conway, pastor, St. Martin de Porres Parish, Chicago, IL

DISCUSSION QUESTIONS FOR BOOK CLUBS

1. Cite three tributes from this book that stand out in your memory. What do your choices reveal about you?

2. What—if anything—distinguishes America's Catholics from those in the rest of the world?

3. Were there any cases where you found the eulogist as interesting as—or even more compelling than—the deceased?

4. Dorothy Day, William F. Buckley, Jr., and Andre Dubus are both eulogists and eulogized in this collection. How did this enhance your understanding of any of them?

5. Many of the deceased were visual artists, musicians, and writers. Does a person's faith—or lack of it—influence their art? Is creativity a spiritual process with or without faith?

6. Among the deceased with a link to the U. S. military are Generals Sherman and Kościuszko, Major David Taylor, "CAG," Joyce Kilmer, and Mary Surratt. Would you have omitted any of these?

7. The Catholic clergy (from priest to Pope) were prominent in this book: as eulogized, eulogist, and as supporter or, in a few cases, antagonist of the deceased. Which ones do you especially remember, and why?

8. Pope Paul VI said that all saints exhibit a humanity and morality "raised to the level of heroism." In addition to Saints Katharine Drexel and Mary Elizabeth Seton, others are either subjects of an official cause or an advocacy movement for sainthood: Cardinal Bernardin, Father Augustine Tolton, Mother Marianne Cope, and Dorothy Day. Do you agree that all saints exhibit heroism?

9. Have you ever been asked to deliver a eulogy? If so, how did you feel about that prospect—before and afterwards?

10. How do you want to be remembered?

ACKNOWLEDGMENTS

I owe a multitude of thanks to all those who helped me compile this history.

First and foremost to Charles Fiore who kept me going and having fun with it. And to Greg Pierce, Cubs fan to the core, who wouldn't let me abandon hope that I'd see the end of this work in my own lifetime. And to my husband, Stan Reinisch, who put up with my obsession with this project. Cheerfully.

This book would not have been possible without: the survivors of the deceased subjects who allowed me to include their eulogies; the publishers who granted permissions; and to the archivists of religious orders who provided information and accuracy checks.

I am ever grateful to Jack Dierks, my first reader—that rare person who knows a Petrarchan sonnet when he sees one—and to Harriett Harrow and Paul MacLean, whose feedback on my works-in-progress has always been valuable.

I thank librarians everywhere: presidential, private and public, especially,

In Illinois: the Abraham Lincoln Presidential Library, Springfield; Michele Levandoski, archivist at the Diocese of Springfield; Patricia Tomczak, at the Brenner Library, Quincy; all of the reference librarians at the Evanston Public Library's Main Branch.

In Florida: Boynton Beach librarians Joe Green, Ellen Mancuso, Patricia Mooar, Bob Heffernan; all those that participate in their Inter-library Lending Program, especially Florida International University and Barry Universities, both in Miami, and Gannon University, Erie, Pennsylvania, for loaning me out-of-print books.

My gratitude also to the archivists at the General Services Office of Alcoholics Anonymous, New York, New York.

Special thanks to those who were valuable resources because of what they found: Carol Pyle, who told me about Robert Redford's film on the Mary Surratt case; Elena Garcia, who led me to Elly Chovel; Barbara Lanctot who led me to Whitefeather, aka Larry Cloud-Morgan; Cathy Pezdirtz, who led me to Liz Christman; Martha Hogarty and Margot Gessler, RIP—who led me to Thomas Lynch back in 1997 with their gift of *The Undertaking: Life Studies from the Dismal Trade*.

Finally, to Anthony of Padua, who helped me find all the rest of these eulogies.

ABOUT THE AUTHOR

Carol DeChant's articles have appeared in the *Miami Herald* and in Chicago's *Tribune, Sun-Times,* and *Reader.* Her earlier book is *Momma's Enchanted Supper & Other Stories for the Long Evenings of Advent,* and she contributed chapters to the ACTA collections *Christmas Presence: Twelve Gifts That Were More Than They Seemed* and *Diamond Presence: Twelve Stories of Finding God at the Old Ball Park.* As founder of DeChant-Hughes & Associates, Inc., a national public relations firm specializing in books and authors, Carol has had a long career in publishing before she began writing books. She and her husband Stan Reinisch live in Sarasota, Florida, and spend hurricane season in Evanston, Illinois.

Her website can be found at
www.GreatAmericanCatholicEulogies.com